CASHING OUT

NEILL LOCHERY

CASHING OUT

THE FLIGHT OF
NAZI TREASURE,
1945–1948

PUBLICAFFAIRS

New York

PublicAffairs

Hachette Book Group

1290 Avenue of the Americas, New York, NY 10104

www.publicaffairsbooks.com

@Public_Affairs

Printed in the United States of America

First Edition: November 2023

Published by PublicAffairs, an imprint of Hachette Book Group, Inc. The PublicAffairs name and logo is a trademark of the Hachette Book Group.

The Hachette Speakers Bureau provides a wide range of authors for speaking events. To find out more, go to hachettespeakersbureau.com or email HachetteSpeakers@hbgusa.com.

PublicAffairs books may be purchased in bulk for business, educational, or promotional use. For more information, please contact your local bookseller or the Hachette Book Group Special Markets Department at special.markets@hbgusa.com.

The publisher is not responsible for websites (or their content) that are not owned by the publisher.

Print book interior design by Amy Quinn.

Library of Congress Cataloging-in-Publication Data
Names: Lochery, Neill, author.
Title: Cashing out: the flight of Nazi treasure, 1945–1948 / Neill Lochery.
Other titles: Flight of Nazi treasure, 1945–1948
Description: First edition. | New York: PublicAffairs, 2023. | Includes bibliographical references and index.
Identifiers: LCCN 2023026022 | ISBN 9781541702301 (hardcover) | ISBN 9781541702325 (ebook)
Subjects: LCSH: World War, 1939–1945—Confiscations and contributions—Europe. | Jewish property—Europe—History—20th century. | Art treasures in war—Europe—History—20th century. | Art thefts—Europe—History—20th century. | Monetary gold confiscations. | Banks and banking—Corrupt practices—Europe—History—20th century. | Fugitives from justice—Europe—History—20th century. | Neutrality—History—20th century.
Classification: LCC D810.C8 L64 2023 | DDC 940.53/18—dc23/eng/20230602
LC record available at https://lccn.loc.gov/2023026022

ISBNs: 9781541702301 (hardcover), 9781541702325 (ebook)

LSC-C

Printing 1, 2023

For Emma, Benjamin, and Hélèna, with much love

CONTENTS

Photo gallery located between pages 122 and 123

PREFACE

I{N 1945, THE ALLIES ESTIMATED THAT THE NAZIS HAD LOOTED}
around 20 percent of European art and treasure before and during World
War II. This figure has fascinated me for some time. Of course, the quantity stolen does not tell the whole story. When I researched the long lists
of artworks that came into the hands of the Nazis, they comprised the
leading artists from throughout the ages and included some of my personal favorites such as Pablo Picasso and Vincent van Gogh. The Nazis'
systematic looting took the form of theft of whole collections, particularly
from Jewish collectors such as the Rothschilds and leading gallery owners
like Paul Rosenberg in Paris. Every incident of looting was a tragedy, and
despite some Allied successes in retrieving pieces—most notably through
the work of the acclaimed Monuments Men—this pillage remains an
unresolved crime in the present day.

The plunder of European art and treasures was not the only theft carried out by the Nazis. The systematic removal of gold reserves from the
central banks of German-occupied countries constituted a heist of massive proportions. On top of this, the organized robbing of gold and other
valuables from the Jewish victims of the Holocaust added to the Nazis'
looted assets. By the end of the war, the Germans had used this gold to
help pay for services rendered by countries that had continued to trade
with them. A lot was left over. Some was buried in Germany, some was
located by the Allies, some was smuggled into Switzerland and deposited

in bank vaults, but a large amount was smuggled out by leading Nazis through what became known as ratlines. Just as the search for looted art and its restitution remain a work in progress, the same is true for the Nazi gold and the investigations into how it was used and where the remainder went.

What continues to intrigue me most about World War II are not the details of the fighting, accounts of the battles that were won and lost, or stories of individual heroism or pure evil; scholars and researchers have little new to add to the copious record that already exists. But the strategic maneuvering of governments in war and the exploration of the basic economic question of who got rich and who was made poor by it are fascinating—the effects lasting into the present. In planning and writing this book, I shied away from previous accounts that highlight the evil opportunism of the Nazis. For me, any debate about the moral actions of the Nazis is a little irrelevant. Nazi ideology legitimizes evil behavior. The Nazis' actions in looting, both collectively and individually, were inexcusable but largely predictable. Yes, there were different levels of sophistication among the senior Nazis, but all wanted to maximize financial gains for the Third Reich and, on a personal level, get rich quickly. The latter was of heightened importance for Nazis who did not come from money and for those like Hermann Göring who had experienced degrees of poverty after World War I.

As World War II came to an end, despite the apparent absence of a collective postwar scheme, many leading Nazis made their own plans for escape. Important aspects of evading the justice of the victorious Allies were selling looted assets, hiding them for future use, and carrying them along the ratlines toward South America. Nazis who escaped Europe were by and large successful at retaining the proceeds from their looted treasure or at cashing it out in one of the European countries that had remained neutral during the war or in South America. On this score, the Allies failed to stem the tide of Nazis exiting Europe along with the loot, and this forms a key part of the book.

The Nazis' robbery of Europe and their attempts at escape do not tell the whole story. What came to interest me most was how the neutral countries profited from their trade with the Germans during the war and, crucially, employed shady efforts to hold on to their profits, including the gold, in the postwar period despite the efforts of the Allies to force them to hand it back. Not only did neutral nations trade with Germany during the war, but also several helped wanted Nazi war criminals escape in the aftermath, sometimes offering semipermanent residence to notorious Nazis. I soon came to realize that none of the so-called neutral countries emerged from the war with any shred of moral credibility. In examining the most important of the neutrals, I include the two Iberian nations of Portugal and Spain (the latter was officially categorized as a nonbelligerent), both led at the time by authoritarian regimes (some historians use the term *fascist* to describe them). Sweden was an obvious country to chronicle, with its close economic ties to Nazi Germany and its postwar economic expansion that was fueled by the windfall from this trade. Unlike Portugal and Spain, Sweden was a democracy, and this raises a set of questions different from those of the Iberian nations.

In South America, it was obvious from the start that Argentina would play a central role in the story. It is worth recalling that Argentina was neutral in the war until pressure from the United States caused it to join the Allies. It declared war on Germany on March 27, 1945. Argentina's historic rival, Brazil, declared neutrality at the start of the war, but following German submarine attacks on Brazilian shipping, it declared war on Germany on August 22, 1942, and the Brazilian army joined the Allies in fighting in Italy in September 1944. Both South American countries were important for escaping Nazis: Argentina was central to the escape plans of leading Nazis such as Adolf Eichmann, the architect of the Final Solution.

The direction of my investigation sent me for different reasons toward these five countries (three European and two South American). I am aware that I have omitted from the story two important neutral countries, Ireland and Turkey. The neutrality of the Republic of Ireland was controversial and a source of irritation to the British, but as far as I am aware few Nazis ended up in an Irish pub enjoying a pint of Guinness. Likewise, the country did not really feature in the trail of looted art, treasure, and Nazi gold. I was initially inclined to include Turkey, given its size and regional importance. As my research for the book progressed, however, it became obvious that the story I wanted to tell took me to the west and north of Europe and to South America. That said, a few Nazi war criminals most probably did transit through Turkey on the way to the Arab Middle East, in many cases, to Syria. The most wanted Nazi to reach Damascus, Alois Brunner, an SS officer famed for his brutality and for being the right-hand man to Eichmann, arrived in Damascus via Italy and Egypt in 1954. Turkey did trade with Nazi Germany, but the impact on its economy did not match that of the other European neutrals. Also, it did not play a major role in the story of looted treasures and Nazi gold. In addition, there already exist several articles and books on the wartime records of these two countries; it is clear they were important exits for some fleeing Nazis, but their significance is dwarfed by the roles of countries with an Atlantic coastline and shipping lanes to South America.

The neutral countries were opportunistic, indifferent to the origin of the gold they were paid; they aided and abetted the international trade in looted art and treasure and were complicit in helping Nazis evade justice after the war. I also believe that several committed major crimes during the war and, subsequently, crimes that to this day have largely gone unpunished. Debates over the restitution of looted art and Nazi gold and implications stemming from them remain to be resolved nearly eight decades after the fighting stopped.

The world now knows of the horrors the Nazis caused and of the lack of repentance shown by senior Nazis who were captured and tried. But the reasons so many Nazis were able to evade justice remain highly relevant. As I discovered, the answer to that question says a lot about the Allies' sorry efforts to cooperate with one another. The specific Allied operation set up in 1944 to deal with the issues of German assets in neutral countries, Nazi gold, and war criminals—Operation Safehaven—represented an ambitious attempt to bring justice and closure to these issues.

Operation Safehaven was the most important of several Allied efforts that aimed to deal with looted goods and war criminals because it focused on the neutral countries. Another important effort that is beyond the scope of this book was the Roberts Commission, or to give its official name, the American Commission for the Protection and Salvage of Artistic and Historic Monuments in War Areas, which was established in

1943 and which did much good work in compiling a catalog of European cultural monuments, museums, and most private collections. This information was passed on to the army and intelligence services prior to the Allied landings in France in June 1944. The commission also helped provide maps, details of looted treasures up to that date, and instructions for salvaging and conserving the paintings and objects. What intrigues me, however, are the looted treasures and gold that the Germans kept hold of toward the end of the war and the Allies' struggle to discover them.

The complexity of recovery and restitution of looted art meant that several times during the war the Allies got it spectacularly wrong: seizing art that had not been looted while letting slip through other paintings that had. Given the scale of the task, this is not surprising, but the consequences of both mistakes were severe.

Throughout my investigations, I noticed that debates about the wartime records of the Nazi-aligned countries are intermixed with historiographical disputes about the regimes in power during the war. This book takes a critical but balanced approach to this thorny problem of different historical perspectives and interpretations. Finally, of all the research I have conducted for my books, the story of the looted treasure and Nazi gold has been the one that has shocked me the most—not the actions of the Nazis but the criminal complicity of the countries involved and their stubborn refusal to comply with the Allies' demands.

World War II was not a catastrophe for everyone. Every cloud has a silver lining, so the saying goes. The cloud of World War II did, too, except that the lining was gold.

INTRODUCTION

In September 1940, the American-owned ocean liner the SS *Excalibur* was busy zigzagging across the Atlantic Ocean between New York and Lisbon—two neutral ports. Its eastbound trips to Portugal were quiet, with few passengers heading toward the war-torn European continent. The crew used these calm crossings to catch up on work on the ship, carrying out minor repairs and cleaning decks. The return voyage was another matter altogether. Since the fall of France in the summer, thousands of refugees had made their way from Paris and the Low Countries through the south of Spain and onward to Lisbon, where they waited to secure passage on liners like the *Excalibur* bound for the New World. The ship, as a result, was crammed to the rafters on its westbound trip to New York. The price of tickets was tenfold prewar rates. Chaos would erupt when the liner slipped its anchor and headed into the River Tagus bound for the Atlantic Ocean. Hundreds of people watched the departures from the quayside, waving Portuguese flags or hankies. Many families could not find enough tickets to sail together and were forced to split, leaving some relatives frantic on the quayside as their loved ones sailed into the sunset and an uncertain future across the ocean.

The multinational crew of the *Excalibur* had greeted many famous passengers. The Duke and Duchess of Windsor were passengers on August 1, 1940, when the duke headed for a new position as the governor of the Bahamas. Prior to sailing, reports surfaced that a bomb had been planted on board to prevent him leaving Portugal, and only after a careful search by the local police was the ship allowed to depart.[1]

The ship's hold was usually loaded with the possessions of refugees, who brought with them everything they could get out of Europe. British agents operating in Lisbon suspected that the ocean liners were also being used by the Germans to smuggle artworks out of Europe for sale in the United States. In London reports circulated of private collectors and galleries in the United States that purchased these works, with the profits going to several leading Nazis in Europe.

Ready to pounce, British intelligence officers linked to the Ministry of Economic Warfare (MEW) waited. For some time, the British had been buying information from local officials in Lisbon that indicated a pattern of both small- and large-scale smuggling. After a series of tip-offs, the British believed they had enough evidence to warrant stopping the *Excalibur* on its inbound voyage to New York. On September 25 in Bermuda, the Royal Navy boarded the *Excalibur*, and after a rigorous search of the ship, authorities seized some 560 artworks. The haul included 270 paintings by Renoir, 30 by Cézanne, 12 by Gauguin, and 7 by Degas as well as works by Monet and Picasso that had been stolen from museums in Paris.[2] These included *Portrait de Paul* by Cézanne, *Femme Bleu* by Picasso, and Renoir's *Fleurs*, the titles given to the paintings by the Allies from the paperwork.[3] The British authorities confiscated the art along with a collection of rare books that was part of the same consignment. The British put together a complete inventory of the seized artworks, and the works were taken to the National Gallery of Canada to be stored for the duration of the war. They were all presumed to have been looted art that would be returned to their rightful owners at the conclusion of the war.

The case, however, was hard to unscramble. The name on the shipment's documentation was Martin Fabiani, a Paris art expert. The works belonged to the estate of the late Ambroise Vollard, who had died in a car accident. Fabiani was the executor of Vollard's will and argued that he was moving the artworks to prevent them from falling into the hands of the Germans. He claimed his plan was to eventually return the works to Vollard's heirs. The Allies viewed Fabiani as shady. Later in the war it was shown that he was working with pro-Nazi art experts and had helped recycle artworks of Jewish collectors in Paris. After the war, he was eventually charged with and convicted of selling art from the looted collections of well-known Jewish gallery owners in Paris, such as Paul Rosenberg.

So, in 1940, the British were convinced that they had seized a major cargo of looted art on the *Excalibur*. The international press was full of stories lauding the British operation. "The Germans apparently recognised the commercial value of what they officially describe as degenerate art," a statement from the Ministry of Economic Warfare proclaimed. The works were classified as enemy exports, and the British press noted "there will be no danger of their again falling into German hands." The seizure was viewed as a great coup for the Allies at a difficult time. The *New York Times* prominently reported the story on page 3 on October 10, after removal of the embargo on the story.[4]

Fabiani, although he was tolerant of Nazis, was in this instance telling the truth about the cargo on the *Excalibur*. In 1949 a British court ruled that the collection should be returned to him. He then handed over all the works to the beneficiaries of Vollard's will. They, in turn, donated a few of the works to the National Museum of Canada in gratitude for the museum's careful preservation of the collection during the war. The rest of the collection soon started appearing in commercial galleries in New York and was quickly sold.

This case exemplifies the murky world the Allies were trying to police in 1940. On this occasion, they were wrong about the cargo, although their suspicions of Fabiani proved to be accurate. The raid on the *Excalibur* was a well-intentioned intervention that was misdirected. It shows how hard it was to interdict illegal trade, let alone tell the illegal from the legal.

As early in the war as the autumn of 1940, the strategic use of neutral ports as exit points for looted art had become established. Lisbon was a favored route for the Germans for several reasons. Berlin believed the authoritarian regime in Portugal to be politically sympathetic to the Nazi cause, despite Portugal's historic alliance with Britain. In 1940, more than one hundred ocean crossings a year between Lisbon and New York occurred. The Portuguese government made it clear to the British

that it was strongly against any enforcement of the naval blockade of
Portugal imposed by the Ministry of Economic Warfare and policed
by the Royal Navy. Besides, several of the liners were registered in the
still-neutral United States, and any stop-and-search tactics by the Royal
Navy would have had to be justified to Washington.

By the early winter of 1940, the British had staffed up their embassies
in Lisbon and Madrid and broadened their searches for looted art.[5] But
many Portuguese were complicit in the trade. Customs officials turned
a blind eye to the lack of correct paperwork for crates. The Germans, as
a result, could move much more looted art out of Lisbon than the British could track. As the war went on, the investigations grew in number,
scale, and complexity. But even after the Americans joined the war in
December 1941, the Allies always appeared one step behind the Nazis,
whose methods of deception grew more sophisticated as the stakes rose.[6]

1

SCHELLENBERG

WALTER SCHELLENBERG HAD FEW REDEEMING PERSONAL ATTRIBUTES and could easily be characterized as just another career Nazi. He owed his lofty position as head of German intelligence to the patronage of Heinrich Himmler, and he remained personally loyal to the Reichsführer until the end.[1] Schellenberg was not a thinker. He was an enforcer, career gossip, and manipulator, and his moves were guided by self-preservation and opportunism that trumped any ideological loyalty to the Nazi Party.[2] He backed winners, and in Nazi Germany they did not come much bigger than Himmler. *Realism* is not a word that can be attached to many of his fellow Nazis, but it was a characteristic ingrained in Schellenberg's personality. While fellow Nazis puffed out their chests and talked of victory in the East or likely failure of the Allied landings in Italy, he was busy preparing for a German defeat. At heart, he was a bureaucrat, comfortable with the details. He was happiest when involved in complex intelligence operations that required precise moves and deep knowledge of his opponents, both German and Allied. The shadows were his natural home. Far from the politics of the High Command and whims of Hitler, he preferred to stay in the background pulling the strings.

He was deeply impressed and envious of the Allied intelligence services. The British agents he respected had been drawn from the top tiers of society, whereas many of his German colleagues came from the world of gangsters and other criminal gangs. The sport of gentlemen, he was fond of saying when asked about British spying. He found the British cold, the Americans brash and easy to con, and the Italians overemotional. Psychology interested him, and his own was far from balanced. He had made a half-hearted attempt to kill himself when one of his missions during the war had gone wrong. This was all erased from his records by his boss and did not impact his ascent to the top of German intelligence.[3]

It was, however, Schellenberg's amazing memory for names and operational detail that made him stand out. If he did not remember something, it was because he chose not to. He became a human reference library of the work of German intelligence agencies in WWII, their agents, and enemies. He watched his rivals self-destruct, and those who did not he undermined with careful calculation and Himmler's support. Preparing for the end of the war appeared a natural extension of the job, so he plotted to save himself from what he foresaw would be the hangman's noose. Germany losing the war would present great difficulties but also offer opportunities to those who had prepared for the inevitable. The postwar era, he thought, could bring benefits to him personally.[4]

However, things did not quite work out as he anticipated. The last one hundred days of World War II were characterized by intensive fighting on the Western and Eastern Fronts as German resistance crumbled after the failure of the Ardennes Offensive (December 16, 1944, to January 25, 1945). While the conflict continued, many Germans firmed up their exit plans to evade Allied justice when the inevitable defeat of Germany finally came. It was a race against time for these Nazis, with the Allies closing in on their exit networks. The German collapse came much faster than Schellenberg's preparations had allowed for, and the peacemaker role he had imagined for himself was overtaken by events on the battlefield and the death of Himmler. Schellenberg, as a result, found himself in something of a jam. Like many senior Nazis, he wished to avoid being captured and handed over to Soviet forces. His two choices to avoid this fate were to utilize one of the ratlines operating out of Italy, Spain, or Portugal to South America, or to take his chances by staying in northern Europe.[5]

No fan of South America, where he had undertaken several intelligence missions during the war, he thought that the best option was to remain in Europe. He believed that his relationship with Swedish officials would help him cut a deal with the British or the Americans. To this end, he was reconciled to singing for his supper by providing the Allies with a detailed account of his work in German intelligence. In his view, this testimony would serve two purposes: spare him from the death penalty and settle some scores with his rivals.[6]

Deep down, Schellenberg believed he had done nothing wrong in the war. He had been aware of the internal decision-making processes that led to the Holocaust and of the practical efforts to exterminate Europe's Jewish population. His involvement, however, was limited to making intelligence assessments about the consequences of the mass killing and listening to accounts about it from fellow senior Nazi colleagues.[7] He understood that several of his peers were doomed if captured by the Allies. Whereas the Americans and the British would go through the nicety of ensuring the due legal process was followed, the Soviets would implement a swifter form of justice. Regardless of the process, the result, he believed, would be the same: death.

Betrayal seemed the better option. Snitching on old colleagues— many of whom he presumed would be in Allied custody and trying to do the same to him—would almost be a pleasure. Schellenberg was smart enough to know that the Allies were desperate for information that would lead to new investigations or confirm existing avenues of inquiry. By being both accurate and detailed about the activities of German intelligence during the war, Schellenberg hoped to buy his way out of jail. There was no topic that he would refuse to discuss.

Once Schellenberg indicated via the Swedes his willingness to share what he knew, he found himself quickly put on a plane out of Sweden. On the morning of June 17, 1945, he was flown to Frankfurt, where he was handed over to the Allied authorities, and on July 7, he was put on an aircraft bound for London. As it flew over London, he stared out of the window. When the plane descended, he could see people going about their daily business. London looked like a city that had begun to bounce back from the war. How different it looked from Germany, from where he had set out. "I cannot understand, no destruction at all," he told his guards.[8] He was very much a man in demand on his arrival: the Allies had argued over who would have first chance at questioning him. As often happened with senior Nazis in the aftermath of the war, a compromise was reached between the British and the Americans. Schellenberg was to be interrogated by British officials, who were responsible for questioning and breaking German intelligence agents operating in Europe, mainly in the neutral countries of Portugal, Spain, Sweden, and Turkey.[9] They would put to Schellenberg a jointly prepared list of questions. It was a race against time—time to interrogate (or break) Schellenberg probably limited by the likely requirement for him to attend the Nuremberg trials as a defendant and a potential witness.[10]

In London, Schellenberg might have allowed himself a nostalgic look back at the handbook he had authored for the German troops in planning for the invasion of Britain in 1940.[11] At that point, he had favored a softly, softly approach, believing that the strong pro-German sentiments among the British aristocracy would trump any anti-German sentiments held by the rabble-rousing Winston Churchill and his small group of victory-at-all-costs mavericks.[12] It was then that Schellenberg found himself at the center of one of the most curious German intelligence operations in preparation for the occupation of Britain, and despite its failure, it made Schellenberg a very sensitive prisoner to the British.

Schellenberg had been tasked with preparing a sympathetic alternative to the royal family—finding a pro-Nazi King of England. Over the boiling hot summer month of July 1940, the Germans hatched a plan to persuade Edward, Duke of Windsor, to return to the throne as a German-appointed king following a successful invasion of England. The Germans believed the duke to be partial to this move because of his apparent Nazi sympathies, which he regularly blurted out when intoxicated.[13] The duke's distaste for Churchill's policy toward Nazi Germany was also well known.[14] Churchill, a warmonger and a man who would demand the total and unconditional surrender of Germany, held views that were certainly far from the duke's own. The final German calculation was that Edward had been left deeply wounded by his abdication and wanted to get back at the royal family.[15] This interpretation was not as far-fetched as it might first appear. His abdication and subsequent exile had created a schism between him and key members of the royal family. The duke barely spoke to any of them, and the alienation was mutual. Both sides went out of their way to avoid one another, such as when Edward's arrival in Lisbon in July 1940 had to be delayed because Prince George, the Duke of Kent, was on an official visit to Portugal. When Edward was asked if he wanted to meet his brother, the Duke of Kent, who had been Edward's closest sibling in the late 1920s and early 1930s, he simply said no.

To carry out the mission that was labeled Operation Willi, Schellenberg traveled to Lisbon on the orders of the foreign minister, Joachim von Ribbentrop, who in 1940 had highly antagonistic relations with Schellenberg's boss, Reinhard Heydrich. It was a difficult balancing act for Schellenberg to manage. He did not want to secure Ribbentrop a major victory over Heydrich but wanted to be seen as having tried to pursue every avenue to persuade or coerce the duke to comply with German wishes. Soon after his arrival in Portugal, however, Schellenberg realized that the prospects of success for the operation were virtually nil.

Spending his days wandering around Lisbon, Schellenberg gave a great deal of thought to how he was going to break the news of the operation's impossibility to Ribbentrop. He shared his concerns with the German ambassador Oswald von Hoyningen-Huene, who concurred and hoped that Ribbentrop would see sense before attempting any clumsy move that could undo the ambassador's long-term work in fostering trade and political ties between Berlin and Lisbon. While giving the appearance of working on Ribbentrop's project, Schellenberg carefully cultivated ties with local Portuguese and Brazilians that helped cement the presence of German intelligence in the city.

Many of his evenings were spent along the Lisbon coastline near the towns of Estoril and Cascais, towns favored by the Portuguese elite. It was in Cascais that the Duke and Duchess of Windsor were staying, at the weekend house of Ricardo Espírito Santo, the head of Banco Espírito Santo. The banker, a leading socialite, liked to give extravagant parties that were attended by both Allied and Axis diplomats and spies. Personally close to the Portuguese leader António de Oliveira Salazar, Espírito Santo operated as his eyes and ears in local society. Much of the gossip that was fed to Hoyningen-Huene and then to Ribbentrop came either directly from or through Espírito Santo. Like many leading Portuguese businessmen, Espírito Santo viewed the war as a golden opportunity to make money for his family's bank. The lucrative trade between Lisbon and Berlin provided great potential for Espírito Santo and others to achieve their financial aims.

As a result, even as early as the summer of 1940, Lisbon was booming, a hive of activity, with the British and Germans competing to gain greater influence with the Portuguese police. Schellenberg would have seen the thousands of refugees wandering the streets, many from France. Among the refugees in 1940 was the famous art dealer Paul Rosenberg and his extended family, who were waiting for passage to New York on an ocean liner. Rosenberg was close to Pablo Picasso, whose works he collected and sold. Rosenberg was one of the lucky ones who was able to get his family out of Europe and into the United States, where he continued the work he had started in Paris. Most were not as fortunate.

On one of his walks around the city, Schellenberg went to the docks where ocean liners were moored and preparing to leave for the United States and Brazil. He watched as the Portuguese customs officials overzealously inspected passenger baggage while crates of cargo appeared not to be inspected at all. The German ambassador had alerted him to the arbitrary nature of the export process and that the Germans had local officers in the export departments on their payroll. Making a note to increase his efforts to recruit Brazilian agents based in Portugal, Schellenberg watched as an ocean liner slipped its anchor and sailed down the calm River Tagus and out into the Atlantic Ocean. It all appeared effortless. Although in the summer of 1940 defeat was far from the thoughts of any German, Schellenberg was impressed by the easy connection between Lisbon and North and South America. Later, back in Germany, he sought additional funding to further increase the number of Portuguese police officers and customs officials on the German payroll.

Despite his useful reconnaissance in the city, Schellenberg grew tired of the fantasy plot of luring the Duke of Windsor into becoming a pro-Nazi king. Looking for a way out of the situation, he dined with a Portuguese friend who was a leading German agent in Lisbon and outlined his frustrations. Together they came up with a way to gently sabotage the whole improbable enterprise. Schellenberg asked for an increase in the number of Portuguese police officers guarding the Duke and Duchess of Windsor. An additional twenty officers assigned to the duke's protection prompted a matching increase in the number of British security personnel assigned to the duke, making any attempt to kidnap the duke almost impossible without a major armed confrontation. For Schellenberg, this was the perfect way to stall the mission, though he made one last attempt to speak to the duke directly, using Portuguese channels. When this failed to produce the one-on-one meeting he wanted, he gave up. The duke left unimpeded to take up his new position as the governor of the Bahamas. Schellenberg watched the duke's ship depart from the tower room of the German embassy atop one of Lisbon's seven hills. The daft scheme had finally unraveled, but he had put in place a new network of agents that would be of great use five years later.

All that remained was to explain the failure of Operation Willi to Ribbentrop. Schellenberg concocted a number of justifications of the failure, including a report that the British Secret Service had planned to bomb the duke's ship a couple of hours before its departure.[16] Other false alarms had been raised to further increase the attention from the Portuguese police, and together they had made it impossible for Schellenberg to get near the duke and duchess. Ribbentrop accepted the assessment and ultimately commended Schellenberg's decision not to kidnap the duke. Even Heydrich called it an "excellent failure" and congratulated Schellenberg on his careful management of the mission.[17]

Once he was back in Berlin, Schellenberg continued to work on developing a new network of informants and useful contacts in the neutral countries. The opportunity for moving goods out of Portugal would increase by the end of 1942 with the opening of a new airport on October 15 located in the Portela district of Lisbon, not far from the city center. Soon a daily flight to Berlin was operating that stopped in either Barcelona or Madrid en route. The cargo on these flights was not subjected to searches by local customs officials, whom Schellenberg had arranged to be paid by the Germans. The Lisbon run would become a favored smuggling route even before the war turned decisively against the Axis powers in 1943. But in 1940, what transited through Lisbon were mainly the products of black market auctions held in private houses specializing in the sale of stolen artworks, silver, and gold. These auctions were used by several diplomats as a means of topping up their salaries or "putting in place their pension plans," as one dealer put it. The Portuguese Secret Police appeared to be aware of much of the activity, but did not intervene.

The British were also aware of the activities, and several of the dealers were on the payroll of the British to provide information about what was bought and sold by whom and for how much. Many auctions featured the sale of artworks and family treasures that Jewish refugees transiting through Lisbon to the New World had been forced to sell to local dealers at rates well below market value. Money laundering was an additional feature of the trade. The Germans had been importing large numbers of forged Portuguese escudos printed in the Low Countries. Schellenberg had used this money to help set up his spy networks in Lisbon, and the counterfeit notes were in general circulation until late 1941, when the Bank of Portugal actively tried to eradicate the forgeries. After the Bank of Portugal informed Prime Minister Salazar of the widespread use of forged currency by the Germans, Berlin was compelled to make payments in gold.

Schellenberg would try forgery later in the war, too. His most ambitious scheme involved flooding the market with fake British pounds that were distributed through Lisbon. The bank notes were flown into Lisbon marked as diplomatic baggage with the intent of transporting them to London by sea using a locally recruited sailor on a Portuguese ship bound for England. The idea was to make the British currency worthless. This plan failed for several reasons, not the least being the poor quality of the forgeries.

When the Germans flew in gold on the Berlin–Lisbon route, the planes landing at Portela airport were swiftly unloaded. British spies watching the airport reported that the heavy crates were loaded into trucks that pulled up next to the plane without any interference from the customs officials. When the British followed the trucks into Lisbon, agents noticed that one truck went to the Baixa area of the city. In the heart of Baixa lay the Bank of Portugal, nestled among the other commercial banks headquartered there. Deliveries to the Bank of Portugal usually took place at night, with trucks backing into the secure compound and gold carefully unloaded and placed in the deep underground vaults.

A second truck following the lead one would peel off to the left before reaching the Bank of Portugal, instead heading up the hill to the German embassy, where it disappeared behind the high gates. British sources had bought information from local builders confirming that the embassy had installed a new large, secure vault that had room to store several tons of gold. As the war developed over the course of 1943, gold continued to arrive at the embassy. The frequency of the flights from Berlin increased and the operation moving the gold became more complicated given the larger amounts involved. British agents operating in Lisbon attempted to buy information from local Portuguese employees of the German embassy regarding the volume of gold being delivered and for what purpose it was being sent to Portugal. Evidence supplied by a female administrator confirmed that the gold had not left Portugal and was being stored in the embassy, but there was little information about its purpose.

The gold trade became further complicated by the scale of the operation and the increasing signs that the gold was not legitimate. "Ill-gotten gains" the British charged, and the Americans soon followed with the same assessment. Tracking the gold became a major Allied operation that soon produced compelling evidence supporting the view that this was stolen gold. The first wave of gold had been looted from the central banks of the Low Countries, Holland and Belgium. Gold was also stolen from the central bank of occupied France. When, by 1943, it was clear that a large portion of the gold had come from the Jewish victims of the Holocaust, the Portuguese deemed the trade too risky. The Bank of Portugal's vault was nearly full, and new, much more discreet ways were needed to import gold. A complex arrangement was put in place with Swiss banks acting as middlemen for the exchange of gold, depositing the value into Portuguese accounts in Switzerland for later transfer to Lisbon.

By 1943, with the help of Schellenberg, Lisbon was a major trading partner with Germany for legitimate commercial activities as well as black market goods. Hundreds of Germans worked in the embassy in Lisbon, the vast majority of whom were spies or employed in trade sections linked to import-export activities in Portugal. Funded by the stolen gold, the web of locally recruited agents increased tenfold as the Nazis further entrenched ties among the Portuguese Secret Police, corrupt government officials, and gossip networks of Portuguese society. Everybody in Lisbon wanted a piece of the German action.

Many payments were made as credit for future information or use. For example, a bribe would be offered to a customs official on the condition that at some point in the future he would be approached for a favor—such as overlooking paperwork on a specific shipment arriving in the country. It became customary for officials to take money from different countries in the war. The Italians, with over five hundred people in their embassy in Lisbon (the largest of all diplomatic representation in the city), were known to be good payers. The British were viewed as more careful in how they spent their money. After the United States joined the war in December 1941, it quickly staffed up its embassy with spies and soon became the most popular payer among the local population. One shady local informant commented that the Americans did not even appear to care if the information they were buying was true.

2

CAMP 020

CAMP 020 WAS SITUATED IN A LARGE HOUSE AT THE END OF A SE-
cluded wooded street near Ham Common in the borough of
Richmond, close to London. Latchmere House was a plain, slightly
austere-looking Victorian mansion that had been used as a military
hospital during World War I. The Security Service, better known as
MI5 (Military Intelligence, Section 5), had carefully chosen it as the
place where alleged Nazis would be interviewed and processed. The
only evidence of it being a prison was the large perimeter fence around
the sizable grounds. The fence served the dual purposes of keeping the
prisoners in and preventing prying eyes of the locals or the media getting anywhere near the building. Two lower barbed-wire fences had
been installed at the request of MI5. Latchmere House was run as a
military camp; British officers wore the uniform of the regiment from
which they had been recruited. There were at least four security checks
to pass from the outside to the inside and vice versa. Passes needed to be
shown and the tight security included the vetting of the local civilians
living in neighboring houses.[1]

During the war, several enemy agents in Camp 020 had been broken—
the term used by MI5 officers—and had confessed to their crimes. A
number were subsequently tried and sentenced to death by hanging.

Others received custodial sentences, and a few were turned and recruited
to work for British intelligence. A steady stream of agents who had operated in the neutral countries were processed through Camp 020. Each
had their own sad story, and many showed a degree of remorse for their
actions. The interrogators' main goal was to discover the extent of the
networks in which the agents had operated. In Lisbon, many enemy
agents were accused of betraying the movements of the convoys of Allied
ships in the Atlantic Ocean. Several agents worked on passenger liners
that transported refugees to the United States and Brazil. In poor countries like Portugal and Spain, money spoke. Indeed, it was the financial
rewards offered by the Germans and the Italians that were the main incentives for recruitment to the Axis side. Many of the enemy agents who
ended up in Camp 020 had little ideological attachment to the Nazis and
instead fit Walter Schellenberg's description of them as criminal and un-
derworld elements who were motivated by money and sex.

The senior officer in the camp was an opinionated extrovert oddball
named Lieutenant Colonel Robin William George Stephens. By nature
a strict authoritarian, he was always immaculately dressed. He was better known in the camp by the name "Tin Eye." Nobody was sure how
he had acquired the name, but it was assumed that it came down to his
"steely glare that emanated from behind his ever-present monocle."[2]
Short-tempered, he did not suffer fools gladly and presumed that almost
everyone who had been sent to Camp 020 was guilty of crimes of working for the enemy. Stephens's hatred of the enemy was clear. It set the
tone for the interrogations and came across in conversations with his colleagues. Blunt and using direct language that often bordered on racism
(notably against Portuguese, Italian, and Spanish prisoners), he was prone
to making sweeping statements about the enemy that were not supported
by evidence.[3] At the end of the war, he faced a court-martial trial based
on claims of ill treatment of prisoners and use of brutality. The charge
sheet stated the following:

1. Insufficient clothing for prisoners
2. Intimidation by the guards
3. Mental and physical torture during the interrogations

4. Prisoners were kept in solitary confinement for long periods with no exercise

5. They were committed to punishment cells, not for any offense but because the interrogator was not satisfied with their answers

6. In the punishment cells, during the bitter winter, they were deprived of certain articles of clothing, had buckets of cold water thrown into their cells and were forced to scrub the cell floor for long periods, and were assaulted and man-handled

7. Medical attention was grossly inadequate

8. Food was insufficient

9. Discharge of prisoners was unnecessarily delayed

10. Personal property of the prisoners was stolen.[4]

Stephens was eventually cleared of all the charges, but his reputation did not fully recover. In a typically robust defense, he addressed those who had accused him as being degenerates suffering from venereal disease. Because they were pathological liars, the value of their Christian oath was therefore doubtful. Charge number 3 was the one that would have wounded Stephens the most. The most important and unbreakable rule he instilled in the camp was that physical violence was not to be used under any circumstances.[5] His distaste for this approach was not on moral grounds but because he thought it was counterproductive to delivering results. It encouraged answers that the prisoners believed the interrogators wanted to hear and lowered the standard of information.

Camp 020 was not categorized as a prisoner-of-war camp, and the treatment of its prisoners was not bound by the Geneva Convention. It was not listed by the Red Cross and was overseen by the Home Office, which categorized it as a civilian or a criminal camp. During its existence, there were three escape attempts; all were unsuccessful. Despite the precautions made to prevent suicide, there were three known cases of prisoners trying to take their own lives. A Norwegian prisoner was the only one who succeeded, hanging himself on the night he arrived at the camp and prior to his first interrogation. Although physical force was not permitted, mind games were part of the methodology employed to break the prisoners.

Central to this was the infamous Cell Fourteen, which resembled George Orwell's Room 101 in his novel *1984*. It was a psychological bluff. Interrogators would threaten to send the prisoner to Cell Fourteen, which would on occasion lead to them breaking down and confessing their sins. The cell had originally been padded when Latchmere House was a psychiatric facility, but during the war the padding had been removed and it was like any of the other holding facilities. Its mythical power and the fear the utterance of its name aroused in prisoners made it a potent weapon that the staff were keen to employ against the enemy agents held in the camp.[6]

The main aim of Stephens and his men was to first prove the guilt of the prisoner and then to extract as much useful information as possible about the enemy and its intelligence network. There was a routine for newly arriving prisoners. Even as the ranks of the prisoners increased at the end of the war, no deviations from the normal process at the camp were permitted, not even for Walter Schellenberg, the most senior intelligence officer to be interrogated in Camp 020. As soon as the prisoner arrived in Camp 020, he was stripped and given a thorough body search. There was a full dental inspection, including of false teeth. On one search, a prisoner had been discovered hiding writing materials in a false tooth. Prison clothing was then issued and the prisoner was put into a solitary confinement cell.

Following a full medical examination and the taking of the prisoner's details, two photographs were taken. The first was of the prisoner wearing his new uniform, and the second, in civilian clothes. The latter photograph was used during interrogations with other prisoners to conceal the fact that the individual was detained at Camp 020. It was also to be used in the event of an escape for recognition purposes. Prisoners who confessed to their crimes remained at the camp and were treated in a reasonable manner, except for those who were sent to trial and possible execution. The death penalty was quite rare for prisoners who pleaded guilty. One Portuguese national who was tried and sentenced to death by hanging was saved by the intervention of the Portuguese government. The importance of Lisbon to the Allied war, espionage, and counterespionage activities meant that it was worth sparing the enemy agent's life to keep the Portuguese onside. Reprieves were granted from time to time for political and not legal reasons. They much angered Stephens, who believed that the enemy agents in his charge deserved to meet their maker.[7]

The modus operandi of the camp was that the first interrogation session was vital in breaking the prisoner. It was a standing-only session for the suspect as a panel of interrogators barked out questions, sometimes interrupting the prisoner midsentence or not waiting for a response. There was no good cop–bad cop routine but instead full-on verbal aggression, with frequent reminders that the death penalty would be imposed if the prisoner tried to mislead his interrogators. Toward the end of the war, the reputation of Camp 020 was well-known to Axis agents and there was little need for the panel of interrogators to make any threats. The intent was to create an atmosphere that resembled an inquisitorial courtroom without the niceties of the presence of a defense lawyer. Testimony from camp prisoners was used against others, with one asked to admit the charges made by the other prisoner or to refute them by making countercharges against his former colleague. Another tactic used with senior enemy intelligence officers was to house prisoners together and record them talking among themselves. It was a crude method, but it was surprising how many Germans were chatty. Exhausted by hours of interrogations, disoriented, and physically weak, the mind played tricks on several of the inmates who previously were savvy to such tactics. Many German agents had received training on how to counter interrogation, including ways to kill themselves. Few tried and even fewer succeeded at Camp 020.[8]

The arrival of Walter Schellenberg at Camp 020 represented an important moment for the Allied investigators. Here was the single man who had controlled most of the German agents held since 1940. Although he did not know their individual stories, he was responsible for the creation of the networks that put the agents in place. Schellenberg's attention to detail and knowledge of specific operations impressed the Allies. His willingness to recount the details of operations, providing lists of names, descriptions of how they were financed, and operational failures, surprised many. It was, however, his apparent lack of knowledge of British intelligence and its operations that most shocked his hosts. The German had little idea about British agents and showed he was unaware that some German agents had been turned by the British.[9] Although nobody mentioned it during Schellenberg's interrogations, the British breaking of the German communication system using the Ultra machine provided its intelligence services with a clear advantage over the Germans. They were able to verify whether the Germans believed the false information they were being fed by double agents. They were able to sense whether a British agent had been compromised and needed extraction from enemy-held territory or one of the neutral countries. The Germans enjoyed no similar insights, and this helped explain why the leading German intelligence officer appeared from time to time to be misinformed about a particular agent in the field or, at worst, a whole operation.[10]

Schellenberg believed that his transfer to Camp 020 was the part of the process of his debriefing that offered an opportunity for him to betray his enemies in Germany. He had prepared carefully for the end of the war, putting himself forward as part of a communication line between the Nazis and the Allies that ran through the office of Count Folke Bernadotte, a Swedish nobleman and diplomat. He had gotten in touch with the Swede while the fighting continued in the belief that he could secure a deal that would recast the war into one between the forces of the anti-communist West and the communist East. He had been received in good faith by Bernadotte, who had overseen his handover to the Allies in June 1945. Prior to arrival at Camp 020, Schellenberg had been treated with kid gloves. Both the American and British intelligence services were aware that their prized asset needed to be made to feel comfortable if he would provide the information they required.[11]

Discussions about whether he should be sent to Camp 020 at all were held. The British were in favor, believing that Stephens and his men had established a good record of persuading and coercing their prisoners to tell the whole truth and nothing but the truth.[12] The Americans were more skeptical, arguing that Schellenberg had indicated he was ready to explain in detail his role in the war and therefore the more direct approach of the British interrogators at Camp 020 was not required in this case. This division of opinion contained all the makings of another mini-crisis in inter-Allied politics until the American officials withdrew their objections. The lack of time available for the interrogations trumped concerns over allowing the British to run them. London insisted that it should have a good shot at Schellenberg but agreed to American input on the questions put to him.[13] Also, several other key Germans who were seen as Schellenberg's rivals were already being held at Camp 020.

The most prominent of these was the once-feared Ernst Kaltenbrunner, a man the Americans believed needed to be broken. He had served as the chief of the Reich Security Main Office (RSHA), which included the offices of Gestapo, Kripo, and Security Service (the Sicherheitsdienst des Reichsführers SS, called the SD), from January 1943 until the end of WWII in Europe. He was eventually executed following his conviction at the Nuremberg trials. It remained one of Stephens's greatest professional regrets that he was unable to break Kaltenbrunner in the short time the Nazi spent at Camp 020 before his presence was required in Nuremberg. The closest Kaltenbrunner's interrogators came to a breakthrough was by using blackmail. The German had become detached from his wife and original family but had taken up with a mistress with whom he'd had twins. He appeared concerned about the health and well-being of this second family and did provide small pieces of information in exchange for information about their whereabouts. But moments of cooperation were fleeting, and soon Kaltenbrunner hardened. He appeared resigned to his fate and refused to cooperate except in offering juicy tidbits of information about Schellenberg, whom he loathed.

Stephens hoped to use Schellenberg's and Kaltenbrunner's mutual disgust of each other to confirm the tales that the former head of intelligence promised to tell.[14] Playing one rival against the other was old school, but the British believed that it could produce results. With this in mind, Stephens gave orders that from the moment of Schellenberg's arrival he should be treated in the same manner as the other prisoners. This came as a great surprise to the German, who believed he would be having a friendly debriefing chat like the ones he had enjoyed with Allied officials in Sweden, where he was first taken for questioning prior to his transfer through Germany to England.[15] As soon as he entered the camp on July 7, 1945, Schellenberg was subjected to the same admission process that every other inmate had been put through. Much to his disgust and bewilderment, he was issued the ill-fitting prison uniform and his photograph was taken.[16] His spirits no doubt rose when he was then told to change back into his civilian suit, white shirt, and black tie and put on his raincoat and out-of-shape fedora. His headgear had taken a battering during his various transfers in Scandinavia and Germany. An additional two pictures were taken, from the front and from the side. The unshaven German looked decidedly angry in both of them.[17]

Huge amounts of paperwork had gone into preparing for the first of his several interrogations. The questions were divided into subsections that were defined by both geography and subject. An additional division of past, present, and future areas of interest was made. The interrogation would start with a chronological approach looking at his recruitment into the German intelligence services and his career progression. Questions were fed in to the interrogators from a wide range of British and American sources. While developing a clearer understanding of the past work of German intelligence was important, there was an equally pressing need to gather information about the present—and most pressing were the efforts of leading Nazis to exit Europe and take ill-gotten goods and money with them to South America.[18]

Different Allied agencies wanted to focus the interrogations on the parts of the testimony that were relevant to their assigned aims. The main distinction came between those investigators looking to the past and gathering knowledge to further Allied understanding of German intelligence during the war and those focused on the future. The past was important not only for the historical record but also potentially as evidence against leading Nazis awaiting trial in Nuremberg. The deep divisions between Nazis held at Camp 020 might be used to persuade one prisoner to give evidence and information on the other. Stephens and his colleagues enjoyed minor successes in persuading the otherwise uncooperative Kaltenbrunner to provide them evidence against Schellenberg. The latter was eager to do likewise against his hated rival by providing the Allies with a more detailed picture of Kaltenbrunner's activities and his role in the Holocaust than they had previously gathered.[19]

The Operation Safehaven personnel preferred to focus on the present and future. In 1945, American and British agents were working around the clock in neutral countries to prevent the most wanted Nazis from escaping Europe and transferring their assets to South America. In 1945, senior Allied intelligence officers suspected that the German exit from Europe was being conducted in an organized manner. Exit plans had been set in place to prepare for the birth of the Fourth Reich in South America out of the ashes of the Third. Argentina had been selected as the central hub for postwar Nazi operations. Officials from Operation Safehaven, as a result, believed that Schellenberg would be able to provide the Allies with information that could greatly assist them in their attempts to stop the Nazi regeneration efforts.[20]

Stephens and his men took an immediate dislike to Schellenberg. On one level, this was strange. The crimes he had committed were of a much less sinister nature than those of the thuggish Kaltenbrunner. Although nobody said as much, there was a degree of grudging understanding of Kaltenbrunner (respect would be an exaggeration). His scarred face and permanent angry expression indicated his commitment to the Nazi cause and his disdain for the Allies. His refusal to break under the fiercest of interrogations at Camp 020 further increased the sense that he was an ideologically motivated Nazi who was resigned to his fate. Schellenberg at Camp 020 was something of a VIP whose credentials and fame among the Allies had come from his peace-feeler efforts and his position as head of German intelligence.[21] The Americans were looking to the future and the likely onset of a confrontation with the Soviet Union. The information that Schellenberg said he was willing to supply would prove useful in any forthcoming cold war. But for the staff of Camp 020, this mattered little. Their job was to deal with the reality of World War II, not the hypothetical Cold War to come.

In the several drafts of the history of Camp 020, Stephens's hardline opinions were increasingly prominent over other authors'. Indeed, Stephens appears to have rejected earlier drafts of the history until he got the version that was most aligned with his own thinking and recollections. His flowery prose laced with hyperbole and strong opinions shows in the summary of Schellenberg's character:

> For a history of Schellenberg much vitriol is required. He was the henchman of Himmler, who made him the chief of Amt VI. In terms it was his

duty, if the word can be coined, to Himmlerise the German Secret Service. Schellenberg accepted the job, and it is true to his character that he disliked the master who fed him.[22]

The narrative then moves to an assessment of the German's character during his time at Camp 020 to gauge how truthful he was being during his interrogations.

> He was a traitor. . . . He contacted Bernadotte while the Germans were fighting and aped the role of a friend of the Allies. All he wanted to do was to save his own skin. In office he would be a vile enemy; in captivity he was a cringing cad. In office, he would ruthlessly cut down his opponents; in captivity he would ruthlessly betray his friends.[23]

From the moment of his arrival, Schellenberg did little to ingratiate himself to his captors. He went into a sulk, complaining about the conditions in the camp. He had not expected to be treated like a common criminal who had to wear a prison uniform, and he found the threatening tone of the interrogations unnecessary. He had, after all, promised to tell the Allies everything he knew about his time in German intelligence throughout the war.

The British considered his attitude to be disrespectful. There are undertones of anti-American sentiment in the assessment of Schellenberg. An extract from his case file, most probably based on Stephens's view, says the following:

> Schellenberg had ratted to the Americans after his failure in his opportunistic mission (peace feelers with Sweden). He was a priggish little dandy, fetched up rakishly at Ham with an assurance born out of extravagant promises in the field. He was shocked by his stern reception and sulked peevishly until he was brought face to face with the reality of British contempt for him and his evil works.[24]

Schellenberg's health was not good, which no doubt added to his sense of gloom. After he had returned from his mission to Portugal during the summer of 1940, doctors diagnosed a poisoning of the liver or gall bladder and could not discount the theory that this had been caused deliberately. The problem did not go away and caused him to seek pain relief treatment for the rest of the war. This brought him into communication with a key player in developing contacts with the authorities in neutral Sweden.

For much of the war, Schellenberg believed that he had been poisoned by British intelligence or the local Portuguese Secret Police.[25] No supporting documents from the British intelligence services mention any such mission against the German. A more likely scenario is that a fellow Nazi enemy tried to poison him or that his health problems had been caused by other factors. Regardless of the reality, it damaged Schellenberg's mental health and his workload capabilities.[26]

3

INTERROGATION

E VEN THOUGH SCHELLENBERG HAD AGREED TO TELL THE ALLIES EV-
erything he knew, verifying what he said was difficult. Interviews of
fellow Nazis at the camp and elsewhere were used to cross-reference and
fill in gaps in the information that Schellenberg supplied. This required
an enormous amount of coordination and cooperation among the Allies, and it was not always successful. Overall, however, the Allies soon
confirmed that Schellenberg was being truthful in his responses, albeit
evasive on some important details. He had few qualms about providing
evidence against fellow Nazis yet at the same time attempted to defend
those Germans to whom he remained loyal. His treason, the British argued, was studied and calculated. His testimony was not that of a desperate man in a state of shock. The opposite was true. He had been preparing
for this turn of events since 1941.[1]

"His judgement was mature,"[2] concluded the British after the first
round of questioning on his personal background and early career development. His detachment from the Nazi cause was clear. Though his
answers were by no means free of Nazi rhetoric and ideology, his understanding of the world reflected a more balanced and analytical perspective than that of nearly all the senior Nazis. The trials and testimonies of
the Nazi leaders at Nuremberg confirmed the cult-like status of Nazism

among those close to Hitler. This was largely absent from Schellenberg's testimony at Camp 020. For instance, at times he appeared to endorse the efforts of Himmler and at other times attacked the short-sighted vision of his commander.[3] "He disliked the master who fed him," the British noted down as he disclosed a typically long-winded explanation of how Himmler's caution and hesitation stopped his effort to secure an earlier resolution of the war.[4] To the last, Schellenberg blamed others for the failure of operations to which he was assigned: the 1940 plan to kidnap the Duke of Windsor was Ribbentrop's mad scheme and never had a chance of success; Himmler's plan to reach out to the Allies in Sweden started too late and did not succeed because he failed to engage with the process as early and fervently as needed.

Officials from Operation Safehaven waited expectantly for the details of Schellenberg's interrogation sessions to reach them. The program had been set up in 1944 once the Nazi defeat seemed both inevitable and imminent. Its main aim was to prevent Germany from financing another war in the foreseeable future. The objectives were divided into short- and longer-term ones. The short-term aims focused on identifying and locating German assets and blocking the transfer of these assets to neutral countries. The long-term aims involved persuading reluctant neutral countries to turn over German assets as war reparations. Safehaven was built on evidence gathered by Allied intelligence operatives that Germany was covertly transferring assets to neutral countries.[5] The Nazi intentions were clear: to escape war reparations and to aid a potential resurgence of the regime in the postwar period.

The director of the Foreign Economic Administration (FEA), Leo T. Crowley, initially proposed the ambitious project on May 5, 1944, when he sent a memorandum on the subject to the secretary of the Treasury, Henry Morgenthau Jr. Crowley followed up with another letter on May 17 suggesting an interagency program that included collaborating with British and additional US agencies related to the program's purview. From the outset, however, US interagency conflicts among the FEA, the State Department, and the Treasury caused problems, with each claiming responsibility and control over the program.

The Bretton Woods Conference, which took place in New Hampshire in July 1944, provided the legal base for the Safehaven program. The Bretton Woods Resolution VI, officially accepted on July 22, stated that neutral nations were to take immediate action to prevent the transfer and concealment of assets from Axis locations to neutral countries.

Although Safehaven was essentially a joint Anglo-American program, it was impeded from the beginning by strong rivalries between London and Washington over its scope and control. Behind the rivalry lay a deep-seated economic competition between the British and the Americans that influenced the policymaking of Safehaven. The British viewed it as an attempt by the Americans to develop economic control over Europe and potentially in the longer run to gain access to the markets of the British Empire. The Americans appeared far more committed to this cause than the British, who were less inclined to risk postwar relations with several of the neutrals over this issue. The American architects of Safehaven saw it as essentially a security-related program, but its emphasis soon shifted toward being a foreign policy–related effort. Central to this was an attempt by the State Department to push American diplomatic and economic influence at the expense of British interests. However, despite the British suspicions of US designs, there was a general consensus that the Nazis must not be allowed to continue their economic activities in the neutral countries, particularly those with pro-German sentiments.

Samuel Klaus, an American lawyer and one of the key brains behind Safehaven, was assigned to the FEA. The FEA was essentially the American equivalent of the British Ministry of Economic Warfare. Klaus focused on the economic details of Safehaven. A dynamic man, he became a frequent visitor to the European neutrals. In Lisbon, he focused on examining the reports the financial attaché James Wood prepared during the last year of the war. The American Safehaven team was largely drawn from the State Department, with the Office of Strategic Services (OSS) providing the intelligence evidence. The MEW led the British response with the Foreign Office, which remained highly skeptical about the whole operation, contributing from London and via its diplomats in the British embassies in the neutral countries.

The scale of the operation and the limited time in which it had to be achieved put great pressure on those charged with carrying it out, like Klaus. The end of the war in Europe increased the stakes. British, American, and French intelligence agencies reported a spike in the number of senior Nazis exiting Europe by way of Italy, Portugal, and Spain. They included Herberts Cukurs, a Latvian aviator and the deputy commander of the Arajs Kommando, which had carried out the largest mass murders of Latvian Jews during the war. It was clear that the war's end had officially halted state smuggling of capital, gold, and looted art out of the neutral countries. It had not, however, stopped the unofficial and private export of items such as gold coins, which were being smuggled into Portugal. Once in Portugal, the coins were sold for foreign currency (often Spanish pesetas that could be wired to Argentina by Basque-based banks). The Nazis, along with their local friends in neutral countries, significantly increased their efforts to get as much out of Europe before the Allies discovered and closed the exit routes.

Ian Fleming of British Naval Intelligence and Walter Schellenberg disagreed on almost everything bar one point: the strategic importance of the Port of Lisbon to both the Allies and the Germans. In 1941, Fleming sent a memo to his boss, Admiral Godfrey, in which he argued that Lisbon was the most important port in Iberia. Fleming had visited the city twice on the way to the United States on the Pan Am Clipper and spent time in London studying Iberian ports and their access to the Atlantic Ocean.[6] As the war progressed, Lisbon's connections to Brazil became increasingly important. Cargo ships routinely sailed between Portugal and its former colony as did passenger liners that linked Lisbon with Rio de Janeiro. Several of the ships made stopovers in the Portuguese colony of Angola, which provided an additional smuggling possibility.

During the initial stages of his interrogation at Camp 020, Schellenberg confirmed the importance of the neutral countries. As well as spending a great deal of time and effort in cultivating relationships in these countries, he had approved a vast increase in the numbers of German agents operating on the ground and provided what he termed generous budgets to help recruit agents. Initially, the German operations aimed to secure the continued supply of important raw materials from these countries for the war effort. The mineral wolfram from Portugal (and to a lesser extent Spain) and ball bearings from Sweden topped the German lists. Schellenberg admitted that a great deal of money was invested in the Portuguese Secret Police and other officials on the premise that they would not intervene in this German "export business." Locals were recruited to help continue the process of getting gold and looted art out after the war ended.

Schellenberg defended what sounded to his British interrogators like defeatism by arguing that the "sudden deterioration of the military situation in Germany in the last months did not allow the German leadership to develop any post-defeat plans." Although he added "every intelligent man saw it coming," nobody was allowed to support a policy of despair, and Nazi leaders punished any overt suggestion of defeatism.[7] Schellenberg claimed that formal discussions about the postwar were instigated among senior Nazis, including Himmler, only in March 1945, at which point the Russians were less than fifty miles from Berlin. Even then, when Schellenberg approached Himmler, the Reichsführer initially rejected any proposals in robust terms, stating that he did not want to be the first defeatist of the Third Reich.[8] But it was clear that individual leading Nazis were making plans to escape. The threat of being captured and put on trial by the Americans and the British or being executed by the Soviets was strong incentive. The major attraction of South America, notably Argentina, was the ease with which Germans and their capital could enter there. Schellenberg admitted that, although few were brave enough to make any institutional plans for the postwar, in private it was a topic that took up many Nazis' attention during the last few frantic months of fighting in Europe.

Schellenberg's comments about the lack of postwar planning among the top Nazis was met with widespread cynicism among Allied officials. The situation on the ground seemed very different from the picture that Schellenberg painted during his interrogations. Of great interest to the Allies was the system that he had left in place in the neutral countries in the event of a German withdrawal or defeat. Though Schellenberg claimed German intelligence had no specific postwar plans for Portugal, Spain, Sweden, and Switzerland, there were, however, *I-Netze*—intelligence networks—set up in the first three countries. These groups were supplied with money and technical equipment such as radios to be employed in the event of a German withdrawal from that country. Personnel were recruited locally to staff them. Their training was minimal, and Schellenberg admitted that the project was beset by major problems. The quality of the people involved was generally not high. Many were unsuitable to the line of work and several lost interest over the years that they were employed.[9] One of the biggest problems was that several members of the network spent the money allocated to them on improving their lifestyle. The purchases of cars, apartments, and other goods raised the suspicion of the local authorities and the Allies. On several occasions the Americans and the British were able to turn members of these networks into double agents.

Schellenberg appeared obsessed with what he charged were the systematic failings of the Germans operating in Portugal.[10] But theirs was not a complete failure. The Germans had secured the services of many locals who aided them with the exodus of goods and personnel from Europe. American and British agents cataloged the extent of German operations in Lisbon during the war, several of which were related to the smuggling of goods. Indeed, one of the first conclusions of Operation Safehaven was that the Germans were extracting gold and looted art from Europe in large volumes from 1943 onward. But, in Portugal, the war was viewed as two distinct phases: from its outset until Operation Torch (the Allied operations in Morocco and Algeria) at the end of 1942, and from the start of 1943 onward. To the Portuguese, the Germans likely would emerge victorious in the first phase and the Allies in the second. Unsurprisingly, the Portuguese provided much more support for German aims during the first phase of the war, when they looked more likely to prevail.[11]

Surprisingly, Schellenberg appeared more distrustful of the Spanish than of their Iberian neighbors. This should not have been the case. The seemingly close ties between Berlin and Madrid were born out of the Nazi support for the Nationalists in the Spanish Civil War. General Francisco Franco leaned much more toward the Axis side than did his Portuguese counterpart, António de Oliveira Salazar. The German embassy in Madrid was heavily staffed during the civil war, and intelligence gathering was at the forefront of its operations. There was much speculation the Spanish would eventually be pressured by Germany into joining the global war. To forestall such a scenario, the young Ian Fleming worked to produce Operation Goldeneye, an Allied plan that prepared various sabotage operations in anticipation of an alliance between Franco and the Axis powers. The Allies believed that the Spanish could be used by the Germans to bully the Portuguese into continuing to supply wolfram to the Third Reich. The possibility of a Spanish invasion of Portugal, backed by German air power flying out of the South of France, was a major threat to Lisbon for much of the war. Like Portugal, Spanish ports enjoyed close links to South America, in particular to Argentina. The Allied navies shadowed Spanish shipping, and intelligence agents were stationed at all the major Spanish ports in the south and in Bilbao in the north. Spanish authorities such as police officers, civil servants, and customs officials were open to bribes, but not on the same scale as those in Portugal.[12]

Internal German politics was at the heart of Schellenberg's preference for Portugal over Spain. The number of *I-Netze* in Spain was high at forty-one, but he questioned their quality.[13] Many of the Spanish-born German agents operating in Spain did not answer to Schellenberg and were widely regarded as close to the Falangist hardliners in Spain. The Falangists were to the right of Franco and called for a greater Spain, one that included Gibraltar and Portugal. Madrid remained a stronghold of German commercial interests, many of which had been built up prior to the outbreak of WWII, and several of these networks would prove useful as the Germans exited Europe at war's end. The individuals involved often enjoyed access to the highest political authorities in Spain, who provided them with the necessary cover and even documents to assist the Nazi exodus from Europe.

4

STOCKHOLM FOG

SWEDEN WAS A VERY DIFFERENT CHALLENGE FROM PORTUGAL AND Spain, both for the Allies and for Germany. Schellenberg's testimony to the Americans prior to his arrival at Camp 020, along with evidence provided by other captured Nazi officers, indicated that the Swedes had not permitted the country's ports to be used for the export of German capital and personnel to South America. But this was not strictly true. Some Germans with strong business ties to Sweden attempted to remain there and integrate themselves into local society. Others exited Europe from Swedish ports on ships bound for Iberia and then onward to South America. Like Portugal and Spain, Sweden was a hotbed of intelligence and counterintelligence operations and Nazi trading in an important ore, with the Jewish question never far from the national debate. Unlike its two Scandinavian cousins, Norway and Denmark, Sweden was not occupied during the war and made a fortune trading with the enemy. It was also a favorite haunt of Schellenberg, who worked hard from 1942 onward to develop contacts with Swedish leaders, diplomats, and businessmen.[1] During his interrogation sessions at Camp 020, he was happy to go into detail on these contacts and the events that led him to try to broker an end to the war.

Schellenberg made clear to his questioners at Camp 020 that Germany's relationship with Sweden was strong and multidimensional. The arrangements between Berlin and Stockholm forbade any Nazi intelligence operations against the Swedes. Officially, this broke down only in the last few months of the war, when Schellenberg had cautiously authorized several missions connected with both anti-Swedish activities and the setup of new *I-Netze* groups that would focus on protecting German assets in the country.[2] The Swedish government had discovered and terminated previous attempts to set up these networks.[3] The absence of anti-Swedish intelligence operations was not a concession by Berlin but reflected a lack of need for them. The Swedish business elites held pro-German sentiments, and several companies were keen to continue their lucrative export business with the Nazis throughout the war. German intelligence still openly operated in Sweden during the war, but its duty was to observe and undertake espionage and counterespionage activities against the Allied spies operating in the country.[4]

The main star of this important story is the Swedish capital city of Stockholm. Known as the "Venice of the North," the city is built on fourteen islands. Stockholm's dark, poorly lit alleys and central shopping areas were the scenes of espionage vital to the outcome of WWII. Winston Churchill eloquently summarized the importance of Sweden in the first volume of his history of the war, *The Gathering Storm*:

> German war industry was mainly based upon supplies of Swedish iron ore, which in the summer were drawn from the Swedish port of Luleå, at the head of the Gulf of Bothnia, and in the winter, when this was frozen, from Narvik, on the west coast of Norway. To respect this corridor would be to allow the whole of this traffic to precede under the shield of [Swedish] neutrality in the face of our superior sea power.[5]

Churchill's assessment of the importance of neutral Sweden's iron ore (and ball bearings) to the German armaments industry was quite correct. Without the constant, plentiful supply of ore, the German war machine would have ground to a halt and the fighting would have stopped much earlier.[6]

The Swedish government argued that if it did not sell iron ore to Berlin, in all likelihood Adolf Hitler would invade Sweden and take it by force.[7] The Allies also understood the importance of preventing the delivery of iron ore and launched several daring military missions to sabotage the supply routes along the Norwegian coast and to Germany.[8] The supply of iron ore to Berlin, however, was merely the tip of the iceberg when it came to Sweden's murky wartime role.

Stockholm was an open city, one in which secret agents of both the Allies and the Axis powers operated in and around its international hotels. The Hotel Grand, perhaps the most prestigious five-star establishment in the city, was used as a base by major spies. The British Special Operations Executive (SOE) was extremely active, employing the city as a center for its agents, who were on missions to destroy the iron ore supply routes to Germany. Axis spies looked to damage Allied efforts and pumped out propaganda, with the intention of convincing Swedes that it was in their best interest to throw in their lot in an anti-communist alliance/pact with Nazi Germany against the Soviet Union.[9]

After the United States entered the war, the Office of Strategic Services (OSS), the British Secret Intelligence Service (SIS, also known as MI6), and the SOE increased their presence in Stockholm, turning their attention to using Swedes for spying missions into the heart of the German industrial lands.[10] On the ground, cooperation between British and American intelligence agencies in Stockholm was far from perfect, but they shared the goal of obtaining information about the locations of vital German war industries to help the Allied bombing campaigns inflict as much damage as possible on the Nazis' ability to keep fighting. The bombing of German industry was viewed as an essential component of Allied attempts to end the war as quickly as possible. There was a strong American community in Stockholm, some members of which were key industrialists in the country. The espionage games created many interesting personal narratives, not least that of the superspy Eric Erickson, played by William Holden in the Hollywood film *The Counterfeit Traitor* released in 1962.[11] Erickson, an American-born Swede involved in the oil business, was pressured by Allied intelligence to adopt a double life, trading with leading Germans while gathering vital information about the German industries and armament factories.[12]

The Americans persuaded Erickson to give the appearance of having strong pro-Nazi sentiments. Being in the oil-exporting business in Stockholm, he was soon contacted by the Gestapo, who were keen to introduce him to suitable German industrialists and to arrange business trips to Germany for him. German stocks of synthetic oil were running out after being sabotaged and bombed, so Erickson suggested a massive synthetic oil production industry be created in Sweden that would supply the Germans. During his many visits to Germany to help set this up, Erickson met with senior Nazis, including Hermann Göring, who introduced him to Himmler.[13] Both Hitler and Himmler approved the ambitious plan, and Erickson was duly granted permission to visit key German industrial sites and meet key German industrialists. During these visits and meetings, Erickson carefully noted down the location of each refinery in Germany.

Each refinery was subsequently bombed in 1944 and then bombed again a few weeks later to cause havoc to the German repair attempts. During one of the bombing raids on the Leuna plant near Merseburg, the Allies inadvertently bombed the building next door to the refinery. Unbeknownst to the Allies, the Germans were using that building for experiments aimed at creating an atomic bomb. After the war, Allied sources suggested that the bombing put the Nazi atomic program back some eighteen months, by which time the war had ended. As for Erickson, at the end of the war, General Dwight Eisenhower lauded him for having played a vital role in helping defeat the Germans. He was also honored by President Harry Truman.[14]

The German invasions of Denmark and Norway had left Sweden at the center of Allied and Axis activity. Divisions within British ranks over how best to manage the Swedes dominated the initial debates in the months following the German invasion. The British ambassador in Stockholm, Sir Victor Mallet, who was close to the British royal family (he was godson to Queen Victoria), pleaded with London not to let the SOE sabotage the area for fear of offending the Swedes.[15] Mallet sensed strong pro-German sentiments among the Swedes and feared that any

British military action would lead to an increase in pressure for Sweden to back the Germans.

From the outset, leading Swedish industrialists viewed the war as a golden opportunity to maximize profits through trade with the Germans. At the time, there appeared little to stop them doing this. There was no blacklist (or proclaimed list, as the United States termed it) that the Allies would use to bar trading with companies and individuals who traded with the Axis powers. Such lists came much later. Naturally, the Germans were keen to exploit trade with Sweden in key areas. Hitler dispatched groups of leading German industrialists to visit Stockholm to develop ties with Swedish industry. He also ordered existing German companies operating in Sweden, such as Krupp AG and Bayer, to expand operations.[16] The key to the trading relationship with Sweden, however, lay in Germany's need for iron ore; its military-industrial complex was totally dependent on it.[17] At the onset of the war, other supply routes for the Germans had dried up, and German planners made the maintenance of the two supply routes from Sweden to Germany an absolute strategic priority. The Germans were even willing to pay Sweden inflated prices for the ore, particularly after their successful invasion of the Low Countries. At this point, the Germans started to pay for the ore with coal exports, currency, and, later, gold bars looted from the central banks of Holland and Belgium.

As soon as Churchill became prime minister, Britain increased pressure on Sweden. Prior to assuming the premiership, Churchill had argued that a neutral country was de facto maintaining the ability of the German war machine to continue fighting.[18] In Stockholm, Churchill's charge was rejected; Swedish leadership, led by the wily and experienced prime minister Per Albin Hansson, argued that Germany was bullying Sweden into continuing with iron ore delivery. By this time, the British were already staging military operations against the supply routes.[19] They judged the most militarily vulnerable of the two trade routes was the overland rail route to Norway used in winter, and then onto ships along the Norwegian coast. The boats carrying the ore were careful to stay within protected Norwegian territorial waters.[20] The Royal Navy shadowed many of the convoys, waiting to stop any of them that strayed into international waters. The game of cat and mouse was a source of great frustration for Churchill, who wanted the supply of iron ore to Germany completely cut off.[21] Operating in Stockholm and using Swedish contacts, members of the SOE were able to identify the timing and amounts of the iron ore deliveries, as well as the route chosen for delivery to Germany. The Allies, despite several military operations, could do little to prevent the iron ore from reaching Germany.

As well as tracking the iron ore, American and British spies gathered information on another key German-Swedish issue. Following the successful invasion of Denmark and Norway, the Germans demanded support from Sweden in allowing their armed forces access to the Swedish railroads to transfer troops back and forth to and from Germany. In a clear violation of its neutrality, Sweden agreed to this demand but tried, unsuccessfully, to keep the existence of the "sealed trains" a secret. The trains were originally meant to transfer only wounded German troops, but it soon became clear that this was simply not the case. By the time the transit agreement ended in August 1943, some one hundred thousand sealed railroad cars had transported over a million German military personnel from Norway to Germany and a slightly higher number in the opposite direction.[22]

The most difficult moment arose in June 1941 when the Germans requested that the entire 163rd Infantry Division be transferred from Norway to Finland on its way to the Eastern Front. The division was combat ready and was allowed to pass through Sweden with all its light and heavy weapons. The request became one of the most controversial moments in the war. The Social Democratic government of Hansson agreed to the request but tried to hide behind the mist of a political situation known as the "Midsummer Crisis." There was little dissention in the government over allowing the German unit to pass. Most of the ministers were sympathetic to the German attack on the Soviet Union.

While the Swedish leadership appeared immune to any moral dilemmas over maximizing the country's war profits, another issue did pose moral questions for the country: the Jews. During the nineteenth century, Stockholm proved to be something of a Scandinavian hotbed of anti-Semitism. Prior to WWII, many Swedes, including members of its ruling Social Democratic Party, argued that the values espoused by the Nazis were healthy and mirrored those of the Swedish national identity. Even the early racial anti-Jewish policies of the Nazis were not altogether rejected by the Swedes. During the war, however, the rescue of and granting of asylum for nearly eight thousand Danish Jews as well as several hundred Norwegian Jews by Sweden helped save them from deportation to Nazi concentration camps. Because German *Schnellboots* (fast boats) patrolled the straits between Denmark and Sweden, the Jews had to be expertly ferried across by Danish fishermen, who took great risks making the crossing in darkness.[23] Much of the credit for the Jews' escape was claimed by the Swedish government, but Sweden's heroism was mainly on an individual basis and did not come down to the state. Most of the Jewish refugees were taken in and adopted by Swedish families. Later, with the war clearly going against the Germans, the Swedes embraced a more active role in trying to rescue Jews. Raoul Wallenberg, a Swedish businessman and diplomat, carried out a mission to Budapest that no doubt saved as many as a hundred thousand Hungarian Jews. By creating a series of Swedish diplomatic safe houses in the city, his team, which numbered several hundred, prevented the Nazis from deporting the Jews to concentration camps.[24] But it was unclear the extent to which Wallenberg was acting on his own initiative rather than under instruction from his superiors at the Swedish foreign office.

A Swedish diplomat with links to the Swedish king, Folke Bernadotte, Count of Wisborg, had originally been chosen to lead the rescue mission in Hungary, but Hungarian rescue groups rejected his appointment on political grounds, arguing that he had links to the Nazis. Instead, Bernadotte was issued a visa by the German legation in Stockholm in the spring of 1945 that allowed him to travel to Berlin, where he met with Walter Schellenberg. During the final months of the war, Bernadotte acted as the negotiator with Schellenberg and later Himmler for a rescue operation transporting interned Norwegians, Danes, and other Western European inmates from German concentration camps to hospitals in Sweden.[25] Folke Bernadotte was an ambitious man. He viewed himself as an important messenger and was made to feel so by

Schellenberg and Himmler when the three men met in Germany in April 1945. Schellenberg was seeking without the knowledge of Hitler to make a separate peace with the West and viewed the Swedish aristocrat as the best man to relay the message via Stockholm to the Americans and the British. Given the state of the war, the mission was hopeless from the start. Bernadotte later claimed he understood that the Western powers would probably not agree to a separate peace, but he duly passed the message on.[26]

At Camp 020, Schellenberg disagreed that the April peace mission was doomed and argued that the outreach he and Bernadotte worked on should have been embraced by the Western Allies. He viewed it as a historic mistake that he and Bernadotte were ignored. He also made the point on several occasions that Bernadotte was extremely committed to the process, believing it could end the war. Indeed, in his diary, Bernadotte outlined in detail his efforts with Schellenberg and Himmler and the conditions he had demanded for going to the headquarters of General Eisenhower with the message, the key one being Himmler's announcement that he would replace Hitler as the German leader.[27] The interrogators at Camp 020 were skeptical: they saw Schellenberg as motivated by self-preservation and thought Bernadotte was an "amateur Swedish diplomat."[28]

During the final frantic months of the war, as a total Allied victory with the unconditional surrender of Germany appeared the most likely scenario, Sweden offered as much help to the Allies as possible.[29] Although they did not have to deploy their forces to the liberation of Denmark or Norway, the Swedes offered the Allies strong logistical support. US planes were allowed to use Swedish airbases during the operation to liberate Denmark. Training camps for the resistance movements in Denmark and Norway were openly operated in Sweden. The Swedes did commit to helping with the liberation of Norway, but as events unfolded this proved to be unnecessary. Swedish intelligence cooperated with the Allies and allowed them access to intercepted German radio communications. It was low-risk assistance.

Churchill's comment that the Swedes had played both sides of the war for profit irked the Swedish government, but Churchill knew what he was talking about. It is telling that many Nazis, including Walter Schellenberg, regarded Sweden as a reliable trading partner of Germany and a potential future strategic partner in the fight against the Soviet Union. Moreover, most Swedes were pleased with the wartime performance of their government.

5

DONOVAN VERSUS MENZIES

As the Nazis fled Europe, the race to capture them was hampered by divisions among the Allies and, specifically, their intelligence services. Much of the focus fell on administering justice to those leading Nazis who were already in custody over devoting resources to chasing those on the run. Although this appeared a sensible distribution of Allied resources, it allowed numerous Nazis to slip through the net and make their escape to South America. The American Office of Strategic Services (OSS) was particularly wrapped up in the efforts to bring captured Nazis to justice. With the postwar future of the intelligence agency still in doubt, the peacetime stakes were just as high as the wartime stakes. The OSS wanted to remain relevant to its political masters in Washington. This became an even greater imperative following the death of President Franklin D. Roosevelt and his replacement by President Harry Truman. The latter was seen as much less supportive of a longer-term intelligence role for the OSS and its leadership. The OSS, as a result, needed quick and high-profile wins to bolster its case for continued existence. At the same time, its wartime record, particularly in the neutral countries, came under greater scrutiny, forcing it to go on the defensive. This was an unfamiliar situation for the OSS, which was better known for being on the offensive and seizing the moment with its operations.

Over the summer months of 1945, William Joseph Donovan, the head of the OSS, was in Germany, there to help prepare for the Nuremberg trials. He wanted the OSS to play a key role in the prosecution of Nazi leaders. The Americans and the British had initially been lukewarm about the establishment of a war crimes trial, and for the court to become a reality it had come down partly to Donovan's efforts in convincing President Truman. The heads of the American and German intelligence services could not have been more different personalities. Whereas Schellenberg was cautious, Donovan had acquired a reputation for being impulsive and gung ho, hence his nickname "Wild Bill."

In Sweden, Donovan and his OSS agents had set out to learn about the Nazis' commercial and intelligence activities in Sweden and across Scandinavia. The German occupation of Norway and Denmark increased the strategic importance of Sweden to America and Britain. Intelligence gathering, however, was not their only task. Donovan wanted his agents to watch the activities of the Soviet Union in the area. In the last year of the war, the OSS's emphasis had already started to shift away from anti-Nazi activities toward a greater monitoring of Soviet actions and, where necessary, counterespionage operations against Moscow.[1] The Cold War had not been declared publicly, but the intelligence services were acting as if it had been. Naturally, this shift impacted the effectiveness of Operation Safehaven. In short, the intelligence wars between West and East started before the end of the conflict with the Nazis.[2]

This was not the only problem facing Allied intelligence agents trying to uncover the Nazi ratlines and exit methods. Donovan had fallen out of favor with his British counterparts, including the head of the SIS (MI6), Sir Stewart Menzies.[3] Winston Churchill placed great trust in Menzies; the two men met over fifteen hundred times during the war. Having Churchill's ear increased the influence of Menzies, who enjoyed near total power over British intelligence gathering. He did not tolerate opposition and regarded the Special Operations Executive formed in 1940 to conduct espionage and sabotage operations in Europe as a bunch of dangerous amateurs. It was his low opinion of Donovan, however, that caused the greatest problems to political and intelligence cooperation between Britain and the United States. At heart, Menzies was an English aristocratic snob who filled the SIS with likeminded men from similar backgrounds. His selection and vetting processes for his agents came spectacularly unstuck after the war, when it was discovered that one of them, Kim Philby, was a Soviet agent. Philby had been the head of the important Iberian Desk during WWII, and his staff had included the writer Graham Greene and the journalist Malcolm Muggeridge.

Menzies operated the SIS with great caution. A deskman, he rarely left England during the war. One exception was a trip to Algiers, the timing of which coincided with the assassination on December 24, 1942, of François Darlan, the Vichy military commander who had defected to the Allies in Algeria and with whom Eisenhower and the United States had been negotiating.[4] The British, however, distrusted Darlan. Menzies's involvement in the killing was privately acknowledged in British intelligence circles. This type of mission was not typical.[5] Cautious, thorough, and rarely moving unless he had adequate political cover—normally, from Churchill in person—Menzies was a strategic calculator. He liked to play out scenarios in his head and enjoyed the expression "read the book to the end." Outcomes and their strategic impact on the war were what interested him. Understated but ruthless and detached, he was often mistaken for arrogant. Fools were not tolerated and rivals who got in his way were dispatched with careful precision.

Relations between him and "Wild Bill" Donovan would never be easy on a personal or professional level. Menzies's cautious nature was in sharp contrast to Donovan's visionary zeal and desire to seize the moment. Menzies, without saying as much, regarded his Allied counterpart as another brash American who could do as much harm as good. For his part, Donovan thought Menzies belonged to a bygone era. Both men had fought and been wounded in World War I, but Donovan believed that Menzies was still fighting that conflict. The newly created OSS that Donovan led in WWII was trying to prove itself. It wanted to find a role that would be converted into a postwar intelligence service that Donovan hoped to lead. Like with all new intelligence services, there were growing pains.

Mistakes were made in Lisbon and Madrid that led one American general to charge that OSS agents were "a menace to the nation." In

Iberia, the OSS was out of its depth against a massive German, Italian, and Japanese intelligence presence. The Japanese were resourceful, their agents posing as tie salesmen, and they provided the Americans with a great deal of false or out-of-date intelligence materials that were of little use to Washington.

Menzies and his British agents operating in Portugal and Spain agreed with the critical analysis of the Americans. Playing catch-up to the British, the Germans, and the massive number of Italian agents who had been operating in the city since 1939, the OSS struggled to make a positive impact. Difficulties between the SIS and the OSS in Iberia and the rest of the neutral countries compounded the lack of coordination in informant sharing. Often, an informant in Lisbon would share different versions of information with the SIS and the OSS, thereby doubling his own financial rewards. This was an even more important tactic in Spain, where chronic food shortages led to massive hikes in the cost of living. Seasoned informants in Lisbon and Madrid soon cottoned on to the initial lack of verification checks by the OSS; agents got much better at verification in the final months of the war. Until then, it was a free-for-all, with information being sold that was of little use. Naturally, this situation greatly infuriated Menzies, who viewed it as a sign of the naivete of the American agents and a sideshow to the important work of the SIS.

All these problems would have been resolvable if not for the more serious ideological differences and varying agendas of the Americans and the British. Schellenberg noted that, on this level, the Americans were much closer to the German intelligence aims than the British were.[6] Here Donovan had a much more future-facing, global perspective than his British counterpart. For Menzies, the SIS, and Churchill, the war was predominately about preserving the British Empire. The global trading empire on which the sun never set had served British national interest. Life without it was unimaginable. It was what made the war worth fighting and dying for and would be preserved at all costs in the postwar order. Donovan, however, thought the empire was a bad idea, an obstacle to democracy and economic development. If Britain's colonies and dominions were to be included in the West's coming fight with communism, then they needed their freedom. Failure to decolonize, in Donovan's view, could make these countries vulnerable to the allure of revolutionary overthrow by communist-supporting groups.

As Schellenberg had discovered from his chilly reception at Camp 020, American intelligence was much more interested in looking at alternative German regimes to Hitler than the British, who favored an unconditional surrender. Menzies went along with efforts to find alternative German leadership without ever believing the efforts would prove fruitful. Donovan devoted a great deal of time and energy to discovering Germans who might challenge the ruling elite. He was much more interested in the peace feelers that Schellenberg offered in 1945.[7] The British regarded them as an attempt to split the Allies and to strengthen the Nazis' position in any negotiations with London and Washington. Menzies recalled the efforts of the Italians to surrender in Lisbon during the summer of 1943 and cross sides to fight for the Allies. The Italian army had dispatched two separate Italian delegations to Portugal to make contact with the Allies with the offer.[8] The result was a furious row within the Allies' ranks over how best to respond. Divisions arose internally in the United States, with Donovan more interested in considering the project and Eisenhower less inclined. In London, the offer led to a rare example of a tussle between Churchill and his foreign secretary, Anthony Eden, with the former wishing to explore the Italian offer and the latter rejecting it. On this occasion, Eden's arguments about the impracticality of the offer trumped Churchill's visionary strategic thinking to explore it further. After the dust settled and the two Italian delegations returned home, the prevailing sense among the Allies was that the proposal had largely been intended to confuse and divide them. Menzies, as a result, was always on the lookout for similar attempts; so, Schellenberg's peace feelers had been received coolly in London.

Relations between the SIS and OSS were strained to the point that Menzies forbade the Americans to carry out intelligence work in any of the nations that belonged to the British Empire. This was a redline that Donovan, for one, found very difficult to abide by. Menzies also barred the OSS from having any contact with the governments in exile in London. Despite the British efforts to limit the scope of American intelligence operations, at the time of D-Day on June 6, 1944, over eleven thousand American agents were operating across the globe in all the major cities of the war. Events on D-Day confirmed the different leadership styles of Menzies and Donovan. The American crossed the English Channel, and he and his commander of covert operations in Europe, Colonel David Bruce, landed in Normandy under heavy German fire.[9] Trapped on a beach, both men noted they had forgotten their cyanide capsules. Donovan joked that if they were captured, he would shoot Bruce first as he was the senior officer.[10] Both eventually got off the beach and joined up with American forces under the command of General Omar Bradley. Quickly transported back to Washington, Donovan met with President Roosevelt and provided him with a field agent's report on the degradation of the German air force and navy, along with the reduced morale of German soldiers in Normandy. Menzies did not actively participate in operations across the Channel; even if he had been fit enough and had wanted to do so, Churchill in all probability would not have authorized it. Menzies was too valuable an asset to risk his falling into enemy hands.

Another area of difference between the SIS and OSS was in their efforts to infiltrate the Catholic Church in the neutral countries: the Americans were more active in recruiting priests as informants. Key figures in the Catholic Church came to play an important role in aiding the German ratlines. Much of the focus on the church was in Italy, where the Vatican allegedly aided several Nazi officers to evade Allied justice. But the Catholic Church, central to life in Spain and Portugal, was a significant challenge to the Germans, too.

German intelligence reports indicated that the Catholic Church was an even bigger obstacle to good relations with Germany in Portugal than in Spain.[11] The church in Portugal was recovering from the period of Republican Portugal (1910–1926), which was characterized by strong anti-clerical policies, including attacks against the church and the seizing of its assets. Salazar, who came to power in 1932, had reversed these policies, placing the church firmly back at the center of Portuguese society. A church in every village and town became a central feature of his regime. Leaders of the church enjoyed a return to political influence. The only factor that was missing was the money. The church, as a result, was on the lookout to improve its financial portfolio, and this point was not lost on Donovan and his OSS agents.

During the war, Donovan authorized the use of priests as informants for the OSS without telling the pope. The network was originally confined to Italy but soon reached Iberia and helped provide key information to the Allies. The perception among church leaders was that, after the success of Operation Torch at the end of 1942, when the Allies landed in French North Africa, an overall Allied victory would follow. This change in the Allies' military prospects helped alter the attitude of key church figures. But it did not alter the political sympathies of many in the Catholic Church. The head of the church, Pope Pius XII, was the king of flexible neutrality. He remained largely silent on the treatment of Jews in Nazi-occupied Europe, and when he eventually spoke out, his statement was deemed not to have been a strong enough condemnation. He half-heartedly supported alternative regimes to the Nazis. He believed the major enemy of humankind was communism and focused his efforts in making it clear that support for communism was incompatible with Catholicism. Widely regarded as a racist, he asked that the Americans not deploy black soldiers when they liberated Rome.[12] Donovan met with the pope in late 1944 and helped shore up the church's public support for the Allied cause. By this stage, the war was heading to an Allied victory, and the friendly meeting of the two men was not surprising. The pope told Donovan to pass along his best wishes to President Roosevelt, whose reelection he supported.

During the meeting with the pope, Donovan did not mention the extensive network of priest informants he had set up. This network proved useful not only during the war but also in the immediate aftermath, helping the Allies track and trace individual Nazis. Father Felix Morlion, codenamed "Blackie," ran one of these OSS-sponsored networks. Even prior to US involvement in the war, Morlion had angered the Gestapo by running a publication that focused on anti-Nazi propaganda and had correspondents in several European countries. He ended up in Lisbon in 1940, where the Portuguese authorities allowed him to continue his work. His propaganda was anti-communist and anti-Nazi, and fitted well with the political outlook of the regime in Portugal.

In September 1941 Morlion departed Lisbon after spending months trying to secure passage to New York on an ocean liner. He feared that the Germans were about to invade Portugal, and his intelligence was based on good sources. Germany did have plans to invade that year but eventually decided against it. Portuguese compliance in supplying wolfram and the German invasion of the Soviet Union earlier in the same year reduced the urgency of attacking Portugal. After his arrival in New York, Morlion founded an information center. By 1944, his activities were funded by the OSS; his network gathered reports from across Europe and handed them to Donovan and the OSS. Much useful information was gained, even though many of the correspondents had no idea that they were in effect working for American intelligence.

British connections to the Catholic Church were much less close. Menzies preferred to use SIS connections with the business and political elite and to let money do the persuading. Since the outset of the war, the British had worked hard to keep Spain—officially a nonbelligerent—from shifting toward joining the Nazis. British intelligence and diplomatic efforts focused on using the British Empire's tried-and-true formula of offering incentives to the Franco regime. The biggest of these backhanders was the supply of bribes to Franco, the generals, and key business leaders in Spain. Millions of pounds were transferred from London through Lisbon and ended up in the bank accounts of the principal personalities of the Franco regime. The first transfer of over half a million pounds took place on June 21, 1940, and was authorized by Winston Churchill, who had become prime minister in the previous month.[13] The aim was clear: to show the leaders of the Spanish regime they would financially benefit from keeping their country out of the war. The payments were made regularly, with agreements put in place as to how the transfers would be hidden.[14] By the end of the war, the British had spent $13.5 million US (over $275 million in 2023) bribing Francoist officials to keep Spain out of the war.[15]

Another inducement was the supply of grain to Spain. Its food shortages had been caused by the Spanish Civil War, and it was not self-sufficient in food staples. The British allowed grain to be imported, bypassing the British naval blockades of Iberia. The import of grain helped stabilize the country and prevented increased calls for foreign intervention. Sir Samuel Hoare, the British ambassador to Spain, banned the SOE from operating in the country for fear of offending General Franco and limited the remit of SIS agents. (Despite these limitations, Menzies and the SIS ran an effective and highly motivated set of agents based in Madrid. Hundreds of local informants were on the books of the British and, as in Lisbon, offered information albeit of inconsistent value.)

But the British and the Americans did not have Spain to themselves. The German intelligence operations run out of Madrid were impressive. German agents developed and leveraged networks with local Spanish officials who aided the Axis campaign. Despite this, Schellenberg confessed during his interrogation in Camp 020 that he was frustrated by the effectiveness of the German intelligence operations in Spain.[16] In the final months of the war and in the postwar period, Spanish officials proved themselves to be more unreliable for the Germans than their counterparts in Portugal. Customs officials at Madrid airport were prone to opening crates and asking for documents from departing Germans. This occurred despite many of them being on the German payroll. At Spanish ports, in the last days of the war, inspections were stepped up; although it was possible for Germans to export goods and personnel from Spain, it was riskier than going through Portugal.

As part of the terms of Operation Safehaven, British and American diplomats requested Prime Minister Salazar allow the Royal Navy to board ships leaving Portuguese ports, but he had refused, adding that any attempt to board ships would be viewed most unfavorably by his government. In 1943, Salazar reluctantly agreed to let first the British and then the Americans use a strategically important airbase on the Azores in the Atlantic Ocean. President Roosevelt and Winston Churchill had worked hard to secure this important concession.[17] Use of the airbase was vital to the supply of American military equipment for D-Day and the final year of WWII. American and British diplomats and intelligence agencies agreed that the airbase would also serve as an important air bridge at the end of the war. The likely need to build up the American garrison in Europe to prevent the Soviets from expanding their spheres of influence in Eastern Europe westward would require continued access to the Azores. Both the British and the Americans, as a result, were aware that this was not a good time to "irritate the wily dictator" in Lisbon. The result was that ships leaving Portugal bound for South America were not stopped by the Royal Navy or escorted to Gibraltar for inspection of cargo holds. Likewise, passenger liners crossing the Atlantic were rarely subject to interventions or checks on passenger identities.[18]

Crucially, the Germans appeared aware of these facts and that is why so many of them were willing to make the longer trip by road, rail, or plane to reach Portugal than to leave Europe from Spain. Despite the presence of hundreds of Allied agents in the city, Lisbon was deemed safer. Besides, within the upper echelons of Portuguese society there remained widespread sympathy for the German cause. This manifested in the close commercial contacts several families enjoyed with the Germans. In private, at family gatherings, pro-German sentiments were openly expressed without fear of reproach. Additionally, Salazar had chosen to ignore the plight of the Jews in occupied Europe, dismissing the question as an "internal issue for the Third Reich."[19] Several of the aristocratic pro-German Portuguese families had close connections with counterparts in Spain (both extended family and business contacts) and with people close to the regime of General Franco. The upper classes in Portugal had supported the Nationalist cause during the Spanish Civil War. They came to see that war as a conflict against communism and anarchy. They viewed WWII through the same ideological prism. In their eyes, the lasting enemy was the Soviet Union and its desire to export communism across Europe and eventually all over the world. In practical terms, the upper classes in Portugal were willing to use their large country retreats to house both Nazis based in Portugal and those coming from further afield. The local secret police, the PVDE (Polícia de Vigilância e Defesa do Estado), proved willing and able to issue new papers to those Nazis who requested them. Several Germans, however, felt secure enough in the country as the war came to an end to not even request new papers. They stayed in plain sight.

The Germans' efforts to ingratiate themselves with the Spanish upper classes were not as successful. In Madrid, Schellenberg concentrated German operations on counterintelligence against the Allies and their activities in Spain. Although he visited Spain on several extended trips during the war, Schellenberg never really understood the regime or the country, which he came to regard as backward and corrupt. The Germans did not realize how big were the bribes the British were paying to the Spanish regime to remain out of the war and to not engage in anti-Allied activities. Schellenberg had, however, noticed the differing attitudes of the Americans and the British toward General Franco and his government during WWII.[20]

On Spain, Menzies and the SIS followed the political lead set at the start of the war by Neville Chamberlain and continued by Churchill. The key man in Spain was Sir Samuel Hoare, a relic of the era of British appeasement who had been made ambassador to Spain in compensation for missing out on a bigger political or diplomatic position. A part of the English aristocratic set, he was educated at Harrow and Oxford, where he was a member of the Bullingdon Club. His mission in Spain was to prevent a slow or a more dramatic drift toward Germany. In public, Hoare tried to charm Franco and his associates. In private, he was party to the scheme of bribing key members of the Spanish elite to remain out of the war. On a personal level, he found Franco severely lacking in political, diplomatic, and social skills. He much preferred Portugal's Salazar, whom he admired as a man of principle. Hoare understood his brief and worked hard not to give Franco an excuse to cozy up to the Germans.

The fallout from Operation Torch, the Anglo-American invasion of French Morocco and Algeria during the North African Campaign of WWII, which started on November 8, 1942, was handled nimbly by Hoare. He managed to prevent Spain from using the moment as an excuse to move to the German camp. It was viewed as a vindication of his policy of gentle persuasion laced with financial inducements. The reality was much more complex and later developed into a war of words between Hoare and David Eccles, the head of the Ministry of Economic Warfare in Iberia. Never a fan of Hoare, whom he viewed as vain and weak, Eccles suggested that the successful handling of Franco was down to Salazar rather than Hoare.[21] Winston Churchill had gone on one of his numerous charm offensives with Salazar to help persuade the prime minister to remain out of the war. Details of Salazar's meetings with Franco, usually held on one of the border towns between the two countries, reveal that Salazar passed on the message from Britain and that Franco was reminded of what London expected of him.[22]

However, in offering Menzies and the SIS limited room to maneuver in Spain, and with the SOE barred for all operations, Hoare severely limited the efforts of British agents to infiltrate Axis operations in Madrid. During the final months of the war, this hindered British efforts linked to Operation Safehaven and other operatives from monitoring or preventing the large numbers of Nazis coming through Spain to exit Europe. From an Allied perspective, this represented a missed opportunity. Most Germans who were apprehended were caught on vessels stopped by the Royal Navy, not lifted off the streets of Madrid or one of Spain's active ports.

At Camp 020, Schellenberg talked of Spain as a missed opportunity for German intelligence, as well, during the war. He struggled to reconcile why the Nazis' large investment in agents and injections of cash failed to produce the level of results that he had expected.[23] Menzies, more pragmatic, viewed Hoare's diplomacy as having achieved its wartime aim, but nonetheless key members of the British team in Madrid, such as Eccles, believed that Britain could have pushed harder and got better results. Franco, in short, had skillfully disappointed both the Germans and the British.

Madrid proved to be a problem station for Donovan and the OSS, too. Initial jubilation following a successful operation to steal Spanish codebooks soon evaporated because of many setbacks. On top of this, a major turf war ensued between the American ambassador in Madrid, Carlton Joseph Huntley Hayes, whom President Roosevelt had appointed to Spain in 1942, and the OSS. Initially, all was fine. Hayes and Donovan were old college friends and both agreed that Spain had become a location of great strategic importance for the Americans.[24] Once Operation Safehaven began, though, relations deteriorated. The ambassador believed that the sixty plus agents the OSS had dispatched to Madrid were not up to the job: they were "amateur cowboys" who had little idea of their remit or of intelligence-gathering techniques.[25] He reported back to the State Department in Washington that many of the agents' top-secret reports had been lifted from the pages of the Spanish press. Defensive of his agents, Donovan accused the ambassador of forgetting why he was in Madrid and of cozying up too much with General Franco. Hayes, he charged, had forgotten that his job was to deter the Spanish leader from siding with Germany even when a German defeat seemed assured. Events on the ground placed a further strain on the relationship between the two men. The ambassador learned in the spring of 1943 that OSS agents had been in contact with Basque separatists in the north of Spain in an attempt to infiltrate them into France. Local OSS leaders had believed it was worth the gamble. Hayes, however, sent off cables to Washington expressing his dismay at the attempts, citing General Franco's demand that the United States not engage with Basque separatist groups.[26]

The anger was not a one-way street. OSS agents, including their station chief in Madrid, Jack Pratt, known by his code name "Silky," found US Ambassador Hayes personally and professionally irritating.[27] To Pratt and the other OSS agents, Hayes seemed out of touch with the world. They argued that he was a hands-on manager whose style suffocated the work of the agents. The ambassador failed to understand that this work involved hosting large parties and handing out large amounts of cash to local informants in exchange for information, even if that information was not always accurate. Also, the Basque issue did not go away. The OSS refused to cede to Hayes's demands to cut all contacts with the separatists. To push back against the OSS, Hayes then set up his own intelligence network run by the military attaché in the embassy. He hoped in bypassing the OSS that he would secure more reliable intelligence without running the risk of offending the Spanish authorities. Cooperation between the two groups was nil. The inevitable clash followed soon after when Hayes wrote to Washington demanding that the OSS stations be closed and his group given sole responsibility for espionage activities in Spain.[28]

The demand reached the Joint Chiefs in Washington, who summoned Donovan to present his case in defense of the OSS. Donovan's report was carefully prepared and contained a mixture of regret—"Madrid is our greatest difficulty"—and combative counterpunching—assertions that the ambassador was more interested in developing closer ties with the Franco regime than in countering Nazi influence in Madrid. The Basques were portrayed as a vital part of American strategy in Spain. It was noted that they would fight the Nazis if the Nazis invaded Spain in addition to undertaking missions against German targets in occupied

France. The Joint Chiefs ruled in Donovan's favor: the OSS operations in Madrid would stay. In their verdict, they did, however, offer him a stark warning in which they noted that many of the ambassador's complaints were justified. This amounted to the first official censure of the head of the OSS.

The American problems in Madrid were similar to the British tensions in the city. What prevented a total breakdown of SIS and OSS operations in Spain was the political support that Menzies enjoyed from Churchill and Donovan from Roosevelt.

During the last months of the war, when German efforts to export their ill-gotten gains from Europe gathered momentum, Allied operations in Spain improved but still fell short of the levels of efficiency that Menzies and Donovan demanded. Germany's main obstacle in Spain was Spanish officials intent on retaining control over the export of German goods.

Schellenberg claimed throughout his interrogations that German intelligence knowledge of the SIS and OSS was minimal. He had little understanding of the political restrictions that the organizations were operating under in the neutral countries.[29] He took little interest in the turf wars between the Americans and the British (or, indeed, the internal conflicts between the British SIS and SOE). For the Allies, his ignorance provided them with an undeserved advantage. Had Schellenberg understood the divisions among the Allies in Madrid at the end of the war, he might have advised his fellow countrymen to make for Spain much earlier than many did. For Germany, the Spanish route was an underexploited opportunity at the end of the war.

6

OPERATION SAFEHAVEN

Tensions within the Allies' intelligence-gathering appara-
tuses, at both the agency level and the national level between the
Americans and the British, impacted the effectiveness of the Allied pursuit of Nazi war criminals and their treasures and Operation Safehaven.
This was not the only problem. During the war, the Allies asked the
neutrals to comply with key requests that clearly favored the Allied side
and that jeopardized the neutrality of those countries. These requests
were hugely unpopular in the neutral countries because they heightened
the chances of German retribution or even full-scale invasion, nowhere
more so than in Portugal, where Safehaven was seen as a step too far
with very little chance of success.

A clear indicator of Operation Safehaven's problems lay in its paperwork. The operation generated thousands of memorandums, reports, ap-
peals to leaders in neutral countries, and interdepartmental arguments.
The bureaucracy connected with the operation was enormous. Officials
felt compelled to write up all their thoughts, plans, and actions. This
group of super-bureaucrats, led by officials such as Samuel Klaus, were
chasing ruthless, rule-breaking Nazis who would stop at nothing to escape. As a result, Safehaven operatives effectively failed to tighten the
noose around the Germans. Playing permanent catch-up, the Allies were

a step behind the fleeing Nazis, arriving a day too late or missing key points altogether.

By the spring of 1945, as the Allies celebrated victories on the battlefield, the fast-approaching end of the war should have increased the Allies' power to force agreement from the neutral countries for stricter operational enforcement. Instead, the opposite happened. Portugal led the way.[1] The British ambassador in Lisbon, Ronald Campbell, asked for a meeting with Portugal's leader to discuss the implementation of Safehaven, but Salazar brushed him off, saying that he was busy dealing with internal Portuguese matters.

When Salazar did consent to meet, Campbell found him in a combative mood with little interest in agreeing to Allied demands. Salazar reminded the ambassador that he had taken a huge risk in allowing the Allies access to the Azores airbase without requiring the necessary reciprocal security guarantees of Allied protection should the Germans take that as a provocation and invade. Instead, Winston Churchill had evoked the ancient bilateral treaty of 1373 in the House of Commons. (The United States diplomat, George Kennan, who had conducted the American side of those negotiations, initially promised Salazar security guarantees, but President Roosevelt had subsequently walked them back.) "Old friends: oldest allies" was how the British ambassador tried to woo Salazar, noting further that the Germans had taken next to no action in response to Portugal granting Allies access to the Azores. No matter, Salazar retorted, the risks had been enormous and the Portuguese had not been adequately rewarded. He then highlighted how Portugal's choice to remain neutral in the war had been based on its lack of ability to militarily defend itself if attacked. He blamed this weak position on Britain's failure to sell Portugal weapons in the 1930s despite endless requests. Speaking slowly, the ambassador provided the rationale that Salazar already knew: Britain did not have any spare weapons to sell.

An astute diplomat, who was regarded by Anthony Eden, UK prime minister in the 1950s, as one of the finest servants of the Foreign Office of his generation, Ambassador Ronald Campbell moved onto the offensive and tried to focus Salazar on the mechanics of Safehaven.[2] He pulled out a balance sheet showing the estimated profits Portugal had made on the sale of wolfram that had been put together by the Lisbon SIS desk in conjunction with their OSS counterparts.[3] Campbell merely mentioned the word *wolfram* when Salazar raised his hand and said that he did not care to hear anymore lectures from the British. "We have stopped selling wolfram to the Germans despite having contracts to continue to do so," he said without raising his voice, but his tone was nevertheless threatening. "You stopped sales on the eve of D-Day, and not before," Campbell responded coolly. The diplomat went on to remind the Portuguese leader that Portugal had continued to sell wolfram to the Germans despite personal pleas from Roosevelt, Churchill, and President Vargas of Brazil to stop.[4] Wolfram, or tungsten, was a vital metal alloy used in anti-tank weapons and machine tools. But Salazar would have none of it and emphasized to Campbell that Portugal had also sold wolfram to the Allies. The trade with Germany had been a legitimate wartime activity, the income from which belonged to Portugal. This was the crux of the problem for the Allies and Operation Safehaven: the neutral countries' insistence that their trade with Germany was legal and payments made should not be returned.[5]

Campbell then discussed the issue of the Nazi gold with the Portuguese leader. From 1941 onward, Portugal had demanded payment in gold for the supply of wolfram. The Allies, Campbell reminded him, regarded the gold as property stolen from the banks of Nazi-occupied Europe and from the Jewish victims of the Holocaust. Salazar regarded the origins of the gold as irrelevant to the legality of the deals for wolfram. Insisting that he regarded the treatment of the Jews as an internal issue of the Third Reich, Salazar made it clear that he would not cooperate with any Allied efforts to convince Portugal to hand over the gold, as stipulated in the terms of Safehaven. An equally pressing issue in the Allies' view was securing cooperation from the neutral countries over war criminals. "The justice of the victors," Salazar called it sarcastically, before outlining the deep legal problems in defining the term "war criminal." For Salazar, so-called justice for war criminals amounted to an unnecessary sideshow, and he advised Campbell to transmit to London the need to focus on the present and the future. This was code for the call to galvanize efforts to deal with the communist threat in the East and prevent it from taking over the whole of the European continent. The threat, Salazar added, extended to Portugal, where the local opposition was dominated by communists with ties to Moscow.

Before Campbell departed, he recalled a story that he regarded as an important sign of Portugal's essential good intentions toward the Allies. Salazar had refused to accept the credentials of the new German ambassador, who had been appointed to succeed the veteran Hoyningen-Huene, who had been recalled (along with the other ambassadors in neutral countries) in 1944. Salazar regarded the nominee as little more than a Nazi thug. It was a strange case that threatened to develop into a major diplomatic incident. The Foreign Office regarded it as a sign that Salazar was positioning himself and Portugal in the winning camp. The Portuguese leader let Campbell know through unofficial channels—the banker Ricardo Espírito Santo—that he would not allow prominent, high-profile Nazis who sought to do so to remain in Portugal permanently. SIS agents in Lisbon, however, pointed out that this did not inhibit leading Nazis transiting through Portugal on the way to Brazil and eventually Argentina. The Portuguese escape route from Europe remained firmly open to all Nazis who could secure the relevant documentation and onward passage on a liner out of Lisbon.

In Spain, Allied diplomats argued similar points, pointing out that the country needed to be seen as on the side of the Allies. The British ambassador, Samuel Hoare, felt uneasy about pressuring the Franco regime too much, claiming that his policy of appeasing the Spanish had produced positive results. Though sympathetic to the lofty aims of Safehaven, the ambassador believed there was little chance of persuading Spain to implement the operation's key points.[6] Networks of German and Spanish military personnel had existed since the Spanish Civil War. Nationalist and Nazi officers had remained in contact, and many of the former were deeply sympathetic to the efforts of the latter to transit through Spain to Portugal or to use Spanish ports to reach Argentina.

Initially, the Spanish refused to cooperate with Safehaven, contending that its remit impinged on issues of national sovereignty. Although this was not a wholly unexpected development, it caused a great deal of concern among officials in London and Washington. The OSS regarded

Spain as the most likely European host for a resurgence in Nazi fortunes. The fear was that leading Nazis would decamp to Spain, where they would be allowed to live and work unhindered by the Spanish authorities. This in turn would lead to the Nazis developing a European power base from which they could prepare for a return to Germany. This assessment was simplistic and not wholly plausible. For a start, the majority of the pro-German members of the regime in Spain leaned toward the Nazis because the Nazis were the most powerful military force in Europe, not because they were Nazis. As the prowess of the German war machine faded, Spain, like its Iberian neighbor, looked more to the Allies and the postwar era. Madrid did not want to be politically and economically isolated on the European continent. But agreement to implementing Safehaven would represent a major political tilt, and Spain was not ready to make it in 1945. After the war, as the United States increased pressure on the country by suggesting that it should be diplomatically isolated, Madrid slowly warmed to Safehaven. On November 3, 1948, it eventually agreed to return around one hundred tons of Nazi gold. This move was seen as vindication of America's efforts to apply strong pressure.

One of the central aspects of Safehaven was dealing with German assets in neutral countries. Though a complex issue, in Portugal and Spain it was seen as a priority. The British SIS believed that Nazis attempting to hide from the authorities in Portugal could use German companies based there as cover. Salazar had been somewhat sympathetic to Allied requests to seize German assets and close German businesses. As the war came closer to a conclusion, the Allies upped the pressure to comply with this demand and others. On March 22, 1945, after a tense late-night meeting with Campbell in the prime minister's office in Lisbon, Salazar issued a law that froze any movable property that was confirmed as looted.

The Allies heightened the pressure on Portugal on May 7, a week after Hitler's death and a day after V-E Day, providing a list of specific demands attached to Safehaven. On this occasion, the Portuguese consulted with both the Americans and the British before passing a decree a week later that complied with nearly all the Allied demands. The decree meant that German assets in Portugal were to be frozen, a census was to be set up to help locate these assets, and the currency exchange between Lisbon and Berlin would also be frozen.[7] These good intentions, which were set out in law, pleased the officials working on Safehaven, who viewed them as a sign of Portuguese acceptance of the new political realities at the end of the war.

They were wrong. Implementation of the new laws was painfully slow. The local authorities offered only limited cooperation. The optimism that had followed the decree was soon trailed by the realization that Salazar might have hoodwinked the Allies into a false sense of belief that Portugal was on board with Safehaven. Events on the ground in Portugal confirmed that business with the Germans was continuing, with German companies handing over management to local Portuguese and registering their businesses in Lisbon.[8]

Leading German corporations such as I. G. Farben, Siemens, AEG, and Roechling that operated large subsidiaries in Portugal, along with other less well-known enterprises, tried to avoid seizure of their assets.[9] Several of the larger companies also owned shares of Portugal's cork harvesting, communications, transportation, and, even, film industries. The Allies estimated these investments at $5 million (in 1945 dollars). There were also German investments in Portuguese colonies, mainly in Angola, that were valued at $2.5 million. Around $5 million in personal property and real estate was owned by Germans in Portugal.[10] Several German property owners attempted to transfer ownership of houses to local Portuguese in case they would be seized by the state.

Adaptability was the key policy as Salazar moved to minimize the consequences of a German military defeat in the Portuguese economy. The war had been good for Portugal, and in government circles disappointment that it was coming to an end appeared. The government also wanted to ensure that the country's gains were not surrendered at the demand of the Allies. Salazar had navigated carefully through the war, playing one side against the other, and he was intent on using all the diplomatic cards at his disposal to make sure all his fence-sitting had not been in vain. In Spain and the rest of the neutral countries, the Portuguese policy of initial compliance but little implementation of Safehaven was lauded as a commonsense approach to a difficult situation. General Franco congratulated his Portuguese counterpart on this careful diplomatic strategy, and even the British ambassador in Lisbon wrote to the Foreign Office suggesting that London should not push Portugal any harder on Safehaven for reasons of future good relations between the two countries.

Equally worrying for the Allies was the cover the financial networks in Portugal provided for German smuggling operations. Every ship leaving Lisbon bound for Africa or Brazil presented an opportunity for the Germans to get goods out of Europe. Salazar made it clear that the part of Safehaven that he was least convinced about was the section that tried to define war criminals. He challenged the Allies to come up with a clear and workable definition. Despite the best efforts of officials in London and Washington, he remained skeptical of both the term and the legality of using it to prevent alleged war criminals from entering and transiting through Portugal.[11] The policy of the Portuguese security police, the PVDE, remained consistent at this point. Intervention and arrest took place when foreigners tried to intervene in matters directly related to the country. All non-Portuguese people were required to register their passport details with the police and complete a location document at the hotels where they stayed. This, however, was not strictly enforced if the person was staying at a private residence or attached to one of the embassies. The police chief reported to Salazar personally and presented a weekly report on the movement of key foreigners in the country.[12]

An early indicator of the problems that lay ahead for the Allies in enforcing an anti-Nazi policy in Portugal occurred near the end of the war. The former German ambassador to Portugal, Baron Hoyningen-Huene, asked for permission to return to Portugal to retire in Estoril. The British did not regard Hoyningen-Huene as a war criminal. Indeed, Ronald Campbell paid tribute to him after his departure as a "worthy opponent." He had almost single-handedly built up German–Portuguese diplomatic, economic, and cultural ties during the prewar period and during WWII.[13] The British viewed him as part of the old German diplomatic school that predated the Nazis. While serving in Portugal, he was mostly seen wearing civilian attire, donning his Nazi uniform only for official events.

The OSS were much more critical of Hoyningen-Huene, precisely because he was the de facto leader of the German community in Portugal.

Much of this group had remained hidden during the war, living in country retreats and not socializing with the local Portuguese society. There was much local gossip about the workings of the Germans and their businesses. Rumors spread of senior Nazis visiting to give talks and drop off looted art, gold, and currency. In Lisbon, the separation between German society and local Portuguese made it difficult to verify these claims, but in 1945 several unrecorded flights did arrive at both the Lisbon airport and the airstrip in Sintra (which was Lisbon's main airport prior to 1942). The Americans believed that Hoyningen-Huene could become a potential leadership figure and an organizer of Nazi efforts to get out of Europe.

Salazar weighed the merits of the case carefully, as he did every decision between the Allies and Axis powers. Because Hoyningen-Huene was not on any wanted list by the Allies and the British did not object to his presence in Portugal, his decision was straightforward. He gave Hoyningen-Huene permission to retire to Portugal and granted him permanent residence, provided he agreed not to undertake any further professional duties. The British did not protest, and the Americans felt it rather trivial in the end to lodge a strong formal objection. Disappearing from the public gaze, Hoyningen-Huene spent most of the rest of his days in Estoril, enjoying his morning promenade along the coastline to Cascais. He remained in contact with many of his wartime friends, mainly Portuguese, and was very much welcomed in the local bridge clubs of Estoril and Cascais. Salazar viewed the postwar conduct of the former ambassador as vindication of letting him remain in the country.

The case of Hoyningen-Huene was not without ramifications. The ambassador, as well as being the de facto leader of the German community in Portugal, was responsible for the building of the large vault in the German embassy in Lisbon. Until his replacement in 1944, he had been at the center of German–Portuguese wolfram trade and the negotiations that determined whether the payments would be made in gold. His connections stretched far beyond diplomatic circles in Portugal. He was known to have close ties with leading Portuguese bankers (not just Ricardo Espírito Santo) as well as the large German commercial community in the country. He had cultivated his relationships carefully and was widely regarded as an astute player who saw little problem in aiding Portuguese companies to profiteer from the war. Portuguese business leaders viewed him as the best route to securing commercial and banking deals with the Third Reich. Initially, at least, they appeared to care little about potential Allied threats of retaliation. Even after the success of Operation Torch in late 1942, trade organized through the German embassy in Lisbon continued to flourish. The Germans were good payers and settled their bills on time; the Portuguese admired both qualities.

When questioned by the Allies after the war about his time in Lisbon, Hoyningen-Huene talked openly about the details of his official duties. He claimed to have been surprised when Salazar ended the sale of wolfram to Germany on the eve of D-Day. Given Portugal's ancient alliance with Britain and the closeness of the two countries' past relations, he believed he had succeeded in creating a strong pro-German sentiment among leading Portuguese people. This could have been even greater if it had not been for Berlin's poorly timed interventions on key issues, which created an impression of bullying. The Portuguese, he conceded, were pro-British in culture and politics, but pro-German in the commercial arena. In retrospect, this is an accurate assessment. But what was absent from his questioning was any in-depth discussion of the unofficial trade that took place in Portugal during the war. He was asked nothing about the contents of the vault in the embassy and the gold bars and artworks that were said to be held inside it. There was no mention of the auctions in Lisbon and Germans' sale of looted goods at these events, goods ranging from jewelry stolen from Jewish victims to so-called degenerate paintings previously owned by Jews. The Allied investigators, while seemingly well prepared on the nuts and bolts of the major events and key issues of the war in Portugal, appeared ignorant, or uninterested, in anything else. Even though Hoyningen-Huene had been replaced before the German exit operation in Lisbon gathered momentum, he had helped put in place a lot of the contacts and intelligence needed to facilitate such an eventuality. For Operation Safehaven, the failure to properly question the ex-ambassador represented another missed opportunity.[14]

While Safehaven officials focused their efforts on gaining support from the political leaders such as Salazar and Franco, on the ground things were moving fast. SIS and OSS agents worked hard to catalog German activities but struggled to keep up with the pace and scale of events as the war ended. During the spring of 1945, the auction houses were extremely busy. The previous year had been quieter for both public and private auction businesses in the city. Most of the Jewish refugees who could had already passed through Lisbon on their way to the New World. Sales had reached a high in late summer 1940 through the end of 1943. During this time, the unofficial price of diamonds, gold, silver, and other jewelry had fallen sharply because of the spike in supply. The price of artworks was depressed in every category of art. Desperate refugees sold everything they could to secure berths on an ocean liner, where ticket prices had increased tenfold since the start of the war. Those ultra-rich refugees who preferred the Pan Am Clipper service to New York were forced to raise even greater amounts of money.

The Lisbon auction houses saw a spike in business again at the start of 1945. This time, however, mainly Axis personnel attended the sales. At first, it was predominantly Italian families doing the selling. The Germans were reluctant to attend public or private auctions in person. Instead, they used official and unofficial brokers to deliver the goods to sell. Although there were no official connections between the German embassy in Lisbon and the auctions, several personnel from the legation were reported as attending the sales. Few records exist of these events. The Portuguese authorities viewed them unfavorably as tax avoidance schemes and havens for the sale of stolen property. The police, however, did little to investigate or intervene. There were two reasons for this lack of activity: many private auctions were held in the houses of people in the upper echelons of Portuguese society, and most of these people had close connections with the Salazar regime.

7

COLLECTORS

THE NAME RICARDO ESPÍRITO SANTO APPEARS MANY TIMES IN THE documents related to Operation Safehaven. Although Espírito Santo was a central participant in the wolfram trade between Portugal and the Third Reich, opinions about his political leanings differed among the Allies. In the months following D-Day, American suspicions of Banco Espírito Santo (BES) increased. Agents supplied evidence confirming that the financial transactions of the wolfram trade continued despite Salazar's official announcement of its ending.[1] These were payments for preexisting orders and deliveries but created the impression that the bank was continuing to profit from sales.[2] The British used Espírito Santo as a means of taking the temperature of his good friend, Salazar. On several occasions the British ambassador Ronald Campbell passed messages to the Portuguese leader through Espírito Santo.[3] London opposed blacklisting BES as a company that would be punished for trading with the Germans. The Americans, who had their own blacklist, were keener.[4]

Ricardo Espírito Santo was a leading banker by day and a passionate collector of artworks and antiques by night. Although Safehaven officials were obsessed with unraveling the complex web of the wolfram trade and the trail of Nazi gold, they largely overlooked the extracurricular activities of many major business leaders. Espírito Santo was not involved in the purchase of stolen artworks and antiques. He did, however, like many others, purchase parts of collections at low prices from distressed sellers. His collection, which he left to the Portuguese state following his death on November 2, 1955, remains one of the most important in Lisbon. The banker was not interested in what the Nazis called "degenerate art."

At the end of the war, in April 1945, Espírito Santo was stopped at the border between Spain and France. The *Times* of London reported the incident on June 16, stating that Espírito Santo had been detained and only released after paying a fine of 250,000 pounds—an enormous sum.[5] The story was not truthful, and Espírito Santo sued the newspaper, which was eventually forced to print a full apology on October 5, 1946, following an out-of-court settlement.[6] The banker had been briefly detained by the French, who then also offered an apology. It was a nonstory. Espírito Santo made regular trips by car to Paris to buy art and antiques for his collection. But the fake story from the *Times* led to a run on the bank in Lisbon when several leading clients (mainly Spanish) withdrew their money.[7] This was the exact intention of whoever planted the story. The story illustrates the vulnerability of people like Espírito Santo to gossip and rumor about their business. In private, he blamed rival bankers in Lisbon for the false story.[8] The other Lisbon-based banks stood to benefit from acquiring the business that Espírito Santo's bank lost.

Another seemingly legitimate art collector in Lisbon during WWII was the Armenian, Calouste Gulbenkian. During the war, the Allies held deep suspicions about his financial dealings and art collection. He remained in Lisbon until his death on July 20, 1955. Gulbenkian's demise helped to transform Lisbon's art scene and led to the construction of the museum to house his world-class collection. It was a hugely important development for a city that had previously lacked any such venue, in contrast to its Iberian neighbor, Madrid. Gulbenkian had made his money in the oil business. At the time of his death, his fortune was estimated to be worth between $500 million and $1 billion (in 1945 dollars). A definitive figure was lacking because of his secretive accounting, which carried on well after his death. Most of his wealth was used to set up a foundation based in Lisbon. He was an avid collector of the arts, and his collection, which originally was kept in a private museum in his home in Paris, was considered to be one of the finest in the world.

He had first arrived in Lisbon in 1942 after leaving German-occupied Paris. According to his son, Nubar, his initial strong preference was to go to Switzerland, but Nubar had urged him to head for Portugal instead.[9] Nubar argued that Lisbon had a better climate, had more "creature comforts," and, unlike Switzerland, was not encircled by hostile countries.[10] In other words, if the need ever arose, the family could always escape to the United States by boat.[11] Nubar was something of a fan of Lisbon and, over the years, spent a lot of time in the capital. He wrote of the city:

> I enjoyed my visits to Lisbon both during and after the war. Before the city began to spread, the countryside was near at hand for hacking; the air is beautiful, the view from the hills overlooking the Tagus estuary and the sea, magnificent. I enjoyed too the highly cosmopolitan company, including that of so many of the exiled royal families of Europe.[12]

Once installed in Lisbon, Calouste Gulbenkian stayed in the Hotel Aviz; his wife, who preferred the sea air of Estoril, took a suite at the Hotel Palácio.[13] *Life* magazine interviewed Gulbenkian in November 1950 for a detailed article entitled "Mystery Billionaire":

> His art collection includes not only paintings but Egyptian sculpture, Persian carpets, rare manuscripts, medals, tiles, tapestries, porcelains, jewels, enamels and miscellaneous objets d'art, in many of which his collections rank as the world's best within their divisions. As one leading art expert had said, "Never in modern history has one man owned so much."[14]

While in Lisbon, Gulbenkian continued his two lifelong passions: making money and collecting world-class art. The latter was more easily available during WWII because of the number of distressed Jews who were willing—or had no choice but—to sell all or part of their collections to help fund their escape from Europe. For these reasons, Gulbenkian acquired several works from the National Gallery in London that were owned by Baron Henri de Rothschild. According to Allied sources, he made three payments to Rothschild that totaled 1,335,000 escudos ($54,200). Though viewed as legitimate purchases, the timing and the relatively low price paid for the artworks raised some concern among the Allies. Rothschild had run out of money in Lisbon and was desperately trying to finance a rather luxurious lifestyle. Most of Rothschild's assets had been seized in France and his cash flow problems in Lisbon became chronic. He approached Espírito Santo to see whether the bank would extend him a loan. Eager to help Rothschild, whom he had befriended in Lisbon, Espírito Santo did what he could. He even raised the Frenchman's case with Salazar to see whether the Portuguese state could offer any additional help. The short-term fixes soon proved insufficient. The artworks in London were one of the few assets that Rothschild could access, and the terms of the sale were quickly arranged with Gulbenkian. The dealer was said to be very happy with his acquisitions. The deal was typical of the times. Among the art Gulbenkian purchased were a pastel by Quentin de La Tour, two Lépiciés, and a Nattier, all of which were portraits, along with a Jasper ewer mounted in gold.

Gulbenkian continued with an aggressive series of opportunistic purchases from around the globe. From his suite in the Hotel Aviz, he spent the afternoons working the international phone lines talking to his contacts around the world. No opportunity for making money was missed. He appeared on the Allies' radar after he attempted to sell his 2 percent stake in the Reichsbank. He cited the reason for the sale as his desire to meet his personal and business needs in Portugal. In reality, he was nervous about holding the stock while based in neutral Portugal. The Allies put the value of the potential sale of shares at 3 million marks. On this occasion, London warned him about his conduct. SIS agents based in the British embassy in Lisbon were deeply suspicious of his dealings, but because the British authorities were unable to put together compelling evidence of wrongdoing on his art purchases, the British Treasury focused its efforts on looking into his complex financial dealings.

After the war, the Americans seemed to welcome Gulbenkian and his family into the fold. The start of the Cold War transformed him, in their eyes, from a shady businessman and dubious art operator into a strategic asset for the Western powers. In an era when the importance of oil was never greater, he suddenly found himself to be a man in great demand. A typical example of this new cooperation occurred when Gulbenkian learned from his son that the plane carrying the crown prince of Saudi Arabia to the United States for his first official visit had been diverted to Lisbon because of engine trouble. As the plane was fixed, the crown prince and his large party checked in to the Hotel Palácio in Estoril, where they remained for two days. Gulbenkian, his son, and the American ambassador headed straight to the hotel to meet the Saudi party. During the impromptu meeting, the discussion moved from recalling old deals to outlining potential new ones. Later the American ambassador hastily arranged a formal welcome dinner for the crown prince at the ambassador's residence. Because it was the weekend, US military and naval attachés had to be hauled off the golf course at Estoril and ordered to return to Lisbon in formal military dress to attend the dinner. Both Gulbenkian and his son, Nubar, were present at the meal when the crown prince offered the ambassador a gold-crusted dagger as a gift.[15] Always the collector, Gulbenkian's eyes lit up when he saw the dagger, but he could not prize it away from the ambassador's firm grip.

Salazar saw a great deal of potential in allowing Gulbenkian to remain in Lisbon after the war finished. The Portuguese fiscal authorities offered him generous concessions on several taxes related to his business. At the center of Salazar's strategy of inducements was his long-term vision that Gulbenkian would be a useful asset for Portugal in both the financial and the art worlds. There is an adage in Portugal that it is easy to invest your money in the country but very difficult to get it out. Looking to the postwar era, Salazar was already planning how to make Portugal attractive to foreigners. Lisbon was short of world-class art and encouraging Gulbenkian to make the country home to his collection made good sense. For his part, Gulbenkian must have been pleased by the Portuguese authorities' lack of scrutiny of the import and export of his artworks. The ease with which he could move his assets was very appealing to him.

Portugal proved to be more willing to accommodate Gulbenkian's wishes than the British, who were keen on having his collection reside in London. The extent to which Salazar went to accommodate Gulbenkian illustrates Lisbon's desire to use the wealth and the art collection for the country's benefit. There was also a degree of opportunism in Salazar's moves. Gulbenkian had been educated at King's College London and retained a great deal of affinity for the British way of life, but not for the British government. The wartime government led by Winston Churchill had taken a robust line with Gulbenkian and his trading with the Germans, categorizing him as an "enemy." Churchill's attitude toward Gulbenkian was consistent with his belief that people and organizations that traded with the Axis powers were untrustworthy. His attitude to the neutral countries that traded with the Nazis was more complicated and considered geostrategic needs in addition to moral issues. For his part, Gulbenkian never forgave the British for his treatment during WWII.

He was awarded a KBE (Knight of the British Empire) in January 1951. This was offered partly as a gesture of goodwill but mainly as an inducement. The Foreign Office believed Gulbenkian important to British oil interests in the Middle East. The oil magnate, however, refused to accept the honor.[16] Nubar Gulbenkian suggested that his father turned it down because, at his stage of life, he did not wish to be known as Sir Gulbenkian.[17] He also suspected that the British's main motive had more to do with the fact that his father had recently accepted the Order of Christ award from Salazar. Gulbenkian, he argued, wanted to turn down the Portuguese award as well but had been advised that, because he was a resident in the country, it would not have looked good to reject it.[18] Eventually, Gulbenkian accepted the award at a private ceremony in Lisbon. The KBE was not the first award from Britain that Gulbenkian turned down. Prior to the outbreak of World War I, his son claimed, he turned down the offer of a peerage.[19]

In the end, Lisbon turned out to be an excellent choice for Gulbenkian to see out his days. For most of the time he managed to remain out of the spotlight, which was very much where he liked to be.

Upon his death, Gulbenkian's will made provision for setting up a type of super foundation in Lisbon that would promote culture and create a permanent home for his art collection. In truth, he did not have much faith in his children continuing his legacy. He remarked that soon after his death his two children, Nubar and Rita, would spend his money on luxury cars at the famous Bentley dealership in Berkeley Square in

London.[20] He left his children $1 million each (current value of $8.8 million) as well as money in trusts.[21] It was the plans for the foundation that were of greater public interest. The Calouste Gulbenkian Foundation's statutes were approved in 1956 and the permanent home for the foundation and a museum opened in 1969. Later, in 1983, a modern art center opened in the same park as the original museum. The Gulbenkian Foundation remains the jewel in Lisbon's cultural crown.

The opening of the museum that houses Gulbenkian's personal art collection transformed Lisbon and helped put the city on the cultural map. The work of the foundation is to develop art and cultural projects within and outside Portugal. But just as elements of Gulbenkian's life were steeped in controversy, so too was the setup of his foundation. Nubar Gulbenkian joked in an interview for *Life* magazine that he had nicknamed the diving board at his home swimming pool "The Gulbenkian Foundation" because he ran and jumped all over it.[22] Negotiations setting up the foundation were fraught with difficulties. Salazar could not resist becoming involved. Issues arose over the payment of death duties. Salazar insisted that no major tax deductions be given on account of the foundation. As always, Salazar was a wily negotiator and gave very few concessions to the family. The Portuguese leader wanted to maximize the financial returns from Gulbenkian's death and to secure the art collection for Portugal.

Initial proposals for more than 15 percent but no more than 20 percent of the outlay of the foundation to be spent in Portugal were rejected by the Portuguese. Disputes arose over the composition of the board, with the Portuguese demanding it include a majority of Portuguese nationals. Nubar's main complaints about the foundation were:

First, that far, far too high a percentage of the foundation's money is spent in Portugal; second; that the foundation is not spending enough money; third, that the trustees are too secretive about the accounts of the foundation. I am not saying that everything the trustees have done, every grant they have made, has been wrong or bad. Far from it. Although they have made grants, especially in the early days, of which my father would have disapproved.[23]

Gulbenkian's son spent much of the rest of his life in increasingly bitter disputes with the trustees of the foundation. In his later years his somewhat extravagant lifestyle caught up with him. He had plenty of time to enjoy what he once famously described as his perfect dinner party; "the best number for a dinner party is two: myself and a damn good head waiter." Nubar died in Cannes in 1972. To the end of his days, he remained dissatisfied that so much of the foundation's money was spent on Portuguese rather than international projects.

Nubar's slightly embellished champagne-fueled recounting of the story of the foundation misses one important point. Salazar and Portugal provided cover and protection for his father to build up the art collection. Gulbenkian's eclectic collection covered various periods and areas, including Egyptian, Greco-Roman, Islamic, and Oriental art; old coins; and European paintings and decorative arts. He bought art through intermediaries, directly from public and private owners, and at auctions. He often took advice from experts such as Kenneth Clark, director of the National Gallery in London from 1934 to 1945, who advised him to buy Manet's *Boy Blowing Bubbles* from 1867. The painting was acquired from André Weil in New York in November 1943. Before World War II, Weil had been active on the Avenue Matignon, Paris, until the Nazi occupation forced him to leave France. He escaped through Lisbon to the United States in August 1941. He subsequently ran the Matignon Art Galleries in New York. Much of his own Paris collection had been confiscated by the Nazis in 1942.

The British ambassador in Lisbon during WWII, Ronald Campbell, carefully navigated the financial, diplomatic, and cultural concerns about Gulbenkian. The SIS wanted to delve deeper into the collector's Lisbon affairs over concerns that he was exploiting the plight of refugees like Rothschild. Buying art at low prices from legitimate owners was not a crime, but there was gossip that Gulbenkian was involved in more sinister acquisitions. The Gulbenkian Foundation claims to have paperwork and receipts for all pieces in its collection, but its wartime acquisitions remain problematic for many experts. Having a powerful ally in Salazar certainly helped the oil magnate navigate the complexities of legitimizing his collection.

The collections of Ricardo Espírito Santo and Calouste Gulbenkian are on display in museums in Lisbon to this day. Much of the art that was sold at the auctions in the final months of the war, however, remains locked away or is displayed in private houses in Lisbon and Estoril. Those works rarely appear on the open market. They are passed from one family generation to another, often merely listed as miscellaneous artworks in wills registered with the state. But the Portuguese families who benefited from sales of arts and jewelry were hardly alone.

In Spain, the Germans and their dealer friends, aware that the war was coming to an end, tried to sell whatever they regarded as too bulky to carry. There was an understanding that the Allies would investigate allegations of looted art after the war, and individuals preferred to sell for cash. Local Spanish dealers moved to hide artworks that could not be sold. The indifference of the Franco regime toward issues such as looted art and Nazi gold and jewelry offered cover and protection to many people involved in the sales. Much of the trade in stolen artworks took place in hotels where internationals stayed. It was a risky strategy given the number of SIS and OSS agents walking the corridors of the hotels. By the end of 1944, it was normal for foreigners to be approached spontaneously about the sale of art. The dealers did their research and knew who was transiting through the hotels. They benefited from the race to get rid of hard evidence in exchange for currency. Gold bars stamped with the swastika were in great demand in the neutral capitals during the war. But in the dealers' view, even these were nowhere near as attractive as hard currency.

One dealer was Arturo Reiss. On December 20, 1944, a stranger approached Reiss at the Hotel Gredos in Madrid and offered to sell him a painting for about $10,000. Reiss suspected that the painting had been stolen from the collection of a wealthy American who had lived in Nice before the war. The British embassy in Madrid passed on the information from Reiss to the Ministry of Economic Warfare in London. They investigated but did little. "This was not based on official information and although parts of it are interesting, on the whole it is not reliable," an official wrote in the margin of the subsequent report.[24] This was a standard response to individual reports of potential looted art. The ministry simply did not have the resources or the networks in neutral countries to pursue individual cases. The Allies were more interested in the big hordes of art and gold that were thought to be in Germany or nearby. This policy proved to be an understandable but nevertheless costly oversight.

8

VICTORY

O N Victory in Europe Day, May 8, 1945, the staff of the British embassy in Lisbon stood on the building's narrow, second-floor
balcony and looked down at the cheering crowd in the street below. Portugal was celebrating as if it had actually been one of the belligerents. The
large crowd outside the embassy chanted pro-British slogans and waved
the Union Jack. Portugal's close relations with the Axis powers during
the first part of the war were largely overlooked as was its wartime trade
with Germany. Portugal's flexible neutrality was deemed a success by the
population, which was grateful the country had been spared the horrors of
war. Locals knew little of Portugal's wolfram trade with the Nazis or the
fact that Portugal held substantial gold reserves, the sale of which could
be used to transform its underdeveloped economy. Even fewer understood
the importance of the country to Nazis fleeing Europe or to the large
amounts of looted art being transited through its ports to South America.

Many hoped that the country would return to the sleepy backwater
it had been in the prewar era. The Portuguese had grown tired of the
thousands of foreigners who packed the streets of Lisbon and Porto.
Restaurants had been booked out by the hundreds of diplomats, spies,
and hangers-on from the embassies. All the best hotels and bars had been
overrun by the foreign crowd and their local friends.

On a diplomatic level, postwar relations between the victorious Allies and Portugal got off to a spectacularly bad start. On April 30, 1945, Portugal, Ireland, and Spain all sent condolence messages to the German population after learning about Hitler's suicide on that day.[1] The Portuguese went further: Salazar ordered that all flags on official buildings be flown at half-mast to mark the death of the German leader.[2] The British were beside themselves with anger. The Foreign Office saw this move as confirmation of Salazar's pro-German leanings, which they had long suspected. Memorandums circulated in Whitehall calling for Portugal to be punished for this dreadful gesture. More importantly, it started a debate that had been absent for much of the war about how to punish Portugal for its wartime trade with the Nazis.

In the immediate aftermath of the war in Europe, evidence of the gold trail to Lisbon grew in volume and quality. Allied intelligence began to not only follow the gold but also provide estimates of the volumes of gold bars involved. The ongoing Allied investigations initially had focused on the official trade between Portugal and the Nazis. Details of known trades and exports were cataloged, but not yet investigated. The Allies' outrage over the condolences and lowered flags changed all that. The shift to a more critical approach to Portugal about its wartime conduct was driven by the Americans. On this issue, officials in Washington fell into two groups: those who favored a closer look at Portugal's relations with the Nazis, and those who prioritized continued access to the Azores and looked more to the future. Similar divisions within the British existed, but there was a consensus that Portugal needed to be punished.

An irritated Salazar failed to understand what all the fuss was about. He reminded the British that the Irish had gone further and declared a National Day of Mourning to commemorate Hitler's death.[3] It was standard procedure for Portugal to send such a condolence letter upon the death of a national leader, he insisted. On May 8, Portugal tried to rectify the impression of pro-German sentiments by sending a letter to Churchill in which Salazar conveyed the good wishes of the Portuguese people on the occasion of the Allied victory in Europe.[4] This failed to improve the mood in London, and Foreign Office officials called for Portugal to be put in its place. Others cited the need to speed up the ongoing investigations into the Nazi gold. They argued that Salazar had been informed that it was stolen gold, and therefore he would not be surprised when the Allies asked for it to be returned to its rightful owners. Anthony Eden, the foreign secretary, adopted a particularly hard line. He called for Portugal to be severely reprimanded for its conduct during the war. Winston Churchill, however, overruled all the advice and sent Salazar a charming and conciliatory note on May 17. In thanking Salazar for the good wishes of the Portuguese people he wrote of the importance of the two countries' ancient alliance and the granting of access to the Azores airbase during the war. The British prime minister's comments indicated that he had an eye on the future as well as the past.[5] The public row was soon put aside. The need for a debate on Portugal's wartime record, however, was gaining traction in London and Washington.

In the late afternoon of V-E Day, Ronald Campbell met with Salazar. To mark the occasion, they posed for a rare photograph together. The wily prime minister and the aristocratic British diplomat had done much good work together during the war. Salazar kept Portugal out of the war, and the physical contrast between the two cities of London and Lisbon could not have been greater. The London bombing had culminated in Hitler's use of the V-2 rockets. Although London was not as damaged as Walter Schellenberg had expected, nevertheless, much rebuilding needed to be undertaken. Lisbon, on the other hand, remained physically intact and showed no outward scars at all. Indeed, in May 1945, the only damage to the city was caused by a hurricane and torrential rains that destroyed much of the city's beautiful outlying gardens and purple jacaranda trees. Although Lisbon lacked a little of its usual color, it could look to the future with a degree of optimism. The food shortages, which were largely the result of the hugely unpopular British naval blockade, were quickly resolved. This contrasted with Britain, where rationing continued on many items well into the 1950s.

During the photo op, Campbell informed Salazar that he would soon be leaving Lisbon. Despite Anthony Eden's concerted efforts to persuade Campbell to take up a major role in the reconstruction of Europe, the ambassador told the Foreign Office that he was tired and wished to retire as soon as possible.[6] The intensive diplomatic activities of the war

years had taken their toll on his health, and Campbell wanted to return
to England to see out the remainder of his days.[7] Salazar told him that his
premature retirement was not only a loss for the Foreign Office but also
equally sad for Portugal. The two men had negotiated hard over access
to the Azores, stopping Portuguese wolfram trade with the Germans,
and most recently implementing the terms of Operation Safehaven. The
Portuguese leader had conceded on all three items but had not delivered
on Portuguese compliance with the final item on the list. In this respect,
Campbell would depart Lisbon with his work incomplete.

Privately, Salazar had mixed feelings about Campbell's departure. He
viewed it as a clear signal of the downgrading of Portugal's importance
to Britain. Campbell's successor was not from the same high-flying pool
of talent as the wartime ambassador. This point both irritated the Portuguese leader, who believed his country would once more be taken for
granted by Britain and confined to the diplomatic backwater of Europe,
and came as a bit of a relief. Campbell had been at the forefront of the
investigation of Nazi gold and looted artworks in Portugal. The Foreign
Office's high opinion of Campbell as one of their best meant that his
comments carried a great deal of weight in Whitehall. His replacement
with a lesser ambassador would mean that any investigations into Portugal would no longer resonate as much. Salazar could see the benefits of
Portugal being pushed further down the diplomatic table of importance.
A lower profile while the Allies investigated the role of the neutral countries in the war was an asset.

Ronald Campbell departed on June 29, 1945, more than four and a
half years after he took up the position in January 1941. His farewell dinner was attended by embassy staff and diplomats from across the city.
Unusually, Salazar also attended.[8] Generous toasts were made. Campbell
confessed in his final telegram to London that he felt his work had been
successful but was far from complete. Touching on a controversial aspect of his posting, he wondered whether he had been overrestrictive of
the activities of the SOE and SIS in the country. He admitted that the
Germans took great advantage of his decision to rein in the activities of
British agents in Portugal for fear of offending Salazar. After the success
of D-Day, he could have unleashed British intelligence. The removal of

his "worthy adversary"—the German ambassador Hoyningen-Huene, re-called after the failed assassination attempt on Hitler—had been decisive for Campbell.[9] To him, it represented the moment when the Nazi state abandoned its operations in Lisbon, even though many fleeing Germans remained. But their objectives were simple survival along with as much as they could safely smuggle; they were not part of a coordinated national threat.

An issue that was unsurprisingly absent from Campbell's farewell re-marks was the efforts of the British government to prevent Jewish refu-gees from entering Portugal. That policy had been in place from the start of the war through much of 1941. Attempts by the Foreign Office to per-suade Salazar not to allow international rescue groups to operate in the country to aid the refugees were documented. In the end, Salazar, who had his own reasons for restricting the numbers of refugees entering the country, rejected the British overtures and allowed the rescue groups to set up shop in Lisbon. Fearing the hidden hand of the Zionists, the For-eign Office believed that the rescue groups would be staffed by members of Jewish extremist organizations. They, in turn, would encourage the refugees not to head for the United States, Canada, or South Africa but instead to set sail for the British-controlled Palestine.

The arrival of refugees in Palestine would have been deemed unac-ceptable by Britain's Arab allies, notably the influential grand mufti of Jerusalem. The Arabs had warned that any substantial number of Jewish refugees in Palestine would lead to a reconsideration of their positions toward the war. In London there was a deep-rooted fear that the mufti, in particular, leaned toward the Nazis. British policy in Portugal was therefore aimed at preventing large numbers of refugees from transiting through Lisbon to Palestine. The fact that no ocean liners made direct voyages from Portugal to Palestine (or indeed anywhere in the Middle East) appeared to be overlooked by British officials. There was no evi-dence to indicate that Zionist groups were developing an on-the-ground presence in Lisbon or chartering ships to take refugees to Palestine. The Foreign Office fretted about it nonetheless.

The British spent much of the postwar period until 1948 worrying about their empire and how best to retain it. India was the most volatile territory, but Palestine was not far behind. Technically, it was not an official part of the empire. The League of Nations had granted mandatory powers to Britain in July 1922. Britain, however, ran Palestine as if it were a colonial outpost. A high commissioner was appointed and the British legal system adopted. Britain had two aims in Palestine: to help find a solution to the violent dispute between the Zionists and the local Arab population, and to retain the important British military bases in the country. Both aims proved hard to achieve. The British control over its territorial possessions started to unravel during this period up until and after the declaration of Israel on May 14, 1948, a development that many Foreign Office mandarins described as the single biggest mistake in British postwar diplomacy.

As one official put it:

> The change in British policy from the White paper of 1939, which attempted to protect Arab rights, to the surrender to Jewish terrorists and US politicians in 1948 lost us an important base (Palestine) and the friendship of the Arab world.[10]

In essence, from the end of WWII through 1948, Britain was distracted by the challenges it faced regarding its place in the world. "Won the war but lost the empire" was the revealing saying employed to describe the reality of the decline of Britain and its role in the world.

So Britain's efforts in Portugal aimed at preventing the transfer of human and material resources that would help facilitate the ability of the Nazis to establish a Fourth Reich in South America, but the country was distracted by events elsewhere in the world and the realization that it was nearly bankrupt. The baton therefore passed to the United States; London was content, postwar, to play a supporting role.

The Americans were undergoing internal changes when on September 20, 1945, President Truman signed Executive Order 9621, which terminated the OSS. With an eye on the future, the State Department took over the Research and Analysis Branch of the disbanded OSS and renamed it the Bureau of Intelligence and Research. The War Department took over the Secret Intelligence (SI) and Counter-Espionage (X-2)

Branches, which were then relocated into the new Strategic Services Unit (SSU). Brigadier General John Magruder, formerly "Wild Bill" Donovan's deputy director for intelligence in the OSS, became the new director of the SSU. Magruder was put in charge of winding up the OSS but maintained some of its clandestine intelligence capabilities. In January 1946, President Truman created the Central Intelligence Group (CIG), the precursor to the CIA. SSU assets, which constituted a streamlined "nucleus" of clandestine intelligence, were transferred to the CIG in mid-1946 and reconstituted as the Office of Special Operations (OSO). The National Security Act of 1947 established the Central Intelligence Agency, which then took over most of the OSS functions. Donovan was overlooked for any role in the new intelligence agency. He fell out with Supreme Court justice Robert Jackson, who served as US chief counsel in the prosecution of Nazi war criminals at Nuremberg. Following a series of clashes over the origination and conduct of the trial, Jackson fired Donovan from the US team. Donovan never recovered politically and spent much of the rest of his days traveling the world. It was a sad exit for a man who had done much for the American war effort.

The end of WWII brought new challenges and changes to Portugal. The last months of the war proved to be difficult ones for Salazar. Sensing an Allied victory as a catalyst for internal political reform, Salazar's opponents upped their anti-government activities with a resulting major increase in industrial unrest. Although in the short term this proved relatively easy for the regime to contain, there was greater concern about Salazar's longer-term ability to deal with potential social and industrial upheavals. Internationally, Salazar was heavily pressured by the United States and Britain to comply with several Allied policies regarding war criminals and to return assets stolen by the Germans. Continuing to find the Allied definition of "war criminal" to be highly problematic, Salazar refused. This was not appreciated by the Allies, especially in Washington, which was much more critical of Portugal than the British. The Americans' attitude toward Portugal would be a crucial factor in keeping Lisbon strategically important in the postwar order.

While the Allies increased the diplomatic pressure on Portugal to comply with the economic and political terms of Safehaven, Salazar was busy reminding the world that Portugal had emerged from the war with its empire intact. The retention of the empire (or the overseas territories, as it became known) was an important ideological part of the authoritarian Estado Novo (New State). The Portuguese leader believed that the British had promised during the negotiations over access to the Azores in summer 1943 to ensure the territorial integrity of the Portuguese Empire. This was not confirmed by London, but the threats to the empire that existed across the globe had receded. Whereas the Portuguese were very vocal in reminding the world of this achievement, they largely swept other issues relating to the war under the carpet. Little mention was made of the wolfram trade, the Nazi gold, or relations with Nazi Germany in general. Rumors of the arrival and departure of Germans in and out of Lisbon were not published in the highly controlled press. Likewise, details of the sales of Nazi looted goods were deemed to be private and did not make it into the press. According to the propaganda department of the Estado Novo, Portugal looked forward to the postwar era with great optimism. The official line was the government would concentrate on internal issues, housing and health care.

On September 3, 1945, the foreign army of a former Portuguese colony made it to Lisbon and paraded through the streets to thunderous applause from large crowds of Lisboetas. The army was from Brazil. The Força Expedicionária Brasileira (FEB) was on its way back to Brazil following a successful campaign against the Germans in Italy. The FEB proudly wore their American-made uniforms and carried their American weapons. The difference between Brazil and Portugal in WWII could not have been more obvious. By choosing to fight in the latter stages of the war, Portugal's former colony received enough weapons and training to be able to effectively defend itself against any military action. Participation in the war brought political change in Brazil as well, albeit short-term change. The authoritarian leadership in Rio de Janeiro was replaced by a new government following democratic elections. Portugal, however, by choosing to remain neutral in the war, received no weapons of any magnitude from either the Americans or the British. Portugal was dependent on other states to defend it. In the immediate postwar era, this was quite a difficult position to be in given that Salazar had lost a lot of his wartime contacts.

The end of WWII brought rapid political change. Even earlier, the sudden death of President Roosevelt on April 12, 1945, led to subtle changes in the attitude of the United States toward Portugal. Though Salazar was saddened by the death of Roosevelt, he was shocked by the electoral defeat of Winston Churchill at the hands of Clement Attlee's Labour Party in Britain. He saw the political demise of Churchill as one of the perils of democratic politics. Salazar insisted that he would not fall victim to the whims of the people. Any thoughts of introducing a form of limited democracy to Portugal were based on the assertion that it would not lead to any change in leader. On his own prospects for retaining power, Salazar was no fool. He sensed that change was sweeping across Europe. There was no certainty that wartime leaders would survive in peacetime. He gave some thought to whether he should continue in office. He viewed leadership of the country as a full-time occupation that did not allow for a family or even a wife/lover/girlfriend. At the end of the war there was speculation in the international press that he was considering marriage, and this was taken as evidence that he might leave office.

It might have been an opportune moment for him to depart the political stage with the sounds of the grateful thanks of the nation ringing in his ears. His popularity never again matched the levels it reached at the conclusion of WWII. In the end, staying on proved to be too much of a temptation for Salazar. The fact that there was no other national leader of his stature helped convince him that he should continue on for the good of the country. The lack of a viable successor was hardly surprising—like many dictators, Salazar did not devote time to devising a succession plan. The people around the regime were essentially second-class versions of Salazar; the brightest rivals had been dispatched into internal political exile.

There was another reason that Salazar decided to remain in power. He understood that Portugal in the postwar era remained extremely important to the outside world, but for very different reasons than during WWII: Salazar knew that as one war ended the likelihood of another starting with the Soviet Union was high.

9

LEARNING CURVE

WHILE LEADERS SUCH AS SALAZAR CONTEMPLATED THE POSTWAR order, many Allied diplomats, government departments, and intelligence agencies engaged closely with the subject of looted treasures. Previously, their focus had been on winning the war. So, many key Allied personnel needed to understand the origins of the issue, the different types of looting, and specific examples of individuals, galleries, and museums that had been placed under investigation. There was a need to go back to the very beginning to search for looted art in the postwar period.

To frame the topic, on May 5, 1945, the Allies produced a detailed preliminary report entitled *Looted Art in Occupied Territories, Neutral Countries and Latin America*.[1] The document was authored by the Foreign Economic Administration, Enemy Branch, based in Washington. It was subtitled a "preliminary report," but it represented a far-reaching effort to define the nature of the problem, provide historical contextualization, and highlight specific cases of looted art.[2] It attempted to supply details of the various networks involved in profiting from the theft and sale of the art. An important step forward, it nonetheless suffered the problem that would blight investigations into tracing the art and making any restitution efforts: the lack of conclusive and damning evidence in the report was made painfully obvious by the legal reminders that the individuals named were suspected of dealing in looted art but that no conclusive proof against them had been provided.[3] This shortcoming aside, the report was a remarkably accurate account of many of the shady networks that had been set up during the war, several of which included dealers and gallery owners of Jewish origins. The report argued that the looting of art had been carried out in a systematic manner and that this was to have a major detrimental impact on the collections and national identities of countries occupied by the Nazis. There was, as a result, a clear and pressing need to address this theft in the postwar years.

The salvage of European art treasures had two priorities. The first was to preserve the treasures for their cultural and artistic value. The second was to recover them and make restitution to their legitimate owners. The Americans and the British had set up independent committees but had plans to convene a Joint Allied committee to deal with restitution issues. The authors of the report were tasked with preservation, recovery, and restitution. They identified the central Nazi objective: "The treasures which are of economic value to the enemy, who is known to have attempted to dispose of them in neutral countries, in order to accumulate foreign funds and securities which might escape Allied control."[4]

It proved difficult to put an exact figure on the value of the stolen artworks. Art markets were fluid and the war had impacted valuations. The British Ministry of Economic Warfare estimated a figure of 36 million pounds, or $144 million. The unofficial figures were much higher. Francis Taylor, the director of the Metropolitan Museum of Art, suggested a number in the range of $2 billion ($3,297,744,444 in 2023) to $2.5 billion ($4,122,180,555 in 2023).[5] These staggering sums constituted more than the total value of artworks in the United States. What was even less clear was the value of the artworks that had been exported to neutral countries like Portugal. This highlighted the crux of the problem for the investigators: they had limited knowledge of which stolen artworks had been exported by the Nazis and to where.

What was much clearer were the Nazi aims: "They realised the importance of securing for themselves stable foreign currency, and the greatest possible financial power abroad."[6] This basic goal of the Nazis was built on their alarm over the economic crisis of the Great Depression that had engulfed the world and made art a safe investment. In times of war, with the value of currency vulnerable, artworks, gold, and silver take on heightened importance as payment methods. Nathan Rothschild, for example, had built the financial empire of the Rothschilds on the use of gold during the Peninsular War. Another problem with currency in times of war is forgery, as the Nazis demonstrated with their fake escudos and pounds.

The long-term nature of Berlin's efforts meant that looting and moving art had started early in the war, prior to the United States' entry in 1941, with attempts made to ship it to Spain and Portugal and from there to the United States or Latin America. Given the establishment of strong German networks in both these areas, the export of art proceeded efficiently and without incident.[7] The art was shipped out of Iberia on ocean liners because these ships were not regularly stopped by the Royal Navy imposing the naval blockades. This in turn further reduced the need for extensive paperwork. When the Royal Navy did intervene, as in the case of the SS *Excalibur*, it was because of a tip-off by a local agent. Prior to the US entry into the war, the New York art market was considered lucrative and discreet by the Germans.[8]

Early attempts to smuggle artworks to Latin America focused on Brazil. The liners connecting Portugal and Brazil were an obvious route. Once in Rio de Janeiro, artworks were cleared through customs with minimal inspections because, as in Lisbon, the Germans had many customs officials on their payroll. Brazil also had a large German immigrant population mainly based in the city of Rio de Janeiro and in the state of Rio Grande do Sul in the south, known as "gaucho country" because of its many ranches. Most immigrants were sympathetic to the Nazis and remained politically and culturally connected with the fatherland. The Brazilian aviation industry was largely owned and controlled by German immigrants, which made it easy to distribute art to the south if required. Rio Grande do Sul borders Uruguay and Argentina, making it straightforward to smuggle works to those countries too.[9]

The smuggling of art from Brazil to Argentina gathered momentum after the Brazilians joined the war on the side of the Allies on August 22, 1942. Residents of Rio de Janeiro confirmed the presence of mysterious artworks that were never unloaded from their crates. In addition to heading to Buenos Aires, a few pieces were smuggled into the capital of Uruguay, Montevideo.[10] From there the trail went cold. American and British intelligence agents based in Rio and Buenos Aires were sure more than art was arriving.[11] When Brazil joined the war, rumors were circulating in Rio de Janeiro that gold was being smuggled out of Europe. Banking records indicate that this gold did not reach Brazilian banks; therefore, it was either re-exported to Argentina (where agents had a harder time gaining access to banking records) or stored in private houses and vaults.[12]

The ocean links between Portugal and Brazil were not always straightforward, but Nazi use of the routes was confirmed in late 1940. On November 19, 1940, the Brazilian liner SS *Siqueira Campos* slipped anchor and headed down the River Tagus out into the Atlantic Ocean. The Royal Navy waited to intercept the ship after it cleared Portuguese territorial waters. Royal Navy patrols were a routine part of the naval blockade of Portugal, imposed by the British Ministry of Economic Warfare. On this occasion, the British acted as part of a wide-ranging intelligence operation tracing the export of German arms to Brazil. British agents had watched the loading of the heavy, unmarked wooden crates from the quayside into the ship's hold. They had noticed known German agents from the embassy present at the docks.[13]

The British knew about the contents of the crates. Earlier in the morning, they had bribed the customs officials for the inventory sheets. The Portuguese officials had no qualms about taking payment from the British for information that the German agents had paid them not to divulge. The crates contained Nazi weapons heading for the Brazilian army. The hardware included machine guns, artillery pieces, and lots of ammunition. The shipment was part of a wider arms deal in which the Nazis would supply the Brazilians with weapons to modernize their armed forces. Brazil's efforts to modernize its military had little to do with WWII at this stage. Like Portugal, the country had formally declared its neutrality at the start of the war. Its need for weapons reflected its deep suspicions that its great rival, Argentina, might use the cover of the war to launch an attack on it in the south.

The British had also been tipped off that looted art stolen from occupied France was aboard the ship but paid scant attention to this information. The search for artworks was not yet seen as important as the search for German weapons. Prior to the *Siqueira Campos*'s departure from Lisbon, a great deal of diplomatic activity reflected the key geostrategic politics of the era. The United States, fearing a backlash against its interests in South America, cautioned the British not to intervene.[14] Ignoring Washington's warning, two Royal Navy frigates waited for the *Siqueira Campos*. The British boarded the ship and then escorted it to Gibraltar, where it was forbidden to dock. Left in the bay during heavy storms, several passengers and members of the crew became sick, adding to the tension of the crisis.[15] Personnel from the navy and the Ministry of Economic Warfare opened and searched each crate in the hold. As expected, they discovered the German armaments but showed little interest in the artworks also on board, which had the relevant paperwork. The political crisis resulting from the ship's seizure dominated the headlines in Brazil. The British were accused of acting like colonialists, and the Americans, dragged into the crisis, were accused of a similar crime.[16]

The deeper issues that lay behind the crisis reflected the fragile nature of American-British relations with the Brazilian government. The outcome of events would have an important consequence not only on the delivery of German weapons to Brazil but also on the subsequent Allied policing of the sea route from Lisbon to Rio de Janeiro. In Brazil, President Getúlio Vargas was away from Rio at his summer retreat, and the two key men left in charge could not have been more different. The minister of foreign affairs, Oswaldo Aranha, viewed the United States as Brazil's most important and natural ally. He had been involved in the negotiations that led Washington to promise to deliver arms to Brazil for internal purposes. Given the shortage of arms in the United States at the time and its commitment to supply Britain, Washington was not making good on its promise to supply Brazil. Aranha's rival within the government was the minister of war, Eurico Gaspar Dutra, who favored more German-centric foreign policy.

Both Aranha and Vargas were gauchos from Rio Grande do Sul and shared a common vision for the modernization of Brazil. The Americans regarded Aranha as a vital member of the government who could steer Brazil toward the orbit of the Allies after America joined WWII. They wanted to do as much as possible to help Aranha survive politically. Like several other internationally known foreign ministers, he did not enjoy a large political following in Brazil, which helped with President Vargas, who did not view Aranha as a threat, but it made Aranha vulnerable to populist leaders linked to Brazil's armed forces, who hated him and everything he stood for. The last thing the Americans wanted was for the British to stumble into the picture with their warships and naval blockades and threaten Aranha's political position. But the minister of foreign affairs was an astute political player, arguably Brazil's leading diplomat of the twentieth century. He survived this crisis. Even though he was later forced from office, he would reemerge as Brazil's representative to the United States and in 1947 was elected as the first president of the United Nations General Assembly.

The Brazilian military, and its representatives in the government, preferred to buy German arms, and politically leaned toward Berlin. Eurico Gaspar Dutra was openly pro-German and was said to have screamed with joy when he was informed the Germans had seized Paris in the summer of 1940.[17] While Aranha was articulate and thoughtful, Dutra was gruff and inarticulate. He rarely finished his sentences and often seemed to lose track of his thoughts. But Dutra understood how to speak to his political base. His supporters were a curious mixture of the poor and right-wing pro-German educated Brazilians. In 1940, most Brazilians believed that the Nazis would emerge victorious in the war. Like the Portuguese, they wanted to back the winner.

The Americans believed Dutra and his supporters would push Brazil into the orbit of German influence during the war. Aranha's removal was a key part of that plan, and the Americans knew it. In December 1940, in Washington, the policy toward Brazil allowed the Brazilians to trade freely with whomever; the Americans would not intervene in any way that would allow the Brazilian military and anti-American politicians to charge that the United States was behaving in an imperial manner. For that reason, the United States had next to no interest in stopping Brazilian shipping on the high seas to inspect cargo for arms or stolen artworks and other goods. When the Americans discovered that the British were planning to stop and board the *Siqueira Campos*, they appealed to them not to do so. The British insistence was deeply disappointing to the American embassy in Lisbon, which reported to the State Department that the Royal Navy should find better things to do with its frigates.

Tensions worsened between London and Washington when, much to the annoyance of the Americans, the British boarded another Brazilian ship on November 27, 1940. The Royal Navy seized several packages they believed originated in Germany. These were not arms but works of art. Once again, it turned out to be a false alarm. The works had proper documentation. By this stage, the Americans had enough of the British shows of naval strength.[18] Popular sentiment in Brazil against the British was threatening to force out Aranha. The final straw for the Brazilians and the Americans came when the Royal Navy stopped a third ship, the Brazilian steamer SS *Itapé*, on December 1 only eighteen miles off the Brazilian coast. The Royal Navy boarded the ship and removed twenty-two German nationals. It turned out that the British acted on poor intelligence and that the ship was traveling between two internal Brazilian ports.[19]

What materialized after complex and bitter negotiations involving officials in London, Washington, and Rio over the *Siqueira Campos* was a compromise in which the ship would be allowed to proceed to Rio with the arms with the proviso that this would be the last shipment of arms from Germany to Brazil. For their part, the Brazilians agreed to seize Axis ships that were in Brazilian harbors. The agreement had far-reaching consequences for the war and the export of looted art to Brazil. The Americans took over policing the South Atlantic routes, with the Royal Navy playing a secondary role. In practical terms, the American Navy was much less inclined to stop and board ships on the high seas. This point was noted by German intelligence, who saw it as a major gain.

The Americans increased their delivery of arms to Brazil, though supply levels were still below what was initially promised. Much was made of the possible German threat to northeastern Brazil. The Good Neighbor policy, launched by President Roosevelt and aimed at developing political, economic, and cultural ties, was stepped up with Nelson Rockefeller at the helm. By 1942, the United States had replaced Britain as the dominant external power in the region. Stopping shipments of German arms was at the top of the American agenda and took priority over everything else.

Overall, the seizing of the *Siqueira Campos* was a disaster for the British.[20] The heavy-handed nature of the Royal Navy's attempts to impose blockades made Britain highly unpopular in both Brazil and Portugal. The Americans were determined to learn from British mistakes and adopted a much softer line to win friends and influence in Latin America. After Brazil joined the war in 1942 following German attacks on its shipping, the Port of Rio de Janeiro became even more strategically important to the Allies. Inspections of freight arriving from Europe became much looser and the potential for smuggling goods much easier. The back door from Europe to South America was fully ajar. Using its embassy in Lisbon as a staging post, the Nazis were able to ship looted artworks out of Europe with ease.

The decline in Nazi influence in Brazil as Brazil joined the war on the Allied side encouraged Berlin to try to develop closer ties with Argentina, capitalizing on the pro-German sentiments in the Argentine military. When Juan Perón came to power in 1946, he allowed Argentina to become a haven for Nazi war criminals.

As long as Washington was encouraging both Brazil and Argentina to declare war on Germany, there was not much interest in what many intelligence officials regarded as small-time German smuggling efforts. This was a costly mistake.

Many Nazis chose to hang on to their artworks until almost the end of the war and to travel with them to South America. Paintings were cut from their frames, rolled up, and then carried in canvas army kit bags. As the officers entered neutral countries, they ditched their kit bags and re-rolled the artworks, tying them with string. Artworks transported by air to Portugal and Spain were carefully packed in crates and covered with legitimate goods that conformed to the customs bill.

The German looting had been carefully planned.[21] Rather than steal from state bodies—national museums and well-known public collections—they chose to predominately rob individuals in the occupied territories. This made Allied attempts at recovery and restitution much more complicated and uncertain. Although there were exceptions, it was a clever policy that added to the scale of the task facing Allied investigators. The looted art was then sold among a small group of leading Nazis.[22] "All high Nazi party members had their teams of agents whose duty it was to look out for important works of art either in dealers' galleries or in private collections."[23] Göring, Goebbels, and Ribbentrop were among the biggest buyers.[24]

Because of monetary restrictions, German bankers and industrialists could not compete with this A-list of Nazi leaders.[25] But German private and semiprivate galleries had their own agents who purchased art from Paris, Brussels, and Amsterdam. Most of these sales were made under duress, and the German state helped to pay for and export the art. To help track-and-trace efforts, the Allies published a comprehensive list of suspected German agents and buyers linked to leading Nazis. Agents for both Göring and Ribbentrop were included. Alois Miedl was one of the most important agents for Göring, working in Holland and Spain for his Nazi master. According to the Allies, Adolf Wüster played a similar role for Ribbentrop and the German foreign ministry. Officially, he was art advisor to the German embassy in Paris during the war. Unofficially, he kept senior Nazis, including Ribbentrop, informed of artworks that were for sale in Paris.[26] It was perfectly common for senior Nazis to have multiple people acting on their behalf. Theft by individual German officers and men was a serious issue, but not as significant as the authorized looting.[27]

The greatest looting, of course, was of collections owned by Jews. The collections stolen from the Rothschild family alone were worth millions of dollars.[28] The Nazis dispersed the works across Germany and neutral countries, where the artworks were sold or stored. Many items from Paul Rosenberg's looted gallery in Paris were traced to Switzerland.[29] Rosenberg and his family fled Paris and spent much of the summer of 1940 in Sintra, near Lisbon, before sailing to New York, but his gallery had been one of

the most prestigious in Paris, the works on show reflecting his close relationships with Picasso and other artists. One hundred sixty-two paintings
and drawings had been deposited at a bank in Libourne, near Bordeaux,
in southwestern France. In May 1941, the total value of this collection had
been put at 7,171,000 French francs.[30] Art from the collection that reached
Switzerland was valued at 300,000 Swiss francs.[31] The list of galleries and
collections raided by the Nazis across occupied Europe was long.

Alois Miedl, Göring's dealer, was an especially notorious peddler of
looted art. A vivacious and well-connected character, he was involved in
the looting of works from the Rosenberg gallery. Walter Schellenberg
confirmed Miedl's connections to Göring, who acted as his protector.[32]
Because he was married to a Jew and had two children, Miedl was in
much need of protection. Born in Munich, he had become a Dutch citizen
after moving to Amsterdam at the start of the 1930s, and there he developed major interests in the banking and financial sectors in his adopted
country. He was a devout Catholic, and rumors circulated that his connections reached high up in the neutral countries and the Vatican.[33] His
arrangement with Göring was both business and personal. Miedl was
thought to have had a long-term relationship with Göring's widowed
older sister, Olga.[34] How that relationship ended remains unclear, but
Miedl's strong Catholicism meant that he was not willing to divorce his
wife, Dorie.[35] Such was his admiration of and loyalty to Göring that he
was said to have detested Göring's rivals, such as Bormann, Himmler,
Goebbels, and Ribbentrop.[36]

Miedl's political views were complex, but according to the Americans
and the British, he was a strong supporter of the Nazis despite having
a Jewish wife.[37] Göring's patronage allowed the Miedl family to be declared as "honorary Aryans."[38] His wife's racial background meant that
Miedl was never officially permitted to join the Nazi Party, nor was he
conscripted into the German armed forces.[39] Naturally, there was a price
for this support. Göring used it as leverage in his business dealings with
Miedl to reduce the price of the agent's commission. Despite this, Miedl's
wily business skills and large black book of contacts meant that he made
a fortune from an early stage. American investigators traced his banking
activities in Holland to funds he had received from Göring in 1937.[40]

Included in his lists of company purchases were art galleries such as the Goudstikker Galleries in Amsterdam following the Nazi occupation of Holland.[41] The invasion of his adopted country opened wide opportunities for Miedl. As a British memorandum outlined:

> He bought many collections for Goring and first choice of any paintings went to Goring. Twelve paintings were smuggled into Spain by him. As Goring's purchasing agent, he bought 17th Century Dutch and Flemish paintings . . . with German marks pumped into Dutch, Belgium and French circulation by the Germans. Other paintings have been paid for in "occupation gilders" or seized as Jewish property. Goring's two most precious paintings, one a self-portrait by Van Gogh after he had cut off his ear, and the other Cezanne's "House in the Park," were brought over to Switzerland by pouch.[42]

Of course, Miedl was only one of many agents Göring used for purchasing art. The Reichsmarschall had a man in each occupied capital city and location of importance in the art world. Two factors, however, made Miedl particularly important. The first concerns Göring's apparent decision to try to smuggle two hundred paintings to Spain in the immediate aftermath of the D-Day operation. The second was Miedl's ability to navigate his way out of tight spots in territory not under German control.[43] The first suggests that, contrary to Schellenberg's claims that there were no postwar plans, senior Nazis like Göring were already preparing for the end of the war. Sales in 1944, the Allies concluded, were made to fund espionage and postwar activities in South America.[44]

It was somewhat surprising that Miedl was chosen for this mission. In May 1944, Miedl's relationship with his protector had already broken down, and the agent and his family left Amsterdam fearing for their safety after a deal he had negotiated on Göring's behalf had gone sour—the works he purchased turned out to be fakes. But Miedl had been preparing for the moment of departure for some time, and Göring must have forgiven him or given him one last chance of redemption in choosing him for this important task. According to Allied sources, Miedl had been smuggling looted art and securities into Spain, where the Port of Bilbao offered easy egress from Europe.[45] His preexisting knowledge of Spain and his support network in Madrid made him the obvious choice, even if Göring no longer fully trusted him. The limited time before the border between France and Spain was closed could have also been a factor leading Göring to rely on an existing agent he knew well.

Over two hundred artworks were carefully packed in two American cars that Miedl and an associate drove through France. Nothing went smoothly for Miedl at the French-Spanish border. He was briefly detained by the Spanish authorities when he entered the country. Using a cunning mixture of support from German intelligence and the Gestapo, along with bribes, he eventually secured his personal freedom and imported some of the artworks into Spain. The intervention of one of Göring's personal representatives on his behalf helped his case. But Miedl was not finished. Upon his release, he slipped back across the border into France to pick up an additional suitcase that contained more loot, including, allegedly, works by Cranach, Rubens, van Gogh, Rembrandt, Anthony van Dyck, Cézanne, Titian, and El Greco. Once again, his luck ran out. He was detained and questioned by the French Resistance operating in the area. A larger-than-life character with a charisma that charmed most people, Miedl somehow talked his way out of trouble. The Resistance released him and the art he was carrying.

The arrival of the art and his family in Spain did not go unnoticed by the Allies. The intervention by the German air attaché, General Kramer, who had told the Spanish authorities that the paintings were the personal property of Göring, alerted the Allies.[46] The SIS and OSS noted that Miedl was most probably part of a much bigger project linked to Göring removing looted art and securities from northern Europe and into Iberia.[47] Not one to keep quiet about his good fortune, Miedl soon touted the paintings for sale in Madrid with a catalog that included them and other paintings he had imported from France.[48] Over two hundred paintings were said to belong to Göring.[49] The majority were valued at between 100,000 and 500,000 pesetas, with five or six listed at even higher prices.[50] The collection was the talk of the town in Madrid's art circles. At parties, "Miedl highlighted his connection to Göring and of the commission he would receive upon the sale of the paintings; German circles in Madrid believed his boasting to be justified."[51] The Prado Museum was said to be interested in purchasing at least one of the paintings by Francisco Goya for a price of 2 million pesetas.[52] That interest cooled, however, when it discovered that Miedl was German (the museum's people had most probably presumed him to be Dutch). The artworks' connection to Göring became common knowledge, and this could also have altered the mood of prospective purchasers. The SIS also let it be known that Miedl's activities were under active investigation. Whatever the reason, the Prado Museum got cold feet. But there were plenty of other buyers in Iberia willing to ignore questions about the origins of the art and its ownership.

Miedl saw out the war in Spain, out of reach of the Allies. Despite American and British efforts to bring him to justice, the lack of Spanish cooperation with Operation Safehaven provided him cover. At the end of the war, he navigated the new political landscape carefully and with a degree of skill that indicated his astute understanding of the Allies' weaknesses on questions of looted art. He cooperated with Allied investigative teams, particularly the OSS officer Theodore Rousseau, who was sent to Spain in December 1944 and who tracked him down. The OSS agent enjoyed some success in getting the Spanish to seize the artworks and briefly detain Miedl, but he never fully got to the bottom of Miedl's story and links to the Nazis.[53] The investigations' progress at least allowed the paintings to be identified and the Dutch authorities notified of their whereabouts.[54] The investigations also linked Miedl to the looting of other artworks held in Switzerland, including paintings removed from Paul Rosenberg's gallery in Paris.[55]

Like many dealers in looted art, Miedl was not subjected to Allied justice after the war. He lost a large proportion of the paintings that he had not sold yet. The Dutch successfully sought restitution of the works he had imported into Spain. But most of his other financial gains from the war were left untouched or undiscovered by the Allies. These were mainly in the banking and commercial sectors. He was even thought to have held on to some artworks that the Allies failed to locate. After living for a time in Madrid, he moved to Portugal and settled in Estoril along the Lisbon coast, where the milder climate and sea air helped him recover from a bout of ill health. He was a popular and well-connected figure in the Lisbon art scene, where he attended exhibition openings.[56] As part of the social scene led by Ricardo Espírito Santo, Miedl was fondly remembered as a man who enjoyed a five-star lifestyle. He talked openly of the good old days of war and his relationship with Göring. Eventually, Miedl returned to Munich; he also spent time in Angola (then a Portuguese colony) and South Africa. He was said to own a large number of shares in South African railways.[57] By any standards he had had a good war.

Throughout Alois Miedl's saga was his wife, Dorie, who appeared to have little problem with her husband's looting of art from fellow Jews. By all accounts, she was not an innocent bystander but more like a business partner and bookkeeper for her husband's activities. She also stored some of his loot in safe deposit boxes in Switzerland. It was only following a marital row that she removed the tags on all the keys to the boxes, which meant that Miedl was unable to discover and open them following her unexpected death.[58] Despite this setback, Miedl was still wealthy enough to see out his days in luxury. He died on January 4, 1990, age eighty-seven, and took many secrets to his grave. He remains an example of a notorious man who got away with the looting of artworks, shares, and financial securities from Jews and the countries occupied by the Germans during the war. His protection by the Spanish authorities and later the Portuguese remains a stain on the records of both countries.

The Germans' efforts to loot art and monuments were relentless. Many leading Nazis, like Göring, regarded this as a once-in-a-lifetime opportunity to add to their wealth and control the historical cultural narrative of Europe. But ridding Europe of what the Nazis saw as the Jewish influence on the arts came a distant second to their desire to make money and prepare an insurance policy for when things went wrong in the war. During his interrogations at Camp 020, Walter Schellenberg asserted that the Germans had not put together a macro escape plan. His argument was that such defeatism would not have been tolerated and ran contrary to Nazi ideology.[59] He did concede, though, that many senior Nazis put in place individual escape plans that were activated as Germany headed for military defeat. Looted art and stolen gold were at the heart of them.

10

BOOKSHOPS AND GALLERIES

To MOVE AGAINST THE POSTWAR EXIT OF LOOTED TREASURE AND Nazi personnel from Europe, Allied officials needed to quickly gather as complete a picture as possible of German activities in Iberia. During the latter stages of the war, the focus was on looted treasure and gold, with gold the greater priority in the short term. In the final weeks of the war, the Allies made greater progress in tracing the complex web of financial dealings involving Germany, Switzerland, Portugal, and Spain than in locating looted treasure. The question of Nazi gold was all the more pressing given the compelling evidence that all parties involved were melting down Nazi gold bars stamped with the swastika and recasting them for resale. Lisbon remained very much the center of the gold trade; the value of gold bars and coins there was up to four times higher than in Madrid. Samuel Klaus from the FEA led a team of key American officials in Lisbon that included Herbert Cummings from the State Department. Together they constituted the team leaders for Operation Safehaven in Iberia. Klaus particularly praised the work of James Wood, the American financial attaché to the embassy in Lisbon during the war, who had used the evidence gathered by the OSS to outline some of the major Nazi schemes in the city and the movement of gold.[1]

Klaus was convinced that Portugal would serve as a financial center for postwar Nazi dealings: "an international free market." He argued that gold would come to rest in Lisbon and monetary transactions would continue to take place in a manner that concealed their links to German interests. The five leading Portuguese banks were all said to be involved in helping Nazis disguise transactions at a time when German assets were officially frozen in the country.[2]

The Allied investigators worked hard over the summer of 1945 putting together more evidence of the existing networks used to sell looted art—including paintings by Picasso linked to the Paul Rosenberg gallery and works and treasures of the Rothschilds. Klaus, Cummings, and their teams pursued three major avenues of investigation in Lisbon: the embassy vault, the corruption in the Portuguese diplomatic service, and a suspicious venue called the New German Bookshop and Exhibition Room.[3] The first effort focused on the contents of the large vault said to have been constructed in the German embassy.[4] It was widely assumed that the Germans planned to empty the vault as the war's end neared. Lisboetas living nearby reported smoke coming from the embassy chimneys and from a fire in the garden on the eve of V-E Day: the last remaining Germans in Lisbon were busy destroying documentation and emptying the contents of the vault.[5]

Residents reported to the Allies that several unmarked trucks had been seen entering the embassy late in the evening on the eve of defeat. They left just prior to dawn and headed toward the city center. They were said to be the same trucks that made regular deliveries of gold to the embassy from the Lisbon airport. There is a palpable sense of frustration in Allied accounts of the German vault in Lisbon. Despite concerted attempts by the SIS and OSS from 1943 onward to find specific details about the vault, they largely drew a blank. The information that they most wanted concerned the amount of gold stored, any markings indicating its origin, and an inventory of the artworks. The most likely reason the Allies failed to secure this key information was that the Germans did not allow locally recruited embassy staff anywhere near the vault. The transit operations were kept secret from the embassy staff. Only a few key personnel had knowledge of them. When the Allies used their tried-and-tested approach of bribing

Portuguese embassy employees, they were met with a wall of silence. British levels of frustration led SOE agents to propose a series of wild schemes to intercept one of the vans making the journey from the airport to the embassy. None of the schemes was brought before Ronald Campbell. Had they been, he would have no doubt vetoed them, arguing that they would have angered Salazar and damaged Anglo-Portuguese relations.

The extent of the Allied failure was confirmed during the interrogation of a former German commercial attaché to Madrid. He confessed to shipping almost $1 million in English gold sovereigns from Berlin to the German embassy in Lisbon. The coins were transferred in small parcels via the diplomatic pouch. They were sold on the Lisbon market for three times the amount they would have fetched in Madrid, and the money was then exchanged in pesetas and used to help finance the German embassy in Madrid. Naturally, the coins had been stored in the vault in Lisbon.[6] According to this former commercial attaché, many other similar transfers of gold and artworks were stored for a time in the Lisbon embassy vault.[7]

The second investigation focused on a delicate issue for the British. A long-held private view among British diplomats and Foreign Office mandarins was that the Portuguese diplomatic service contained many corrupt individuals. Schellenberg hinted at this without going into details. Several Portuguese diplomats were suspected of being on the Germans' payroll. Even Prime Minister Salazar suspected a corrupt Portuguese diplomatic service, one having been influenced by the period of the Republic in Portugal; he did not trust that his regime enjoyed its complete support. Much of the diplomatic service was drawn from the aristocracy who needed money to maintain their country estates and lifestyle. In key legations, such as in Madrid, Berlin, and London, Salazar was especially careful with his choice of representatives. The problems arose at the consul level, where officials had been appointed by the Ministry of Foreign Affairs in Lisbon.

The consul that the Allies were most interested in was Adelphe Weiss, who had served as the Portuguese consul in Switzerland before returning to live in Estoril.[8] The Americans claimed that Weiss was selling the Portuguese government art that had potentially been looted through Switzerland.[9] The items in question comprised a famous series of eighteenth-century Gobelins tapestries given by the French queen Marie-Antoinette to her sister. The series contained seven pieces that depicted the Story of Esther.[10] Weiss, in his deliberations with the Portuguese government, was said to have made no reference to the real owner of the tapestries and failed to explain how they came into his possession.[11]

The third line of Allied investigation focused on finding out more about the "New German Bookshop and Exhibition Room," located at Avenida da Liberdade 50 in central Lisbon. The SIS had devoted much time and many resources to watching the shop. Originally, British agents believed the bookshop to be a hub for meetings involving German intelligence and their local informants. Karl Bucholtz in partnership with two local men named Henrique Lehrfeld and Wilhelm Gesseman opened the bookshop in late 1943.[12] Bucholtz was a well-known dealer in looted art, with a record going back as far as 1938 of selling art for the benefit of the Nazis. The German had arrived in Lisbon with approximately half a million marks' worth of art, books, and sculpture from Germany.[13] The items fetched high prices at the shop. OSS records indicate that the bookshop was in regular contact with dealers in looted art from Switzerland from D-Day until the end of the war. There was a marked increase in the turnover of the shop during this period, with a regular group of buyers from Portugal purchasing directly from the shop or from one of the private auctions that the Americans believed were hosted outside of its regular operating hours. Several employees from the German embassy in Lisbon were frequently spotted entering and leaving. Allied agents watching the shop reported that on several occasions they carried a diplomatic bag.

Bucholtz had strong connections to gangs of suspicious, opportunist Nazi art dealers, including local people working with German art agents linked to the trade in looted art. He said he was a refugee in Lisbon, in effect having been expelled by the Germans. His frequent journeys from 1943 until the end of the war contradicted this claim. He was a regular visitor to, among other places, Berlin, Geneva, and Zurich. Bucholtz hosted a number of exhibitions in the shop that attracted publicity. The British, while strongly suspecting his links to the trade in looted art, devoted more time to investigating the Germans and locals who visited the bookshop. After the war, Bucholtz disappeared and eventually resurfaced in Colombia, where he lived until his death on January 6, 1992, in Bogotá. There remains much mystery about the artworks that were sold in the shop in Lisbon (he opened additional branches in other European cities, including Madrid). The bookshop he left behind eventually moved to another location close by. During the global economic crisis that hit Portugal in 2010, the bookshop was declared bankrupt and sold to LeYa, the biggest publishing group in Portugal.

Bucholtz's shop was among a roster of names and places that the Americans and British believed traded looted artworks in Lisbon. Several inter-Allied problems arose when the Americans and the British came to different conclusions about particular individuals. Mistaken identities were commonplace, as was differing knowledge of the social and art networks in Lisbon. In some cases, the Americans considered a Portuguese person to be guilty of peddling looted art, but the British regarded them as innocent. Communication between the Allies was not always efficient and systematic. Trading information often depended on personal relationships between the Allied agents in Lisbon and their administrative support staff. Tensions heightened as competition between the Allies grew. The British were regarded as upper-class twits by a few on the American team, and the British viewed the Americans as dangerous cowboys who splashed handfuls of dollars around the city in exchange for information of questionable value.

Similar problems appeared in gathering evidence against local Portuguese. Some marred Allied attempts to create a blacklist of Portuguese companies that had traded with the Nazis. Ricardo Espírito Santo found his bank under serious pressure from American (and later French) demands that it be blacklisted largely as a result of information provided by business rivals. In the art world, rival galleries were keen to spite one another by supplying false stories to the Allies about alleged works of art being sold. It was commonplace for gallery owners to be paid to inform on other galleries and exhibitions. They did this willingly. It was the season for score settling and bloodletting in the Lisbon art world. The Americans lacked a good historical knowledge of the market that would have prevented many of the mistakes that ruined their efforts. The British, with their large ex-pat community in the city and close links to

Portuguese society, were at least able to dismiss many of the wilder allegations made by local informants.

The British ambassador, Ronald Campbell, was never enthusiastic about the use of local informants as sources of reliable intelligence. He argued that the SIS and SOE had enough agents operating in the country to secure more accurate information through their own efforts. His one exception was the attempts to bribe PVDE agents into providing news of the Germans' activities and Salazar's attitude to the events of the day. But Salazar and the head of the PVDE, Captain Lourenço, had almost no interest in the art world. Salazar viewed art as part of the propaganda sector, and under his regime there were strict (albeit not always successful) attempts to control the cultural sector. He failed to understand the relationship of art to money, wealth, and power.

For Salazar, art, looted or otherwise, was not an important issue. He found the Allies' near continuous hounding of his office bizarre. He wondered why the Allies wasted time on the issue when they should have been devoting all their time and attention to the coming conflict with the forces of communism. When Campbell pressed him on the possible role of the Portuguese government in acquiring looted art, he claimed with justification that he knew little about it and suggested that the Allies might be looking in the wrong direction in focusing on Portugal. António Ferro, the director of the Secretariat of National Propaganda (SPN), whose remit also included culture, knew more, but this complicit, cagey man who was loyal to Salazar was smart enough not to divulge anything to the Allies. Ferro's extended visit to Brazil during the war had raised eyebrows in British circles as to what he was doing there in addition to the advertised furthering of Luso-Brazilian cultural ties. For political reasons linked to the Azores agreement, Campbell never called for the SIS to question Ferro at the end of the war. Salazar would never have agreed to it.

The evidence gained during the British investigations was never complete enough for the relevant case files to be marked "proven" against Ferro. The American report of May 1945 and an updated version published later in August 1945 did contain specific names. The cases, however, were preceded by a warning:

Following is a list of other individuals whose activities appear suspicious. It should be emphasized that positive evidence against them is lacking, and that they are reported here only as a suggestion that their operations may bear watching.[14]

The list of cases was, however, suggestive:

- Albuquerque, F., Rua Nova da Trindade 1E, Lisbon. Interior decorator and antique dealer. Said to have been in close contact with Italians prior to the defeat of Italy. Pictures which may have been looted have been reported in his shop.
- Eisen, Margarete (Mrs C Duarte). A German reported to have smuggled Titian's "Salome" from Portugal to England. Said to be selling diamonds for the Germans.
- John, Conrad. Partner in the Galeria de Arte, Rua Nova da Trinidade 3A, Lisbon, which has been reported to be handling looted objects.
- Josipovicci, Leon. Rua de Santa Marta 45, Lisbon. German or Rumanian art dealer. Partner of Conrad John in Galeria de Arte. Suspected of handling looted pictures.
- Kugel, Jacques, Calendas Galleries, Rua da Chagas, Lisbon. Probably German refugee art dealer, operating the Calendas Galleries, twice reported to be working for the Germans. Has a reputation for shady dealing.
- Ostins, Jean Rolland. Avenida Palace Hotel, Lisbon. Intermediary for communications to enemy countries. Known to have dealt in art objects from enemy territory and to have sold works from confiscated Jewish collections.
- Perreira, Elfrida Marques, Galeria de Arte . . . Is suspected of handling looted art pictures.
- Raposo, Paiva, Rua de Ataide, 1, 2nd floor front, Lisbon, she has offered art objects for sale, claiming they come from Portuguese families in need of money. Would be an excellent front for the disposal of looted pictures.

- Wohwill, Mrs. F. Estrada de Benfica 463, Lisbon. Reported to be
  trafficking in visas and works of art, and to be in touch with enemy
  nationals.[15]

Although far from comprehensive, the list served as a sample of the
bigger picture of what was going on in Portugal during this time. It was
a similar story in Spain, where the Americans listed a series of suspects
with the same caveat that good-quality evidence was hard to come by.
Both the Americans and the British failed to penetrate into the upper
echelons of Spanish society as they had been able to do in Portugal.

Allied efforts in Sweden at monitoring the sales of looted art during
the war proved to be more successful. The OSS viewed Sweden as a natural venue for these activities, and the embassy in Stockholm devoted
greater resources to this issue than the embassies in Lisbon and Madrid.
As part of Operation Safehaven, the Americans reported the following:

> Certain members of the Nazi Party, whose names have not yet been re-
> vealed, are beginning to send their valuables from Germany to Sweden,
> where they are to be sold to form a capital investment in Sweden. Bu-
> kowskis, the well-known Stockholm Auction Rooms, have received two
> cases of valuable pictures from Germany during the last two weeks but the
> consignor is unknown.[16]

Subsequent reports outlined similar activities throughout 1944 and
into 1945. Artworks owned by the Italian state were turning up for sale
in Stockholm. For many Nazis, who believed that Sweden was at heart
pro-German, the movement of goods to Stockholm was ideal.[17] There
was little prospect of getting the loot out to South America, but they
were able to convert goods into local currency, which they believed to
be safe in Sweden. Given the high volumes of art flowing into Sweden,
the Allies believed that it was being sent by senior Nazis or was part of a
grander centrally orchestrated scheme from Berlin.

Toward the end of the war, as a result, the auction houses in Stockholm were doing brisk business. In 1945, several exhibitions took place
in Stockholm that are said to have included looted artworks. The Gallery

Saint Lucas, Struregatan 3, hosted an exhibition of Flemish and Dutch paintings whose provenance could not be fully established. When questioned, the director of the gallery refused to discuss their origins. He did admit that several of the paintings came from "poor Jewish refugees."[18]

The biggest black hole the Allies encountered in the track-and-trace operations was naturally in Switzerland. The secrecy surrounding the Swiss banking system and the availability of safe deposit boxes and vaults made Switzerland an attractive destination for looted art. Sending stolen artworks to Switzerland was different from moving them to other neutral countries. Despite detailed investigations and studies, the Allies found it hard to calculate the value of looted art.[19] In 1945, Allied sources suggested a figure between 100 million and 300 million Swiss francs but admitted that this was little more than a calculated guess. Apart from a few cases of individual smuggling via the German diplomatic pouch, little was known about the amount of art in the country. The Allies believed that Swiss museums and leading art dealers were not involved in the looted-art market. There were a few exceptions to this rule, but in 1945 the Allies thought most museums and dealers were clean. It was common for local authorities to ask Swiss dealers to produce certificates confirming that paintings offered for sale had been in Switzerland for several years. This helped limit the circulation of stolen art.

It did not, however, address the main problem, which was that the vast majority of looted art secretly imported into Switzerland was not for sale. It was in storage in the country's legendary bank vaults. The rest was sent to forwarding agents or private hands. Works of art that were sent from Germany to Switzerland could remain there undisturbed for five years under the name of the addressee. Under Swiss law, these were not considered imports. The Allies claimed that the shipments of art from Germany to Switzerland were handled by a Swiss company named Brenner, which was based in Basel, and the German company Schenker, which had several branches in various Swiss cities.[20]

Throughout the war, a number of well-known Nazi art agents and buyers, such as Alois Miedl, visited Switzerland on a regular basis. There was evidence that these individuals were engaged in the traffic of looted art objects, and these networks also involved several Swiss art dealers.[21]

Leading Nazis were at the German end of the supply chain. Allied intelligence agents were extremely active in Switzerland but found the gathering of accurate and compelling evidence even harder than it was in Lisbon and Madrid. The scale of the Swiss export route was confirmed by the specific case studies the Allies examined at the end of the war. Fifteen major networks were found, although the Americans did not term them "investigations" out of fear of offending the Swiss authorities.

From this accumulation of admittedly incomplete Allied evidence, a picture of the movement of looted art emerges. As German losses on the battlefield worsened and the momentum of the war swung toward an Allied victory, the movement of looted art increased across Europe. There was no centrally orchestrated German escape or exit plan, so the transport of art came down to specific individuals. These leading figures in the Nazi Party acted mainly out of selfish personal gain and for some higher purpose. The number of shipments and the arbitrary nature of the art looted (shipping of whole collections was rare) made tracing the treasure all the harder. Switzerland was considered a temporary refuge or safe haven (as Germans called it, ironically, given the Allied Operation Safehaven). Sweden was selected because of the deep-rooted German belief that the country's political, commercial, and banking leaders were pro-German, if not always pro-Nazi.

The slight miscalculation the Germans made regarding the Stockholm route was to underestimate the scale of the British and American intelligence operations in Sweden. The British SIS and SOE along with the American OSS operated in Sweden with fewer political restrictions than those of their colleagues in Portugal and Spain. As the war drew to a close, the Americans and the British reinforced their intelligence operations in Sweden, mainly to watch for Soviet moves in Scandinavia, but the same agents proved useful in tracking and tracing looted art. The Americans wanted to adopt a hard line toward Swedish networks. The British prime minister Winston Churchill singled out the country for special scorn in his speeches. He argued that it had gotten rich from the war and that its commercial elite had much to answer for because of their extensive trading relations with Berlin for the entire duration of the war.

All the Allied scrutiny of Stockholm placed the Swedish authorities under far greater pressure than that of their Portuguese and Spanish counterparts to cooperate with Allied investigations or to conduct their own inquiries. This made moving art out of Sweden nearly impossible. The Swiss also came under similar pressure but hid behind their strict banking rules that ensured the secrecy of transactions. The contents of their banking vaults remained firmly closed to Allied investigators during and after the war.

For that reason, leading Nazis who wished to disappear in South America needed, as a practical matter, to transit through Portugal and Spain. Any looted art or other stolen items could either travel with them or be sent separately through established semiofficial networks. Allied agents recorded a massive increase in the number of flights from Germany entering Spain through Barcelona. After refueling, the planes flew on to Madrid and Lisbon. At the start of 1945, the Allies discovered fake import licenses for goods entering Spain from Germany.[22] The import licenses were for pharmaceutical products with the value of 7 million pesetas for a period of less than two months. The German pharmaceutical trade with Spain was a cover for the export of other items, including gold and looted art. The strong connections between German pharmaceutical companies and Spain and Portugal, where they dominated the market, was a successful cover.[23]

Once again, the efforts to trace enemy assets in Madrid were set back by the different priorities of the Allies devoted to the task. The Americans led the way, trying to motivate their Allied friends to act. The British response was to provide information when requested, but not to take a major lead in investigations. The French professed interest, but, in reality, Paris was apathetic. On top of national divisions, various rivalries arose between legations in different capitals. A few appeared interested, and others thought it not a priority. One such example is the Dutch legation in Madrid, which showed little interest in following up on an Allied lead that pictures looted from the Netherlands by Göring were at the free Port of Bilbao awaiting export to South America.[24] In the end, the British legation in Madrid was forced to inform the Dutch legation in London and complain about their counterparts in Madrid.

Much of the lengthy correspondence among the Allies focused on creating a unified body through which issues regarding enemy assets, including looted art and Nazi gold, would be investigated. Suggestions included delegating the work to the future United Nations. It was hoped that neutral countries would then take the problem more seriously. In the short term the neutral countries displayed a distinct lack of enthusiasm for cooperating with Allied investigations.

The Spanish proved to be the most frustrating. When approached with specific requests for information, Spanish officials shrugged and wondered why the issue was important to a war that had now been decisively won. In Lisbon and Madrid, the authorities did not consider it likely that many Nazis would exit Europe and move to South America to prepare for the rise of another Reich.

Both Franco and Salazar had a deep-rooted fear that the Allies would bring a great deal of pressure to bear to prevent the neutrals from holding on to the proceeds of wartime trade with Germany. In Portugal, there was an additional reluctance to allow the Allies complete access to records concerning the assets of German companies that had been frozen. Frustrations among Allied officials and diplomats had been building for a long time. At the center of everything was a lack of understanding of the Allies' main aims and the purpose of Operation Safehaven. As one official in Madrid pointed out:

> My feeling, however, is that though much effort is being expended, we are not getting anywhere because neither we nor the consular posts have been given the slightest indications of the objects who London have in mind in compiling these lists. We have not even been told whether the main object is to confiscate German assets to use them to pay reparations, or whether it is to prevent the Nazis from using their assets in neutral countries as a means of perpetuating their power.[25]

To make matters worse for the Allies, an overfocus on specific cases was not producing the desired results. In Iberia, much of 1945 was spent checking the allegations against individuals whose names had been placed on the lists. One of several U-turns featured the case of Margarite Eisen and concerned a work by Titian of Salome, which was said to have been smuggled into England.[26] Eisen was thought to have been a member of a Nazi looted-art network in Lisbon. The Ministry of Economic War-fare visited the National Westminster Bank branch where the painting was said to have been deposited. They discovered that the bank only held in Mrs. Eisen's name a cash balance and a large flat container, which had been deposited there before the war. The case against Mrs. Eisen was dropped, and the ministry wrote to the source of the information instructing them not to waste any more of their time.[27] Because the original allegations had come from the Americans in Lisbon, this added to the inter-Allied tensions.

It was not all mistakes and failures, but the Allies were lost in sinuous paper trails that kept them far behind the activities of a cunning and elusive enemy. While the race to discover looted art and gold shifted eastward, and delivered major finds across Germany and beyond, the back door to escape Europe remained ajar. The failings that took place near the end of the war in the neutral countries, mainly in Portugal and Spain, continued through the summer of 1945. As the world's attention turned away from the European theater toward the decisive battles in the campaign against the Japanese, senior Nazi officers like Herberts Cukurs were quietly leaving Europe.

Lisbon was a hive of activity for the smuggling of Nazi gold and looted art. The Portuguese police turned a blind eye to much of the activity.

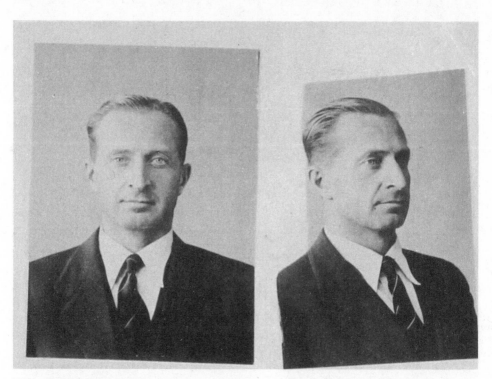

Walter Schellenberg controlled almost all German intelligence activities in the neutral countries. A man who preferred to remain in the shadows stepped forward at the end of the war to try to secure an agreed German surrender with the Western allies. These two photographs are from his Camp 020 interrogation file.

Continued on Page 5   Continued on Page 4

FRENCH ART TREASURES SEIZED IN BERMUDA LAST WEEK

LONDON, Oct. 9. (BOP).—The transfer of French art treasures, by the sale of which in the United States Germany hoped to secure dollar exchange, has been frustrated by the Bermuda contraband control authorities.

It is authoritatively stated that information had been received that a large consignment of French pictures had been shipped in the vessel Excalibur to the United States by A. M. Martin Fabiani of Paris, described under the dual title of art expert and expert adviser on customs questions.

The British authorities had good reason to believe he was acting as a German agent. That the Germans realised the commercial value of what they describe as "decadent art" was shown by the fact that the collection, consisting of over 500 paintings and drawings, included 270 works by Renoir, 30 by Cezanne, 20 by Gauguin and 4 by Degas, with others by Monet, Manet and Piccasso. The pictures were seized as enemy exports at Bermuda, where there will be no danger their again falling into German hands.

According to the B.B.C. report last night, the consignment is valued at several hundred thousand pounds.

Extract from *The Royal Gazette* newspaper in Bermuda published on October 10, 1940, of the British operation to board the SS *Excalibur* and seize alleged looted art being transported from Europe to New York.

The American Export Lines SS *Excalibur* arriving at the Jersey docks in New York. The ship spent the war crisscrossing the Atlantic bringing refugees and looted art to the United States.

The dock's activity in Lisbon harbor with a Spanish cargo ship recently arrived from Bilbao during World War II. Many crates remained unchecked and unopened by the local customs officials. The Bilbao to Lisbon to South America shipping route was a lucrative one for smugglers of looted art and later used by Nazis as an escape line.

Lisbon airport with the daily Lufthansa flight from Berlin (middle) displaying the swastika on the tail. It is in front of the regular Spanish airlines flight from Madrid.

Nazi officials in Paris removing confiscated works of art from galleries and collectors, including some pieces from Paul Rosenberg and the Rothschild family. They are being loaded onto French trucks for transport to Germany.

The Nazis seized the gallery of prominent art dealer Paul Rosenberg at 21 rue la Boetie in Paris, and in 1941 created the Institute of the Jewish Question in the building. The institute would be the center of anti-Jewish propaganda, creating a series of exhibitions, such as "The Jews and France," which were held across the city.

Portugal's dictator António de Oliveira Salazar posing for his sculpture. Ironically, Salazar showed almost no interest in the arts generally or the looted treasure passing through the country during and after World War II.

Wild Bill Donovan (pictured third from the left), the charismatic head of American intelligence during World War II. He was ousted at the end of the war, which had a negative impact on Allied efforts at tracing looted treasure and Nazi fugitives.

Sir Stewart Menzies, the director of British Intelligence, could not have been more different than his American counterpart. Calculating, elitist, and with a strong belief in the British Empire, he enjoyed the full support of Winston Churchill. He ran British intelligence like a gentlemen's club and came spectacularly unstuck with the exposure of Kim Philby as a Soviet spy.

Livraria Bucholtz, located at Avenida Liberdade, 50 (the Champs-Élysées of Lisbon). The bookshop was a front for the sale of looted art and treasure. German intelligence agents were regular visitors, often carrying overstuffed diplomatic bags into the shop.

Private auctions of looted works of art took place in a room behind the curtain of the bookshop, Livraria Bucholtz, where there was a dedicated space for invited guests only. British intelligence agents watched the bookshop but were never able to see behind the curtain.

The Spanish capital of Madrid was the center of smuggling and attempted sales of looted treasure. It was also a ratline for Nazis who wished to escape. Argentines, who had been dispatched to Madrid, helped facilitate the exit of many Nazi officers who were willing and able to pay.

The beautiful city of Stockholm, Sweden, witnessed much unsavory activity in World War II and beyond. The major trade ties that developed between the Swedes and Nazis were utilized by the latter to escape after the war. The profits of war were used by Sweden to launch its economic miracle in the post–World War II era.

The Azores airbase, with its long runway, was vital to the Allies for D-Day, and remained of enormous strategic importance to the Western powers from the outset of the Cold War. Salazar cleverly leveraged continued access to the airbase against Allied demands to return the Nazi gold Portugal had acquired during the war.

The White Buses of the Swedish Red Cross in the mission organized by Count Folke Bernadotte at the end of the war. The operation, and Bernadotte's role in it, remained highly controversial in the postwar period.

Count Folke Bernadotte, the United Nations mediator in Palestine, preparing to give his report to the UN in 1948. His role was complicated by the fact that many Zionists regarded him as anti-Semitic.

The body of Bernadotte returning to Europe following his assassination in Israel. Bernadotte was never able to escape the shadow of allegations made against him that centered upon his contacts and negotiations with Walter Schellenberg and Heinrich Himmler at the end of World War II.

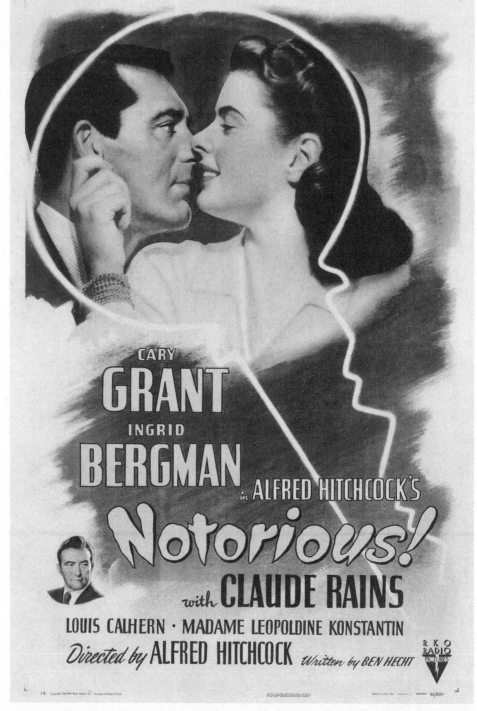

CARY
GRANT
INGRID
BERGMAN
in ALFRED HITCHCOCK'S
Notorious!
with CLAUDE RAINS
LOUIS CALHERN · MADAME LEOPOLDINE KONSTANTIN
Directed by ALFRED HITCHCOCK   Written by BEN HECHT

R K O
RADIO
PICTURES

Alfred Hitchcock's box office hit, *Notorious!*, made Brazil famous in the postwar era for all the wrong reasons: it portrayed Brazil as a home for Nazi war criminals. Brazilian leaders argued that the film should have been set in Argentina, the country where the majority of the Nazis were fleeing.

Juan Perón and his wife, Eva, were two highly populist leaders in Argentina. President Perón took a strategic decision to encourage Nazis to emigrate to Argentina. He hoped to use them to strengthen the country's military and economic positions.

Eva Perón on the Lisbon leg of her Rainbow Tour of Europe to help promote Argentina. Photographed having lunch hosted by Portuguese leader Salazar (seated near left). Evita, as she was known, wanted to talk about fashion; Salazar wanted to talk about the state of the Argentine economy.

While the Allies discovered large amounts of gold stolen by the Nazis in World War II, today significant amounts still remain unaccounted for or were not returned by the neutral countries (especially Portugal).

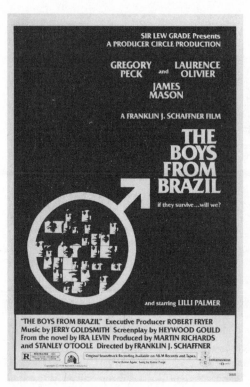

The Hollywood film *The Boys from Brazil* was meant to be based, in part, in Paraguay but was actually shot in Lisbon. The story moves once again to Brazil, citing the country's alleged hosting of Nazi war criminals in the postwar period. This added to the perception of Brazil, not Argentina, being the major destination for escaping Nazis.

The lights shone brightly in Buenos Aires during the post–World War II period. The city was regarded as the most European in South America, and its neighboring towns became very popular with those Nazis who managed to escape and who enjoyed the healthy climate.

The fake passport used by Adolf Eichmann to enter Argentina. These passports were not cheap to buy, but by 1947 there was a strong network and well-organized support structure to help Nazis escape Europe to Argentina.

After World War II, the streets of Lisbon emptied as foreign spies, diplomats, and refugees had all left. There remained big questions over Portugal's Nazi gold and the amount of looted treasure that had passed through the country. Portugal remains the neutral country that got away with the most.

11

POSTWAR LISBON

IN THE IMMEDIATE AFTERMATH OF THE WAR, LISBON REMAINED VERY much on the watchlist of Allied intelligence agencies. American embassy officials were trying to finish the work financial attaché James Wood had started, piecing together a comprehensive picture of the illicit goings-on in the country during the war involving the Nazis. There was a new set of priorities, however, and these involved looking for fleeing Nazis who were trying to escape through Lisbon on an ocean liner. The cooperation of the Portuguese authorities was sporadic and dependent on the mood of Salazar. In South America it was the same story. Nobody except the Americans and the British appeared interested in devoting sizable resources to catch Nazis.

Allied agents in Lisbon posted reports of several Germans with newly issued Argentine passports traveling on ocean liners to South America after the war ended. The documents were claimed to have been issued by the German embassy in Madrid and subsequently by the embassy of Argentina in Lisbon. Descriptions of the Germans were not precise and little additional evidence was offered to support the claims. The British Ministry of Economic Warfare ordered a tightening of surveillance of passenger and crew lists on ships departing for South America. As a safety precaution, it ordered an increase in the boarding and searching of ships sailing from Spanish ports as well, although there remained a reluctance to board ships sailing from Portuguese ports. The British continued to use a softly, softly approach with Lisbon. The Americans, while expressing concerns about the strategy, allowed the British to take the lead in Portugal.

Reports of Germans escaping with fake Argentine passports originated in the State Department and were transmitted to the British through the American embassy in London.[1] Although the reports had started in the autumn of 1944, the British were slow to react because of a lack of proof.[2] Despite this shortcoming, British agents in Lisbon continued to monitor and investigate the issue throughout the summer of 1945. The State Department claims led the British passport control officer to tighten monitoring of crew and passenger lists in Lisbon. This had previously been identified as a weak link in the efforts to thwart Nazis escaping Europe because the holding of a passport (real or fake) was enough to guarantee boarding. Predeparture background checks were only sporadic as a result of the pressure they put on British resources in Lisbon.

At the South American end, the Allies increased surveillance of Brazilian passport control and soon discovered major gaps in Brazilian controls at the ports. Brazilian officials' lack of interest was identified as a major weakness in Allied attempts to prevent Nazis from entering the country. Brazil's war participation on the side of the Allies meant that there were political niceties to observe. London felt it unwise to apply strong pressure on the Brazilian government to put its house in order in this key area. Instead, the strategy of the Americans, with the British lining up behind, was to highlight the positives of Brazilian efforts in the war. The State Department and the Foreign Office believed it would be counterproductive to the political situation in Brazil to make demands about internal security issues. The situation in Rio was fragile. The success of Brazil's transformation from authoritarian rule to democracy was at the heart of American policy toward Brazil. This was a seismic shift that could help modernize Brazil economically and politically but also lead to positive reforms across the South American continent.

This was not the only reason for holding back on Brazil. During the war, President Roosevelt made a number of private promises to help persuade Brazil to join sides with the Allies. These included American contributions to the development of the Brazilian economy and construction of much-needed infrastructure to link the vast country internally and with the outside world. Arguably, the biggest promise that President Vargas believed he had been made was over the United Nations. Brazil was under the impression that it would be given a permanent seat on the Security Council of the UN. Whether Roosevelt made such a definitive offer on this point is not clear. Discussions surrounding the promise stalled after Roosevelt's death. The new president quietly reined in many of the promises his predecessor had made, believing him to have been overgenerous. Brazil, in the aftermath of the war, was about to discover that it had been misled by the Americans.

As Nazi escape attempts increased in frequency and number, the Portuguese tried to ignore the implementation of Allied measures aimed at counteracting the Nazi exodus to South America. Frustrating as this turned out to be for the Allies, it did not mean that the Portuguese authorities were necessarily endorsing the efforts of the Nazis. Notoriously a man who worked at his own speed, Salazar slowed the pace of the negotiations with the Allies about allowing Portuguese shipping to be regulated and boarded when necessary. He argued that after spending five years dealing with the war on a daily basis (serving as minister of foreign affairs and defense in addition to prime minister), his priority from V-E Day onward was internal issues. The convenient refocus was part of a strategy of nonconformity with Allied postwar goals related to Operation Safehaven. The absence of the newly retired British ambassador Ronald Campbell was a significant factor that enabled Salazar to dictate the agenda with the Allies and the speed with which it was—or, more likely, was not—pursued. Both the American and British ambassadors who arrived in Lisbon after the war were midlevel diplomats whose abilities and understanding of Salazar fell far short of Campbell's.

Salazar's chief of the PVDE, Captain Lourenço, proved to be equally elusive. Immediately after the war, opposition groups, many of which were communist, increased civil disobedience across Portugal. Watching events in Brazil closely, they believed that the Salazar regime would be vulnerable in the peacetime era. Calls for democratization and the holding of free elections escalated.[3] Salazar took some comfort in the fact that the opposition forces were deeply divided and lacked a significant unifying figure who could present himself to the public as an alternative leader.[4] Lourenço, however, was taking no chances, and after a brief flirtation with holding free elections, Salazar ordered his chief of police to increase levels of repression.[5] Allied attempts to engage with the PVDE on the issue of Nazis entering or transiting through Portugal were largely ignored.

Most senior officers in the PVDE remained sympathetic to the Nazi cause. Contacts with Germans working at the embassy that had been developed during the war did not fade when the war ended. Isolated cases arose of PVDE officers helping former German diplomats receive fake documents. Germans whose presence in the country could draw unwanted attention were provided with new identities and residency permits and, if required, Portuguese nationality. The police additionally ran protection rackets to provide security for Germans who moved to the countryside. It remains unclear who, if anybody, in the political sphere authorized these actions by the police. Although Salazar had given permission for the ex-ambassador to live in Portugal, this was only agreed after Hoyningen-Huene had been interviewed by the Allied war crimes unit and given a clean bill of health. It is likely that Salazar did not know about the other individual cases that his police force authorized. Captain Lourenço, an astute leader of the Secret Police, was loyal to the Portuguese leader, and therefore if he knew about these cases, then likely Salazar would have been informed. A "don't ask, don't tell" policy is the most probable explanation of individual police officers helping out their old German paymasters in exchange for more money.

The Allies were not unaware of the political leanings of the PVDE. They tried to work with members of the force, including Lourenço. But most of their efforts fell on deaf ears during the crucial summer months of 1945. During this time, Lourenço worked on one of Salazar's internal policies, the reform of the police and the replacement of the PVDE. Its successor, Polícia Internacional e de Defesa do Estado, better known as PIDE, took over the duties of the PVDE on October 22, 1945. The main roles of PIDE were border control, immigration and emigration control, and internal and external state security. The force was based on the British model of Scotland Yard, and over time PIDE developed many informant networks that helped keep Salazar in power. Its increasing use of repressive measures became a feature over the years. PIDE was initially led by Lourenço, and this offered the Allies a degree of continuity, but it did not transform Portugal's willingness to support the Safehaven investigations.

Lourenço was playing a wider-ranging game and not merely carrying out the reforms of the Secret Police requested by Salazar. The PVDE was a forerunner of the German Gestapo in terms of organization (and not the other way around, as is often recounted in Portugal). German officers traveled to Lisbon during the 1930s to study the force's structure and workings. What impressed them the most was its ruthless streak and results-oriented culture. The close links that developed between the PVDE and the Nazis were a product of the original linkage of the two organizations. During the war, members of the PVDE, though probably not Lourenço himself, supported the Nazis by passing information to German agents about the workings of Allied intelligence. On occasion, cooperation was extended to joint operations against individuals.

The most notorious example of overt cooperation came in 1941 when Gestapo agents operating openly in central Lisbon with PVDE support arrested the German Jewish pacifist refugee Berthold Jacob in broad daylight.[6] His detention and subsequent quiet deportation to Germany, where he died in a concentration camp, sent shockwaves through Portugal. Links between the Gestapo and the PVDE became even closer as the war progressed and the Germans increased the number of Gestapo-associated personnel in the German embassy in Portugal. As the war ended, these links were utilized to help fleeing Nazis and their looted goods and capital escape justice through the production of false papers and the provision of suitable accommodation away from the major cities. As Schellenberg recounted, the Germans continued to pay handsomely for the supporting services of the PVDE, which explained why the Allies were unable to make much headway in penetrating the police force.[7]

As a result, reform of the PVDE was needed after the war. Salazar understood this, as did Lourenço, who had additional motives as well.

The police chief viewed the end of the war as an opportunity to purge the PVDE of its pro-Nazi officers, who were not invited to join the more Anglo-centric PIDE.[8] This nicely served the purpose of removing all of Lourenço's internal rivals and allowed him to appoint loyalists to key positions. The creation of PIDE signaled a shift by Salazar. Putting aside his hostility to Operation Safehaven, and his fears that the Allies would demand the return of Nazi gold from the wolfram trade, he needed to reposition himself and the country. The Scotland Yard–style setup of PIDE was meant to send a message to the Allies that he was embracing change, albeit on a relatively superficial level, and that he would be a sophisticated postwar player in European politics. His main motive was to make sure Portugal was not left out of the very negotiations that would determine its fate in Europe. He wanted no rerun of the mistakes his Portuguese predecessors had made at the end of World War I, when they allowed the country to be overlooked in the postwar political settlement despite its participation in the fighting.

Salazar's short-term aim was to comply with aspects of Safehaven to alleviate Allied pressure on the country. His ambassador in London, the Duque de Palmela, had been sending him the coverage of Portugal in the British press; it was unfriendly. Salazar was accused of being pro-Nazi, and reports of specific help Portugal was alleged to have given Germans evading justice were highlighted.[9] The reports, which tended to be wide of the mark, were fed to the media by British intelligence sources. The American coverage was kinder and reflected the start of a shift in the State Department's attitude toward Lisbon. The increasingly influential diplomat George Kennan played a key role. During WWII, Kennan outlined his position on the menace of the Soviet Union to the postwar order. During his posting in Lisbon during the war, he met with Salazar on many occasions while conducting the sensitive negotiations of American access to the Azores airbase. The two men had bonded, not over the Azores but in their joint belief that the Soviet Union was likely to prove the major challenge to Western hegemony in postwar Europe.[10] Never keen to outright oppose the Allies, Salazar played a complex game of evasion, postponement, and seeming compliance without actually implementing Safehaven or returning the Nazi gold.

The medium- and long-term goals reflected the Portuguese leader's belief that pressure on Portugal to negotiate over the Nazi gold would in time recede as the American-led Western powers came to terms with the military and security threats posed by the expansionist agenda of the Soviet Union. Central to the strategy—the ace of spades, as far as Salazar was concerned—were the negotiations over continued American access to the airbase in the Azores. Simply by looking at a world map, it was clear that the Americans would need the Azores base in the Atlantic Ocean if it was going to build a major and long-term military garrison in Europe.

The British, he understood, were economically broken by the war, and the Labour government led by Clement Attlee would focus on domestic issues such as the creation of the welfare state.[11] The advice Salazar was receiving from London was that, despite the unflattering press coverage, Britain cared less about Safehaven than its American and French colleagues. Although this might not have been strictly true, Salazar's belief that this was the case helped him to call London's bluff on many of the postwar activities related to Safehaven. By the autumn of 1945, Salazar was a man who had ridden out the internal and external political storms that threatened his leadership and, in his view, Portugal and its empire.[12]

Captain Lourenço worked in the shadows to reposition Portugal among the victorious Allies without publicly changing the country's policies toward Safehaven. Following instructions from Salazar, he quietly cooperated with British intelligence to help keep the situation in postwar Portugal under control. The chief of police made an important distinction between those Nazis transiting through Lisbon to a destination in South America and those trying to remain in the country permanently. The former group were not bothered by the authorities, provided they caused no trouble and had plans to exit the country. The extent to which the police force, amid organizational reforms over the summer of 1945, had knowledge of the German ratlines through Lisbon remains unclear. British intelligence kept a close watch on the ports of Lisbon and Porto but struggled to prevent Nazis from slipping through the net using false papers and freighters rather than passenger liners.

Lourenço showed scant interest in exiting Germans. It was the second category—those who wanted to remain in Portugal—that attracted his attention. At the center of this group were personnel from the German embassy who had strong connections to the SS-linked intelligence service known as the SD.

12

ON THE RUN

THE SICHERHEITSDIENST (SECURITY SERVICE), OFTEN KNOWN BY ITS full title, Sicherheitsdienst des Reichsführers SS (Security Service of the Reichsführer SS), or the SD for short, was the intelligence agency of the SS and the Nazi Party. Founded in 1931, the organization was the first Nazi intelligence agency. The Gestapo was formed two years later. During WWII in Lisbon, several SD personnel in the German embassy were tasked with intelligence roles. From 1943 until the end of the war, the head of the SD in Berlin was Ernst Kaltenbrunner, the great rival of Walter Schellenberg. The Portuguese authorities viewed the SD as troublemakers. Although Lourenço and Salazar tolerated much of the activities of the Abwehr (a German military intelligence service), they regarded the SD agents as little more than thugs, intent on making mischief in Portugal and beyond. The SD's view of the PVDE was equally low. The first thing their agents wanted to do following a German invasion of Portugal was to fire Captain Lourenço and replace him with a more ideologically friendly officer.

In Lisbon, the SD's chief for most of the war was Adolf Nassenstein. Born in London in 1911 to an English mother, he lived in the British capital until 1931.[1] He spoke perfect English without an accent and, unlike many of his colleagues in the SD, he was a careful and calculating

strategist who could be charming.[2] He possessed a deep understanding
of Britain and its limitations and believed that it should have come to an
accord with Germany to avoid the war. Like Salazar, he viewed the common enemy as communism and the Soviet Union. His desire to find an
accommodation between the Nazis and the Allies did not end with the
outbreak of the war in 1939. He retained a strong belief that the war was
a mistake that could have been avoided and called on the Allies to join
the common struggle against the Soviet Union following the German
invasion in 1941. Above and beyond everything, he was a diehard Nazi.
His loyalty was to Kaltenbrunner and the service of the SD even after the
German intelligence services were unified in the latter part of the war. It
will not come as a surprise that Schellenberg offered faint praise of Nassenstein in his interrogations at Camp 020:

> In general, Nassenstein's professional qualities are regarded as mediocre.
> To be sure, his long experience as an agent abroad is valuable to him.[3]

Indeed, Schellenberg said one of his biggest regrets about his management of the German operation in Lisbon was that he was not able to get
rid of Nassenstein:

> I was unable to dismiss Nassenstein at the time of his wife's suicide, al-
> though this was an obvious necessity. . . . It was evident from this small
> illustration what a sorry outlook there was for the service in spite of all my
> efforts.[4]

Within the SD, Nassenstein was originally seen as a highflier with a
good record. He arrived in Portugal on May 4, 1942, with the main role
of recruiting agents for the Americas among the Brazilians living in Portugal.[5] Soon after his arrival, he moved to rented accommodation in Estoril along the Lisbon coast. There he socialized with the wealthy classes
of Portuguese society, many of whom he conversed with in flawless
English. A popular figure among the locals, he made connections with
several Portuguese families that had links to Brazil. He enjoyed minor
successes in recruiting Brazilians based in Lisbon. His main contact was

Plínio Salgado, who led the Brazilian Integralistas and who had been exiled to Portugal by the Vargas regime in Brazil.[6] Salgado retained good connections with Brazilian fascists and helped supply the SD in Lisbon with current political literature and press summaries from Rio. Nassenstein sent these on to Berlin along with assessments of the possibility of overthrowing the Brazilian government and replacing it with a pro-Nazi administration.[7] The majority of these far-fetched plots centered on the political orientation of key figures in the Brazilian military and defense establishment. Salgado was largely politically isolated in Portugal, but his connections in Brazil provided Nassenstein with an opportunity to please his masters in Berlin with the supply of colorful information.

The structure of German intelligence in Lisbon was not as rigid as it was in other countries.[8] The distinction between Gestapo intelligence, led by Emil Schroeder, and Nassenstein's division was not great. As a result, Nassenstein, like Schroeder, was interested in obtaining political information about Portugal, mainly through agents who held official positions in the Portuguese government.[9] In this area, he enjoyed some successes, but with the local perception from 1943 onward that the war was going in favor of the Allies, it took increasing amounts of money to bribe government officials. He was involved in two important escapades. The first was the attempt to flood Britain with fake currency, much of which was initially distributed in Portugal. The second was the distribution in Portugal of what the Allies called Nazi terror funds that would finance sabotage of the Portuguese infrastructure in the event of a German expulsion from the country. Some of these funds might have been used to help Germans transiting through the country or those trapped in Portugal at the end of the war to escape.[10]

As German defeat appeared inevitable, Nassenstein tried to make his move and leave Lisbon. He made plans in March 1945 to head to Argentina using false papers and disguising his appearance with a fake beard and glasses. British agents from the SIS had him under surveillance. When he had previously left Lisbon to holiday in the Algarve to the south, his absence and travel movements were carefully monitored.[11] Rumors of his permanent departure from Lisbon reached British intelligence in the middle of March 1945 by way of a local informant in the

German embassy. The SIS alerted London about the likelihood that Nassenstein was about to flee Lisbon.[12] The SIS requested any ship that Nassenstein sailed on be intercepted and taken to Gibraltar, where he would
be arrested.[13] The intelligence service consented to his detainment and
transfer to Britain for interrogation. Nassenstein was accused of recruiting agents in Portugal who were sent to England.[14] If captured, he would
have ended up in Camp 020 alongside Schellenberg.

In the end, Nassenstein chose not to flee to Argentina for a number
of potential reasons. It was perfectly possible that he knew he was under
daily surveillance and this made an escape too dangerous. Despite the
vast amount of financial resources at his disposal, he might simply have
had difficulties securing passage on a liner. Ships sailing from Lisbon to
Brazil in March and April 1945 were full, and posing as a crew member could have offered the best possibility of securing a berth. A more
likely scenario was that Nassenstein, who enjoyed good contacts with the
PVDE, believed that the Portuguese police would protect him at the end
of the war. He hoped simply to disappear in Portugal in all the chaos,
using either his own identity or fake papers issued by the embassy or
agents in the PVDE. He would plan to settle permanently in the country
or wait in Portugal and then head to Argentina via Brazil later. He also
had connections in Spain if the Portuguese authorities proved hostile to
his remaining in the country.

When the war ended, Nassenstein was abandoned by his PVDE
agents, many of whom fell prey to the purge of the police force by Captain Lourenço. Instead of hiding out in the country, he was eventually
interned at Caldas das Taipas near Guimarães in northeast Portugal.[15]
Prior to his arrival at the detention camp, he was ordered to report to an
internment camp in Vila Almeida along with some less significant members of the German embassy in Lisbon.[16] Vila Almeida is close to the
city of Guarda and the wolfram mines, not far from the Spanish border.
Nassenstein tried to escape to Spain, but despite using country back roads
he encountered a manned border post where the Spanish guards refused
him entry.[17]

In June 1945 he was then taken into custody while the Portuguese authorities debated what to do with him. On November 17, 1945, PIDE

decided to hand him and four other Germans over for repatriation. The five were released pending arrangements being made for their return to Germany. Two days later, on November 19, the four other Germans appeared to begin their repatriation, but Nassenstein was absent.[18] He went on the run in Portugal, hiding first in the countryside and then moving to Lisbon with his close friend and colleague from German intelligence Herbert Wissmann, whose official title at the embassy had been press attaché. The two men hoped to lie low until the Allies simply stopped looking for them.[19] Nassenstein believed that his wartime contacts in the now-defunct PVDE would stop the local authorities from pursuing any case against him or, more likely, handing him over to the Allies for interrogation and possible charges.[20]

Unbeknownst to them, the two Germans stumbled into a toxic arrangement in Lisbon with the family they rented an apartment from. Neighbors recounted that the men moved into the apartment on the third floor of Avenida António de Aguiar, 7, at the start of 1946. The tenant of the flat, the owner's daughter, Cacilda Figueira, had agreed to shield the Germans in return for a considerable amount of money.[21] Her lover, a local man, António Nunes dos Santos, discovered the arrangement and demanded a share of the money for himself.[22] Cacilda refused. A series of heated exchanges followed during which Nunes dos Santos threatened to inform the police about the Germans' presence if she did not share her ill-gotten gains with him. After she threw him out on the street, Nunes dos Santos carried out his threat: he wrote an anonymous letter to the Portuguese authorities stating that Cacilda was hiding two Germans.[23] The police ignored the letter. Their lack of action further infuriated Nunes dos Santos, who then made further financial demands on his mistress. When she once again refused, he pulled out a revolver and shot her dead.[24] After his trial, Nunes dos Santos was sentenced to life imprisonment (there was no capital punishment in Portugal). During his time in prison, he provided the police with information about the two Germans and the address where they were staying. The case was quickly passed on to the PIDE and Captain Lourenço.[25]

On the morning of January 14, 1947, officers from the PIDE raided the apartment. The police action followed a lengthy investigation into the whereabouts of Nassenstein and Wissmann. The officers attending the scene were given instructions to arrest the two Germans with the view to questioning them about their disappearances after the war.[26] Senior PIDE officers knew both men personally, and Captain Lourenço had attended social events with them during the war. Nassenstein regarded the captain as a personal friend and had written of his great respect for the officer during WWII. It was thought that the raid would therefore be relatively routine and that the Germans would not offer any resistance. This proved to be wrong.[27]

PIDE officers entered the apartment without incident. As the officers read out the arrest warrants, everything changed. Wissmann pulled out a gun and fired at the policemen. The gun jammed. He fired again. The same result. After firing for a third time with the same result, Wissmann put the gun to his own head and pulled the trigger. The gun did not go off for a fourth time. At this point he dropped the revolver, reached into a trouser pocket, and pulled out a poison capsule, which he swallowed. He died within minutes.[28] At the same time Wissmann took out his gun, Nassenstein produced a revolver and held it against his temple. Looking into the policeman's eyes, he pulled the trigger. The gun went off, but the chamber was empty.[29] At this point, one of the policemen seized the gun before Nassenstein could pull the trigger again. Nassenstein was taken into custody for questioning.[30]

The PIDE was not interested in the wartime activities of either Nassenstein or Wissmann. Their inquiries solely concerned the men's whereabouts since the end of the war and the names of people who had helped hide them. Prior to his return to Lisbon, Wissmann had been living in Madrid, where he had been sheltered by the local pro-German groups.[31] His return to Lisbon was the first stage en route to Argentina.

Nassenstein refused to cooperate with the police. He made two further attempts on his life while in his cell, which resulted in him being put into a straitjacket. Nassenstein assaulted his guards on at least two separate occasions; his violent temper shocked even the seasoned PIDE officers. "We can't keep him in a straitjacket forever," Captain Lourenço told his political superiors at the Ministry of Foreign Affairs.[32] There was a fear that if Nassenstein took his own life in custody, it would not look good for the PIDE.[33] A third German agent had died in a shoot-out with the police just prior to Nassenstein's arrest. "This will look like we have assassinated all three men," a worried Lourenço told the Portuguese minister of foreign affairs.[34]

To avoid Nassenstein succeeding in taking his own life on Portuguese soil, Lourenço contacted British intelligence through the embassy in Lisbon.[35] Citing the strong political reasons for Nassenstein's departure from Lisbon, he asked the British whether it would be possible for them to remove Nassenstein within twenty-four hours.[36] It was an unusual, highly unofficial request from the head of the PIDE. The British jumped at the offer. It gave them a chance at a diehard Nazi who had been based in Lisbon and had aided the escape of other Nazis and their looted treasures. Arrangements were made for the secret handover, which took place at 10:00 a.m. on January 16 at a quiet cargo area in the Lisbon airport. A British aircraft to take Nassenstein to Gibraltar landed on time, and the van carrying the German arrived soon after. In a sign of Lourenço's concern, a total of thirty-eight police officers had been assigned to escort Nassenstein.[37] After a quick handover during which the senior Portuguese officer briefed the British on the German's mental state, the aircraft took off at 11:30 a.m. and arrived in Gibraltar in the early afternoon.[38]

The handover was the start of a sinuous route to get Nassenstein to Germany for his interrogation by British and potentially American intelligence. Upon arriving in Gibraltar, he was transferred to a Royal Navy ship that was sailing to Glasgow.[39] The British authorities worked to move him on as quickly as possible "in view of his suicidal tendencies and the unpleasantness that would ensue should he do away with himself whilst here."[40] From Glasgow, he was sent by train to King's Cross in London and then driven out of London to the coast and taken on a troop ship to Germany.[41] Throughout the entire journey, Nassenstein, who thought he was going to face a firing squad, pleaded with his guards to make sure his gold watch was handed over to his children and that his family was informed about his fate.[42] By the time he arrived in Cuxhaven, near Hamburg, where he was to be interrogated, his fears had been calmed. Once he decided to cooperate with the Allies, he appeared keen to tell his side of the story. The Americans wanted to interrogate him but, as in

the case of Walter Schellenberg, allowed the British to conduct proceedings. Several questions were sent by Washington for the British to put to
Nassenstein.[43]

In preparing for the interrogation, the British noted Nassenstein's
change of mood. They hoped that he would prove to be a useful source
of information on the wartime workings of German intelligence in Iberia. The camp at Cuxhaven, however, was very different from Camp 020
at Ham. Whereas interrogators such as Stephens and his fellow staff at
Camp 020 used fear as their main weapon, proceedings at Cuxhaven
were undertaken in a much more gentlemanly manner. On February 26,
1947, Nassenstein was interrogated by British intelligence, who sought to
extract the names of any German agents who had been dispatched from
Portugal to England during the war. Nassenstein's memory was rather
fuzzy.[44] He was then pressed on the recruitment of enemy agents operating in the neutral countries. Again his recollections were vague and
nonspecific. He claimed that this was not part of his role in Lisbon.[45] He
said that most of this kind of work had been undertaken by Sturmbann-
führer Erich (Buero) Schroeder, who was the senior SS officer in Portugal.[46] Nassenstein suggested two other names—Major Franz Cramer and
Oberstleutnant Alois Schreiber—who might have knowledge of enemy
efforts. But unlike at Camp 020, there were few follow-up questions.

Nassenstein either deliberately misled his interrogators or more likely
could not remember the very detailed points of information he was being
asked about.[47] Any expectations that the Allies had that Nassenstein
would meaningfully assist Operation Safehaven were soon disappointed.
When asked about his work regarding the Americas, Nassenstein denied
the recruitment of either local or outsider agents. He claimed that his
prime source of information about South America came from the newspapers that he had delivered to Lisbon from South America. Regarding
contacts with the PVDE during the war, he was more open and talked
warmly about several of the leading officers in the police force.[48]

Its deputy head, Paulo Cumano, was singled out for special praise. The
German viewed him as a reliable and good friend of the Third Reich who
could be entrusted to deliver what was needed for the German embassy
in Lisbon.[49] Nassenstein implied that the PVDE was sympathetic to the

German cause and keen to receive the financial contributions the Germans made to selected individual officers. Christmas gifts in the form of cash bonuses were particularly appreciated, as were gifts for wives and girlfriends of the officers. In return, the officers did not investigate the arrival of goods and personnel in Lisbon from Berlin or from the German legation in Spain.

In the spirit of cooperation with Captain Lourenço and the newly established PIDE, the British chose not to pass on these allegations to the Portuguese police. Given Salazar's failure to act against similar claims made by the British and supported by strong evidence during the war, it would have made little difference.[50]

For their part, British intelligence became defensive of Captain Lourenço in the postwar period. He was increasingly viewed as a reliable partner in the struggle against the Soviet Union and communism in general. Privately, he supplied the British with the names of Soviet agents, both foreign and Portuguese, who worked in Portugal after the war. There was an obvious motive in giving up the identities of the latter group because they were the leading political opposition. The former group, however, helped the British because several of them had been posted in Portugal during WWII and had connections with British intelligence. The exposure of Kim Philby, the head of the SIS Iberian Desk, was, however, still a long way off.

British intelligence put forward a case that Lourenço had acted in a pro-Allied manner and should be rewarded for his actions. His postwar record in handing over Nassenstein, albeit with ulterior motives, was flagged as a further signal of good faith.[51] There were also recorded cases in which the PIDE handed over information to the British (not to the Americans) about German individuals whom they believed would be of interest. There was always a degree of mutual self-interest in such dealings, but nevertheless it was again understood that Salazar was quietly communicating with the British about issues related to Operation Safehaven. On a personal level, Captain Lourenço reaped his reward when in 1956 he was appointed president of Interpol. The appointment to this prestigious role was warmly welcomed by Salazar as a sign that Portugal had been readmitted to the international fold, a reward for the continued discreet cooperation of the PIDE and the intelligence and security services of the North Atlantic Treaty Organization (NATO), of which Portugal was an original member. Lourenço served out a full four-year term prior to his retirement.

In Cuxhaven, Nassenstein presented himself as an intelligent man, albeit a "diehard Nazi," to his interrogators, who were poorly prepared for the interview in contrast to the agents working at Camp 020.[52] They accepted his narrative of being a middle-ranking officer involved in mainly bureaucratic work during his time in Portugal. Bizarrely, at no stage during his interrogations was he subjected to questions about his knowledge of German attempts to get personnel and looted works of art out of Europe through Lisbon. The interrogation team had very limited knowledge of events in the Portuguese capital during the war. Its main source of information was cut-and-paste extracts from interviews with other Nazis who had served, or been responsible for, German policy in Iberia. Little mention was made of Safehaven; instead, the interrogators focused mainly on Germany's efforts to recruit enemy agents in Britain. As a result, the testimony of Nassenstein was almost worthless and represented a clear missed opportunity for the Allies to develop a deeper understanding of how the Germans used Portugal as the back gate of Europe.

The British SIS believed Nassenstein, along with Erich Schroeder and his team, was involved in postwar planning for the Iberian Peninsula.[53] The failure of the Allied interrogators to pick up on this key point initially, despite having both men in custody after the war, was a major oversight. Though the topic was brought up vaguely in Schroeder's interrogation, the German's denial was not challenged or put to any kind of test.[54]

Schroeder's arrival in Allied hands was much less dramatic than Nassenstein's but equally important. A muscular man of medium height and thinning brown hair, Schroeder had small dueling scars on the left side of his face.[55] He had arrived in Lisbon in March 1941, ordered to Portugal by Heydrich, the head of the German Security Police.[56]

The official title of his posting was police liaison officer, but his duties went far beyond this role. His office was not based in the German embassy but, to separate himself from the embassy, in a rented premises

at Rua de Buenos Aires, 25, in Lapa, near the British embassy.[57] He lived
in Estoril at Chalet do Reis on Rua António Martins and each day made
the forty-minute drive to work along the picturesque marginal road. Socially sophisticated, he believed that a central part of his duties was to
wine and dine local Portuguese who could be useful to the Nazi cause.
He was in charge of checking up on the local German population in Portugal, making sure they were complying with the Nazi party line and
obeying regulations such as draft duty. He was a diehard Nazi whom
the Allies regarded as central to the illicit activities of the Germans in
Portugal.[58]

Schellenberg recalled Schroeder with mixed feelings. He thought his
work to be efficient but his personal life a mess and his character a little
unbalanced. Schroeder, he had been informed, drank heavily.[59] During
his time in Lisbon, Schroeder seduced his secretary and got her preg-
nant. When Schellenberg recalled him to Berlin to explain himself and
to receive a reprimand, Schroeder showed up in his office in a state of
emotional distress.[60] As Schellenberg told him that he was aware of the
situation in Lisbon, Schroeder drew his pistol and proposed to shoot himself then and there.[61] A little taken aback, Schellenberg told him this was
not necessary but that he should give up drinking and mend his ways.[62]
When Schroeder returned to Lisbon, according to Schellenberg, he became a more temperate man.[63]

Like Nassenstein, Schroeder developed close ties with the PVDE. In
organizing joint police conferences, offering to supply the local police
with sophisticated radios and other equipment, he regularly met with senior PVDE officers. His brief was to make the police believe they would
be a valued part of a German-dominated postwar Europe.[64] The flat-
tery was sincere. Schroeder confessed to being impressed by the ruthless
methods that the PVDE used against the local communist opposition.
He estimated around twenty thousand Portuguese were either directly
or indirectly linked to the opposition.[65] He studied and discussed interrogation techniques with the PVDE and the suppression of much of the
judicial process in cases involving political dissidents. The dispatch of
convicted prisoners into exile in Africa for Schroeder was a logical and
smart move. At social events he organized for the PVDE officers, he

enjoyed listening to stories of their successes. He came to view the police force as a reliable ally of Germany.

One of the major problems the Allies had in untangling the German operations in Portugal and Spain was the overlapping nature of job responsibilities in each country.[66] Walter Schellenberg told his British interrogators at Camp 020 that there was a lot of crossover in the division of responsibilities in the embassies.[67] In Lisbon, the situation, he argued, led to inefficiencies and turf wars between individuals.[68] The British spent much of their time cross-referencing interrogation reports with captured German officials from the embassy. The Allies in general focused on procedural processes and missed the bigger picture. Interrogators understood that Nassenstein and Schroeder were underplaying their roles and responsibilities—each man argued that the subject in question was related to the other. Both presented themselves at their interrogations as middle-ranking bureaucrats. This was far from the truth, but by the time the suspicions of the Allies were aroused in the case of Schroeder's postwar planning operations, it was too late. The first red flag on this topic did not appear until an internal British memorandum was sent on July 9, 1946, over a month and a half after his interrogation had taken place on May 27, 1946.[69] To make matters worse, the interrogation file appears to have been misplaced or incorrectly filed, and it was not until October 1946 that there was any follow-up activity on whether to reopen his case.[70]

Schroeder, one of the most important German intelligence agents in Lisbon, successfully slipped through the net. His case was not formally reopened and his wartime record remained unchanged following his interrogation in May 1946. Schellenberg's vague testimony at Camp 020 on the problems of the German operations in Portugal and their overall organizational shortcomings probably contributed to the lack of Allied interest.[71] The oversights should not disguise the centrality of Schroeder to events in Portugal. The PVDE reported that Schroeder was central to most of the German intelligence and counterintelligence operations that took place in the country. He was known as a fixer. When Salazar decided to expel German members of the embassy for spying, it was Schroeder who made the necessary arrangements for their departure.[72] Smoothing over the damage caused to relations between Berlin and Lisbon was left largely to him, and to a lesser extent Nassenstein. This involved the presentation of evidence of Allied espionage activities in Portugal to the Portuguese authorities.

The wolfram trade became one of the most important aspects of Schroeder's responsibilities. It also gave him a part in the financial dealings between Berlin and Lisbon. His department was financed directly from Berlin with payments made through the Bank of Portugal to a local Lisbon-based bank, Banco Pinto e Sotto Mayor.[73] Keeping up the supply of wolfram to Germany was a job that Ambassador Hoyningen-Huene led politically and financially.[74] Schroeder's role was to ensure the practical side of the supply chain. He regularly visited mines and appointed German technicians to oversee the extraction of the ore in an efficient manner. Security of the mines was a high priority given the attempts of the Allies, mainly SOE agents, to sabotage them.[75] Schroeder paid local units of the PVDE to act as security guards at many mines, whose remote locations made them vulnerable to attacks.[76] Despite Salazar's nationalization of the mines at the start of the war, German companies held interests in many of them and made direct and indirect financial gains from the operations. As a result, Schroeder became involved with German companies and their representatives in Portugal.[77]

Despite his strong denials during interrogation, Schroeder and his office were thought to be involved in the issuing of fake passports to Germans. He did admit that on one occasion in 1943 his office had issued false passports to the sailors from the *Admiral Graf Spee*, who had made their way from Argentina to Lisbon.[78] The celebrated pocket battleship had inflicted heavy damage on the Royal Navy before being confronted by three British cruisers at the Battle of the River Plate on December 13, 1939. The ship was damaged in the battle and was forced to put into port at Montevideo, Uruguay. Convinced by fake reports of superior British naval forces gathering outside the harbor waiting to attack it, Hans Langsdorff, the commander of the ship, ordered the vessel to be scuttled on December 17. Schroeder insisted, nonsensically, that was the only time his office committed the crime of issuing false passports.[79] This was a flagrant lie that made little sense because the *Admiral Graf Spee* was scuttled three years earlier than he claimed.

SIS agents operating in Portugal believed that issuing fake passports was a routine operation in the German embassy that greatly increased during the first months of 1945. Given Schroeder's centrality to intelligence operations at this time, his denial of involvement appears far-fetched. Cooperative and, on a superficial level, compliant with the Allies, he tried to persuade them that he had not attempted to evade capture.[80] He was interned at the end of the war in Portugal before being transferred first to Paris and then to Germany, where he was questioned. It was clear that he anticipated that he would be interrogated as a middle-ranking official with little to hide. His questioners, though far from satisfied with his answers, did not have enough evidence against him to delve deeper. He guessed they would go lightly on him. The report of his interrogation shows that Schroeder had guessed right:

> It is highly probable that Schroeder in depicting his office as merely a mailbox and himself as completely innocent is seeking to cover himself and is concealing at least part of the truth. Although this Centre recognises this possibility, the absence of complete briefs has made it impossible to refute the prisoner's story, despite intensive interrogation.[81]

The failure of the Allies to connect the dots on Safehaven was never more apparent than in Schroeder's case. During his interrogation, the German bragged about how well-connected he was to leading members of Portuguese society, whom he knew from social events in Lisbon and Estoril. Many of these people were the very same individuals who were buying looted art at private auctions and displaying it in their homes. Unbeknownst to the British, the auctions were not advertised but took place under the cover story of dinner parties or soirées for a select group of invited guests, all drawn from well-established pro-German networks that included leading bankers. The majority took place in private homes, often on remote properties near Estoril and Cascais. Even the clubhouse of the golf club in Estoril, which was founded by the banker Ricardo

Espírito Santo, hosted an event. It was not ideal—a number of the British embassy personnel played at the club—but it served as a reserve venue. The club had a reputation for attracting the top end of Portuguese society.

Part of Schroeder's duties included producing German propaganda in Portugal.[82] By 1943, the propaganda wars between the Allies and the Axis powers had reached sophisticated levels. Earlier efforts had focused on the production of printed materials such as posters and postcards highlighting each side's basic messages. The Germans and Italians emphasized the threat of the "common enemy" of communism, while the British promoted the idea that London was the best friend to its oldest ally. Later in the war, a greater sophistication developed in attempts to win over the Portuguese. The British dispatched the Hollywood idol Leslie Howard to do a one-man Shakespeare performance at venues in Lisbon and Madrid. Howard was killed on the return flight to Britain when his plane was attacked by the Luftwaffe over the Bay of Biscay.[83] Not wishing to be left behind, the German embassy sponsored a series of art exhibitions at various venues, including the bookshop and gallery at Avenida da Liberdade 50 in central Lisbon. The calculating hand of Schroeder was involved in these activities, even though he had shown no previous interest in art. By all accounts, the exhibitions were a great success; moreover, they served as perfect cover for the import of artworks into Portugal (both legal and smuggled).

The British interrogators who questioned Schroeder after the war were deeply suspicious of bank accounts related to his department in Lisbon. The balance of the main account at the end of the war in 1945 amounted to 1,750,000 escudos ($60,870 at an exchange rate of 28.750 escudos to a dollar).[84] The account, along with other German assets, was blocked by the Bank of Portugal on the orders of Salazar in compliance with Operation Safehaven.[85] However, the Reichsbank continued to transfer funds to Portugal, to this account and to other personal accounts linked to Schroeder.[86] The Germans adapted to the new financial situation swiftly and nimbly, using local proxies for the transfer of funds, much of which was directed through Spain. The German "terror funds" continued to be sent to Lisbon, where they were dispersed into locally held accounts.[87]

Although the Allies were pleased that Salazar had eventually acted against German assets in the country, they appeared not to grasp the point that money was quite literally flooding into Portugal in diplomatic bags and in the form of Nazi gold, which was smuggled to the vault at the German embassy. Seizing German assets did not decrease the pace of German investment in Portugal; it had the opposite effect. The only difference was that importing assets shifted from legitimate banking channels to smuggling and the black market.

13

GOLD BARS

THROUGHOUT 1946 AND INTO 1947, THE PORTUGUESE AUTHORITIES continued to show little concern about issues connected with the German presence in the country during and after the war. They were more concerned with proposals to develop the country for international tourism. Portugal received a lot of favorable coverage by the international press during the war and into 1946. American publications like *Life* magazine focused on the exiled royalty of Europe, including the Spanish, Italian, French, Bulgarian, and Romanian royal families living in Estoril and Cascais. It was a nice story that highlighted two key positives about the country, the weather and the high level of personal safety. Headlines like THE ROYAL GRAVEYARD OF EUROPE put a more downcast spin on the situation, but the majority of the royals were happy to live in a small country on the western edge of Europe and visit the leading five-star hotels along the Lisbon coast to attend balls and weddings. Much of the coverage devoted to Portugal during this time focused on these events. Less attention was paid to the other, less glamorous developments taking place in the country.

The former German ambassador to Portugal Hoyningen-Huene felt little need to fade into the background. Socially well connected in Portuguese society, he was not shunned by the people he mixed with during the war. He was a regular guest at lunch and dinner parties organized by prominent Portuguese commercial and banking leaders. At the center of much of this activity was Ricardo Espírito Santo, who personified the postwar era in Portugal. He, like Portugal, had experienced a good war. His bank, BES, and other banks in the country, made enormous amounts of money from the wolfram trade and other wartime commercial activities. At the apex of the banking system was the Bank of Portugal, which had also enjoyed a very good war. Its officials made the right call when they smartly identified the Germans' use of forged currency to pay for wolfram.[1] The shift to payment in gold was a masterstroke. Portugal had amassed hundreds of tons of gold reserves that would prove very difficult for Allied officials to trace.[2]

The bankers privately debated how Salazar would choose to use the gold. There was little discussion about any prospect of handing it over to the Allies or any moral concern over its origins. The details of the Holocaust that were published in the Portuguese media, from the summer of 1945 onward, were met with indifference. Though the Portuguese population was concerned about Holocaust survivors being held in detention camps in Europe in the postwar period, few made any connection between these people and Portugal. The government was keen to flag its own policy of tolerance toward Portugal's small Jewish population as an example of the country's strong social cohesion. Few Portuguese knew about or understood the Allies' concerns about the origins of the gold bars that were carefully stacked in the Bank of Portugal's vaults, deep under the streets of Baixa in downtown Lisbon. Even fewer cared. For the Portuguese, once the war was over, the country was ready to swiftly move on.

There was little mention in the media of the continued activities of Germans or of the sales of looted art. The Allies were happy in public to play along. Portugal's and Salazar's favorable international press coverage in 1945 and 1946 were part of the strategy of the Americans and the British to take a hard line against General Franco's Spain. Portugal was cast as the contrasting good example of a neutral country. Despite Portugal's message of condolence to the German people on the death of Hitler, Salazar was viewed as a man who had come on board with the Allies at a key juncture in the war. As Winston Churchill had reminded the Foreign Office, the country took risks for the Allies even when its security could not be guaranteed.[3] The Americans were keen to publicly laud Salazar to illustrate to the Spanish how wrong General Franco's decisions were during the war. The Portuguese were happy to bask in the glow of this public adulation given to them at the expense of their Iberian cousins.

However, from a practical perspective, the postwar lap of honor granted to Portugal complicated progress on Operation Safehaven and its search for evidence regarding three key areas related to Portugal:

1. The numbers and seniority of Nazis who escaped Europe for South America
2. The assessment of the amount of Nazi gold that entered Portugal during the war and was deposited in the Bank of Portugal
3. The movement of looted Nazi treasure, such as stolen gold and artworks, into and out of the country during the war and crucially in its immediate aftermath.

Choices had to be made regarding which of the three issues to prioritize. Intelligence sources from both American and British agencies noted significant activities in numbers 1 and 3 in different parts of Europe. Reports from Italy outlined the existence of a major ratline for escaping Nazis in that country. Suspicions, later confirmed, of the role of senior members of the Catholic Church in these activities added credence to the reports. Southern Italy was seen as a likely point of departure for Nazis who were able to escape amid the chaos and confusion that characterized the immediate aftermath of the war in Italy.

The Monuments Men were already hard at work tracking and tracing large collections of art and gold in this key zone of Europe. Their successes were spectacular. Because Allied commanders wanted to laud and publicize the achievements of the Monuments Men, they helped create two misleading impressions. The first was that the majority of the art and gold that the Germans had looted in the war remained in Germany and nearby countries. Not all of it did. Second, the focus on large-scale finds of paintings ignored the amount of art, gold, jewels, and other valuables that individual Nazis extracted from Europe near the end of the war and in its aftermath. The result of the deployment of Allied intelligence resources targeting ratlines in Italy and the concentration of the Monuments Men in the north was that the Allies left Lisbon neglected again.

Naturally, this situation suited Portugal because Salazar wanted to retain the large amounts of gold deposited in the country as well as what was owed to Portugal but still in Swiss vaults.

In Spain, ports in the north of the country such as Bilbao continued to be watched as did a number in the south.[4] Allied agents in Madrid monitored the Spanish banking system—a large section of which was based in the Basque territories—for dealings with banks in Argentina.[5] A number of leading Spanish bankers were, according to the British, sympathetic to the Nazis and responsive to requests to transfer funds out of Europe into the Argentine banking system. They did this under the cover of regular Spanish–Argentine ties involving German companies and commercial enterprises based in Spain. The Allies followed a number of these transfers but appeared ignorant of the extent of the banking activity taking place between Madrid and Buenos Aires.[6] The British were hampered by Ambassador Hoare preventing the SOE and SIS from operating in Spain. After the war, several Nazis who were later interrogated by the Allies presumed that Spain offered a temporary sanctuary for Germans, who could blend in to this large country where bureaucratic chaos—a feature left over from the Spanish Civil War—still reigned.[7]

Allied officials devoted a great deal of time to building a case against Spanish actors during WWII. Franco was regarded as an unrepentant fascist who represented a movement that was alien to the new Western Europe that the Allies aimed to create. Although evidence was scant, there was a strong feeling among members of Operation Safehaven that Spain had helped protect a number Nazis in the latter part of the war. The State Department called for caution in assessing what to do with Spain. The three questions Safehaven posed about Portugal were also relevant to Madrid. With a view to the medium and long term, officials looked to bring Spain in from the cold to play a key role in the newly formed Western alliance. Its geographical position lent it a great deal of strategic importance that could not be indefinitely ignored. It was too early in 1946 to forgive Franco; nor did the Allies want to humiliate him.

In Lisbon, Salazar took a calculated gamble that, in the postwar world, the newly created United Nations would not be interested in pursuing old Nazis or rumors of their treasures passing through his country. There was little hard evidence to suggest that Portugal had been systematically involved at a collective level in helping Germans escape Europe. There was no financial paper trail linking Portuguese officials to the sales of fake passports or the awarding of export permits for goods with suspicious origins. To add to the inability of the Allies to make a case against Portugal, for the duration of the war the records of the Alfândega (Portuguese Customs) were placed in storage, from where they eventually disappeared. The official line from the government was that Portugal had complied with the terms of Safehaven from late 1944 onward. The freezing of German assets in Portugal in 1944 was put forward as proof of the country's good intentions. When pushed in private by American and British diplomats, Salazar reacted in a prickly fashion, arguing that any cases of looted art and goods exiting through Portugal must have been illegally exported and that his government was doing all it could to make sure that such instances were investigated and charges brought when laws were broken.

The Nazi gold was another matter. Here Salazar concentrated on first dispersing the hard evidence. Gold bars were sent to Portuguese Timor, Goa, and other locations across the globe. The chief concern centered upon the gold bars that had been stamped with the swastika. Attempts by the Bank of Portugal to exchange these prior to the end of the war had met with limited success. Part of the stock was sent to the Catholic Church in Portugal for storage. The church eventually used the gold to help modernize the shrine at Fatima and improve facilities for pilgrims visiting the site.[8] In addition to the government's stash of Nazi gold bars, Lisbon was awash with unofficial gold bars that had most likely been traded by Germans from the embassy or those transiting the country. Tracing the origins of this gold trade required the dedication of resources that the Allies simply could not spare in 1945 and 1946. Only decades later was the amount of unofficial gold in Lisbon estimated, and the number was much higher than the 356.5 tons officially held by the Bank of Portugal; the State Department reckoned that an exact figure would never be known.

The contents of the vault in the German embassy in Lisbon remained a mystery. Interrogators of Germans who had worked in the embassy missed questioning about this key area.[9] They had other priorities— building a more complete assessment of the workings of the German operation in Portugal. After the war, the Portuguese police confirmed the existence of the large vault, and that it was bare, emptied at the very end of the war by German officials.

During his postwar interrogation, the former ambassador Hoyningen-Huene was questioned at length about the official role of the embassy and the aims and objectives Berlin had set for it. A complex picture emerged of a legation split into two sections, diplomatic and intelligence. The ambassador made it clear that he had little time for the intelligence personnel. And because he along with the other ambassadors in neutral countries had been recalled in 1944, following the attempt on Hitler's life, he was not pressed on the increasingly dubious operations that centered on the embassy toward the end of the war. This was another mistake. Hoyningen-Huene must have authorized the construction of the vault. Intelligence reports had noted its existence as early as 1942—an important date because this was when Berlin started to pay the Portuguese in gold for the wolfram exported to Berlin. The ambassador would have known how much gold was in the embassy in 1944; but no one asked him.

Postwar Lisbon and Madrid had no local appetite to dig up the wartime workings of the German embassy. The social, financial, and commercial interactions of German personnel and leading members of society made any investigation potentially uncomfortable. In Portugal, many of the major beneficiaries of the Nazi trade in looted treasures and gold were government officials and police officers. The Portuguese state was not the sole beneficiary of the wartime trade. Several banks, companies, art galleries, and other cultural institutions gained much from their contacts with the Germans. Hoyningen-Huene had set out to deepen and entrench German–Portuguese ties well before the outbreak of the war.

Several Portuguese, as a result, owed their good fortunes to their network of relationships with the Germans. During the war, money became no object for the Germans operating in Portugal. Stolen gold, looted art, and forged currency were all in circulation. Nobody wanted to ask questions of ownership or discuss authenticity. It was a boom time and almost no one wanted to miss out.

After the war, Operation Safehaven officials continued to look at the operation of the Banco Espírito Santo. There were unproven suspicions that the bank had been involved in illegal activity at the end of the war. Ricardo Espírito Santo's private collecting was considered a separate issue altogether, but the Allies wanted to know if the bank had been laundering gold from individual Germans in Portugal. The black market trade in gold, the Allies believed, must have been linked to institutions that were financially capable of buying it and storing it. No new evidence was gathered about Espírito Santo personally, and he was soon removed as a suspect in the investigation.

By 1946, Espírito Santo, like many Portuguese, was enjoying his wartime fortune. Lisbon had emptied of the foreigners who had staffed the embassies. The Jewish refugees had long departed, and the Germans who had mysteriously arrived at the end of the war had moved on to South America. The only outsiders in Lisbon, in addition to exiled royals, were the remaining diplomats and a few tourists. Lisboetas had not forgotten the war, but the country moved on very quickly. Portugal had not suffered any physical damage from the conflict. No rebuilding projects were required, and the shops were full of foodstuffs and other household goods. Little had changed. It was as if the clock had been reset to 1939.

In villages in the northeast of Portugal, where the wolfram mines were located, the signs of the inhabitants' newly created wealth were on show: new cars, large houses, shops selling expensive items, and a general sense of increased income. Salazar had nationalized the industry at the start of the war, but not before the locals had gotten rich on the back of the sale of wolfram to Germany and, to a lesser extent, the Allies. For many people in Portugal, the war was an opportunity to improve their financial position. From the peasant farmers in wolfram villages to the smartly dressed bankers and gallery owners, the war brought benefits—a once-in-a-lifetime chance. Rumors of the illegal nature of trade or the dubious origins of gold bars, diamonds, and artworks were met with silence. Even if the Allies had been able to find the resources to interview the many local beneficiaries of wartime trading with the Germans, few would have cooperated with the investigators. There is a certain irony in that Portugal benefited much more financially from the war than the Spanish did, yet it was the latter country that found itself diplomatically isolated by the Allies in the postwar era.

Salazar presented his nation as culturally rich, with a strong national identity linked to the historical importance of Portugal and its empire to the world. His aim of developing the country was not fully realized until the 1960s, by which time Portugal emerged as a venue for mass tourism. Salazar wanted the world to forget about the country's wartime record and massive trading profits. When the State Department in Washington asked for negotiations over the potential return of Nazi gold, Salazar stalled.

The postwar media in Portugal airbrushed out the country's relations with the Nazis. Newspapers like *O Século* and its weekly magazine *O Século Ilustrado* highlighted Portugal's close connections with Britain and the United States.[10] Articles reminded readers of the historic links between Lisbon and London dating back to 1373 and the signing of the first major treaty between the two countries. Despite Salazar's best efforts to keep out the influence of American culture in Portugal, Hollywood movies were hugely popular in Portuguese cinemas. In 1943, Lisboetas attended the European premiere of *Casablanca* and cinemas in Portugal were full through the war. Then people were banned from showing support for one side or the other. In cinemas they rectified this by cheering loudly for the British newsreels that preceded the main film. By the start of 1946, Portugal sat culturally and politically in the Western Allied camp.[11] Reading publications like *O Século* during the latter part of the 1930s and from 1946 onward was like looking at two completely different publications.[12]

The Allied investigations, however, did not completely go away. Slowly, building on work undertaken during the war, a more complete picture was created of the trade in looted gold. Central to the process was

Germany's export of gold to neutral countries from around 1942 onward. At the end of the war, two issues dominated the Nazi gold trail: how to identify and take control of the gold in Germany and other countries, and, after that, what to do with it.[13] Neither of these tasks proved to be easy.[14] Equally problematic was convincing the neutral countries to cooperate with the investigations and consider returning the gold. The Allies were determined to pursue the Nazi gold but were unsure how best to deal with the beneficiaries of the trade. There were no easy answers.[15]

Portugal was not the only country that had moved on. The position of the Swiss was to offer friendly cooperation publicly while in private making it clear that it would not be party to any activities that would infringe upon its strict banking privacy laws.[16] Franco and the Spanish failed to see what, if any, benefits cooperating with the Allies would bring. In its view, Spain was singled out for special postwar punishment by the Allies and had little to gain from complete cooperation with Allied investigators.[17] Likewise, the Swedes proved to be reluctant partners in the investigations. Its leaders followed the line that trade with the Nazis had been legitimate for a neutral country and the profits from these activities belonged to Sweden.[18] The Allies regarded all the policies of the neutral countries as opening positions in a longer-term negotiation.

In trying to piece the jigsaw puzzle together, a dedicated group of Allied personnel from multiple agencies worked around the clock. Information was drawn from the intelligence services, the British Ministry of Economic Warfare, the Bank of England, HM Treasury, and British legations in the neutral countries. Attention focused first on the triangle of activity between Germany, Switzerland, and Portugal from 1942 onward. The second factor was harder to unravel and concerned the unofficial trade in Nazi gold.

As Portuguese bankers were sipping gin and tonics in the postwar Lisbon sun and enjoying the fruits of their wartime bounty, they likely did not know how close the Allies were to unraveling the details of their wartime deals. The Allies had cracked the code of the Bank of Portugal's workings and its dealings with the Nazis. Understanding how the Bank of Portugal used the three accounts it held with the Swiss National Bank proved vital. The first account carried gold earmarked by the Swiss

National Bank for the Bank of Portugal account and held against escudos in Lisbon. This represented Switzerland's purchase of escudos.[19] The
second account proved much more interesting. It was thought to be part
of the highly complex procedure for converting German gold. Allied investigators summarized the process as follows:

> The sale of German gold to Swiss banks, who then bought escudos from
> Portuguese commercial banks and transferred them to a Reichsbank ac-
> count in Lisbon; the Portuguese bank then surrendered its Swiss francs
> against escudos to the Bank of Portugal which used the Swiss francs to
> buy gold from the Swiss National Bank and feed it into the Bank of Por-
> tugal's account.[20]

A third account was used for gold earmarked by the Swiss National
Bank for the account of the Bank of Portugal at the direct order of the
Reichsbank.[21]

On top of these complex banking activities was the use of the direct
route: the physical movement of gold by road and air to Portugal and the
other neutral countries. This was riskier from a security perspective, although there were no reports of attempted robberies of these shipments.
With the cooperation of the corrupt customs officials in Lisbon and elsewhere, cargos of gold left little or no paper trails for investigators.[22] Despite Allied protests, the movement of gold, in addition to the complex
trades managed by the Swiss National Bank, continued right up until the
end of the war.[23] The most likely motive for the continued use of air transport was that the gold being exported did not form part of official trades
between Portugal and Germany.[24] Instead, its export to Portugal and onto
ships bound for South America was part of an improvised effort to get it
out of Europe for future use. Schellenberg was dismissive of the idea of
systematic postwar planning by leading Nazi personalities.[25] But that left
room for what he himself described as individual actions.

It appears inconceivable that, while Schellenberg and other Nazis were
putting out peace feelers to the Allies before the war was over, no consideration had been given to postwar activities and how to finance them. In
1946 the Allied investigations were sifting through enormous amounts of

materials: enemy intercepts, interrogations of German officials in Lisbon, and on-the-ground Allied intelligence reports based on information from paid informants.

In Lisbon, the only German based in the embassy who talked about postwar activities in his interrogation was a low-level Abwehr agent, Frank Koschnick, who operated in Lisbon from the start of 1943 until the end of the war. As with the rest of the Lisbon operation, Schellenberg was not impressed by Koschnick.[26] His responsibilities included the transfer of German assets to Portugal and Spain. When the PVDE subjected his accommodations in Lisbon to a routine search at the end of the war, officers discovered locked metal boxes that contained shares that belonged to the Companha de Bains de Monaco and a South African company. All were bearer shares, which made them untraceable.[27] The British believed Koschnick to be the man responsible for a series of attempts by the Germans to peddle foreign securities in Portugal.[28] He was questioned after the war and repatriated to Germany in 1946, where he was held in an internment camp until his release on November 29, 1946.[29] As Allied investigations continued, he was rearrested and questioned for a second time.[30] The British intelligence created a dossier on Koschnick:

> It transpired that the subject was known to be in a position to throw full light on the looted origin of thousands of securities then identified and located in Portugal. He was re-interrogated by representatives of the British, but proved uncooperative although he admitted that whilst in Portugal he had been engaged in peddling foreign securities.[31]

Koschnick had been a frequent traveler to Madrid, where in January 1944 he started talking to German representatives in Spain about the organization of postwar activities in Iberia.[32] Although he failed to provide the Allies with details of this and subsequent meetings on the same subject, Koschnick's interrogation helped confirm that the Germans were giving a great deal of thought to Iberia at the start of 1944.[33] This time frame coincided with the significant increase in the volume of air traffic from Berlin via Barcelona or Madrid to Lisbon.[34] OSS and SIS agents watching the Lisbon airport reported that the daily flights carried several unmarked crates that were not inspected by local customs officials at the airport. The rest of the cargo was subjected to routine customs inspections. This indicated that the Germans had established a secure route to import gold and looted property.[35] During his interrogation, Koschnick refused to answer any questions about the process of importing looted securities into Portugal; British intelligence suggested that these likely entered the country in the diplomatic pouch of the German embassy.[36]

The noncooperation of Germans interrogated about their activities in Lisbon prevented the Allies from putting together a fuller picture. Although the OSS and SIS had notable success in tracking and tracing parts of the German activity, resources were not available to reveal everything. An added problem was the unreliability of the information supplied by local informants. On several occasions tips turned out to be false or misleading, causing the Allies to waste resources on investigations that led nowhere. Several British spies in Lisbon suspected that the Germans were deliberately feeding false information to people they believed to be American informants to throw the Allies off the scent of German activities in Iberia. Whatever the reason, the Allies were inundated with information from local informants from January 1945 until the end of the war, so investigators had a difficult task working out which leads to investigate and which they should dismiss. German activities in Lisbon during the latter stages of the war, as a result, retained a degree of mystery.

14

STORY BUILDING

A MID THOUSANDS OF INTERNAL MEMORANDUMS THAT CIRCULATED among Operation Safehaven officials was a short intercept saying that if the Germans could not get their looted goods out of Europe through Lisbon, they might try Sweden.[1] It was an alert for agents working in Stockholm and the Swedish ports to be vigilant for Nazi activity. With Lisbon open, along with Italy and Spain, the Swedish exit was underused by the Nazis. Nevertheless, Sweden's ambiguous role in the war came under increased Allied scrutiny. The Swedes proved to be the most direct of the neutral countries in their rejection of key parts of Operation Safehaven. Salazar and Portugal played a much more sophisticated strategy of promising much and delivering little. Franco and Spain simply tried to ignore Safehaven, except for offering tacit support in specific cases that suited the regime's ends. The Swiss smiled and embraced the "vitally important" operation, but did little other than make false promises. It was the reaction of Sweden that antagonized the Allies the most and explained why Churchill felt more personally irate with Sweden than with any of the other European neutrals. His swift removal from power after the war spared the Swedes the wrath of his fiery oratory. His successor, Clement Attlee, adopted a more diplomatic approach based on his assessment of the strategic importance of the country as the European continent headed into the Cold War.

Sweden was empowered by WWII. Unlike its two Scandinavian neighbors, Denmark and Norway, it had not been occupied. Instead, as a major trading partner of the Nazis, it had grown rich from its trade in ball bearings and iron ore. The supply of ball bearings became more important to the Germans after the US Eighth Air Force successfully bombed the SKF plant at Schweinfurt (ironically owned by the Swedes) in August and October 1943. Toward the end of the war, the Germans turned to Sweden for additional resources. Swedes felt little discomfort in trading with the Nazis. Despite their liberal democratic traditions, the Swedes had few qualms about receiving payments from Germany, which the Allies later claimed were from dubious origins. From the perspective of London and Washington, the Swedes benefited from ill-gotten gains, which they should have handed over to the Allies at the end of the war.[2] When officials from Safehaven made this appeal to the neutral countries, Sweden, with Switzerland close behind, declared its rejection the loudest. Later, when Safehaven officials suggested that the neutral countries could face political and economic sanctions if they did not comply with the terms of the operation, the same two countries argued that this would amount to a violation of their national sovereignty.

In Camp 020, Schellenberg stated that Sweden was one of the more reliable neutral countries in its relations with Germany.[3] Although he was not the only senior Nazi to attempt to ingratiate himself with key political and commercial personalities in Sweden, it was obvious that he saw an opportunity to utilize the country as a point of contact between Germany and the Allies.[4] Schellenberg sought out Swedes who would at the very least pass messages to London and Washington in the early years of the war.[5] Later these contacts acted as conduits between Himmler and the Allies in the hope that the Reichsführer could negotiate the surrender of Germany in the West and a continuation of the war in the East against the Soviets.[6]

Personal relationships and chemistry matter. In times of war they can generate strange friendships that on the surface appear little more than marriages of convenience. Schellenberg's relationship with Folke

Bernadotte is a case in point. The German was looking for a serious interlocutor with the Allies and the count appeared a natural choice. He had
organized prisoner swaps in 1943 and 1944 and his lofty personal ambitions meant that he was looking to play a role in helping to mediate the
end of the war. Over time, Schellenberg came to trust Bernadotte, especially when Germany suffered military defeats in the final months of the
war and his options were limited.[7] In retrospect, Schellenberg's attempt
to negotiate a German surrender to the Allies and not the Soviet Union
was doomed to failure. Himmler's reluctance to act without the knowledge and backing of Hitler slowed negotiations to the point that they
became irrelevant. Events on the ground moved faster than Himmler's
deliberations.[8] During his postwar interrogations, Schellenberg was naturally keen to talk up the potential this channel provided for altering the
course of the war, but it was an exaggeration; Schellenberg was boasting
of his own importance in the story of the last days of WWII.

Two interesting questions were not posed by Schellenberg's interrogators at Camp 020. The first concerned Himmler's possible motives for
seeking an accord with the West. There were two. One, it was a strategic move that Himmler believed the Americans and the British might
embrace given their deep military and political tensions over the leadership of the Soviet Union. In meetings with Himmler, Schellenberg fed
him countless stories of the splits in the ranks of the Allies, including
those between the Americans and the British.[9] His intention was to convince Himmler that all was not lost and that there could be a viable route
forward for the Nazis in a post-Hitler era.[10] The extent that Himmler
was taken in by these arguments is not clear. He did, however, authorize
Schellenberg to meet with Bernadotte, and, after an initial reluctance to
meet with the Swede in person, Himmler eventually sat down with him.

Two, it was a way for the Reichsführer to demonstrate his pragmatic
side, and at the same time save Schellenberg's life. At that late stage in the
war, while several leading Nazis were putting finishing touches on their
escape plans through Italy or Iberia, others were looking to win favor with
the advancing Allies. Between the lines of Schellenberg's self-serving
answers at Camp 020, there is a large measure of self-preservation evi-
dent in his efforts to encourage mediation with the Allies through Folke

Bernadotte. He was not the only Nazi trying this. Even Schellenberg's great rival, Kaltenbrunner, who had threatened him after learning that he was discussing postwar planning with other senior Nazi officers, had tried to open a back channel. Kaltenbrunner's refusal to cooperate during his interrogations at Camp 020 and his eventual death sentence at the Nuremberg trials concealed the fact that he, too, had tried to engage with the Americans at the end of the war.

Whatever Himmler's motives, even with the eventual failure of the peace mission by Schellenberg, Sweden proved to be a lucrative country for German commercial and military interests during the war. Bill Donovan, head of the OSS and a late convert to the usefulness of Operation Safehaven, wanted to target Sweden and Switzerland particularly. He believed that he could justify the continued importance of an American foreign intelligence service like the OSS during peacetime—in Sweden for its commercial links to Germany and in Switzerland for its banking activities. Although justice in terms of restitution would be hard to achieve, forcing the neutral countries to look at their unsavory trading activities during the war was worth a fight.

Internal changes in both the American and the British intelligence services in the postwar years had an impact on the search for Nazi personnel and looted goods. The legacy of wartime successes was not enough to guarantee a place in the new dawn of 1946. In America, Donovan's efforts to use Safehaven as an argument for the continued relevance of the OSS failed. His participation in the Nuremberg trials turned out to be his last major act as head of the OSS. On September 20, 1945, Truman signed the executive order abolishing the OSS.

A new leadership for the newly created Central Intelligence Agency was introduced. Several ex-OSS men who had worked closely with Donovan played leading roles in the agency, such as Allen Dulles, who served as its director from 1953 until 1961, and William Casey, director from 1981 to 1987. But the American intelligence service became a more bureaucratic structure after the war. The reduction of the gung-ho approach that had characterized much, though not all, of the Donavan era was replaced with a more cautious tone and modus operandi. The major shift, however, was that the intelligence service was driven by present-day and future threats. This meant checking the ongoing threat of Soviet expansion, not tracing erstwhile Nazi assets and personnel. This had a marked effect on the negotiations with the neutral countries about issues related to looted gold and art.

In Britain, unlike his political master, Winston Churchill, Stewart Menzies survived the changes at the end of the war. He was allowed to reorganize British intelligence to face the challenges of the Cold War. He was never given the access to Prime Minister Attlee that he had enjoyed with Churchill, however. Menzies had met Churchill on nearly 1,500 occasions, equivalent to five times a week for the duration of the war. Senior figures in the ruling Labour Party made it clear that they regarded him as an aristocratic dinosaur from a bygone age and that he was well past his sell-by date. He quickly came into political conflict with the fiery Labour foreign secretary Ernest Bevin, whose foreign policy Menzies did not always understand or approve of. It was his carefully honed bureaucratic skills and a deep sense of conservatism about British intelligence services that helped Menzies survive the postwar cull.

Much of the initial work of the postwar-rebranded MI6 was hindered by the presence of Soviet agents in the organization—Kim Philby and George Blake. Menzies's recruitment policies came under scrutiny. He was accused of running MI6 like a gentlemen's club, drawing almost exclusively from the English aristocracy. The Soviets targeted this group and Menzies was held accountable for many of MI6's failings and the deaths of several agents whose identities had been compromised by moles inside the organization. Menzies enjoyed a good WWII, but was never as relevant afterward.

The rapidly evolving new realities of the Cold War meant a shift away from seeking justice for Nazi crimes committed in WWII toward focusing on the present and future. In 1946 the majority of the political, military, and intelligence leadership of the Western powers believed that a confrontation with the Soviet Union was imminent. World War II had barely ended before there was talk of World War III beginning.

Operation Safehaven was not killed stone-dead because of these political and intelligence changes; it was, however, no longer at the top of the American and British list of priorities in 1946. That is why Swedish officials were able to brazen out the investigation, insisting without any basis that they had complied with the majority of the terms of Safehaven. In April 1945, the Swedes had promised to restore looted treasures and freeze German assets in the country. But they rejected the key point of Allied control over the external German assets.

At the start of 1946, under the pretext of cooperating with the Allies, the Swedish parliament passed legislation to control German property in Sweden—but the cooperation never really happened. In July 1946 an agreement was reached in which Sweden handed over $12.5 million of German assets to the Intergovernmental Committee on Refugees to help rehabilitate and resettle the nonrepatriable victims of the Nazis. Sweden also agreed to hand over an additional $54 million to the Allies and over $8 million in gold that had been looted by the Germans from Belgium.[11] Agreements were one thing. Implementation was another challenge altogether. It took eight years for the Swedes to pay up. Even then, they did not pay everything they had promised in 1946.[12] Swedish officials haggled over the payment terms of each part of the agreement. They did hand over the $12.5 million to the Intergovernmental Committee on Refugees, but everything else was delayed. It was not until 1955 that agreement was reached on $18 million that had been promised for reparations.[13] The payment of $8 million in Belgian gold to the Tripartite Gold Commission—established in September 1946 by the Allies to recover gold stolen by Nazi Germany and to return it to the rightful owners—was held up by Sweden until December 1959, nearly fourteen years after the agreement had been reached.[14]

In between this time, the Dutch made a claim against the Swedes for the return of $9.7 million of their gold. Negotiations started in July 1946 and carried on until 1955.[15] The Swedish defense was that the gold had been acquired before the 1943 London agreement on looted gold and art forbade countries to keep it. In April 1955, Swedish and Dutch officials came to an accord that saw Sweden transfer about $6.8 million in gold to the Tripartite Gold Commission.[16] None of the statistics reveal the true extent of Swedish trade with the Germans during the war. They do not account for the unofficial and black market commercial trade that provided Swedes with much-needed additional income. The extent of

Nazi smuggling operations from the start of 1945 could not be included because no reliable figures on the value of this trade were available. Interception of messages between Sweden and Germany during the latter stages of the war indicated that the smuggling of artworks, gold, and other looted items was frequent.

Swedish narratives of the war and the postwar period were still very raw and primitive in 1946. The government essentially suggested that the country was a victim of the Nazis, not a country that had profited from its wartime trade with Berlin. Several high-profile cases add to the sense that we will not ever know the whole story when it comes to Sweden. The example of Raoul Wallenberg, a Swedish businessman and diplomat, is one of the most baffling. Despite his heroic rescue missions to save Hungarian Jews, Wallenberg's story is complicated by his family's business links with Nazi Germany. Wallenberg's justification for his connections with the Nazis was that his frequent business trips to Berlin were useful in helping him become acquainted with the working practices of the Nazis. This, he argued, proved important during his rescue efforts. The reality was that his family financially benefited from trading with Nazi Germany. His story and eventual disappearance are a sad example of both the good and the shady elements of Swedish activities during the war.

Another story with two sides is that of the many Swedes who took in Danish Jews who had been evacuated between October and November in 1943 during the German occupation. Sweden was proud of its record of helping the Jews during the war, but even here the facts were much more complicated than the banner headlines. Despite its rescue missions and the housing of thousands of Danish Jews, the Swedish government did little about the Holocaust. News of the concentration camps was reported in Sweden but was often met with indifference, particularly in conservative rural areas. Details of the horrors of the Holocaust were not disseminated in the press until the end of the war, after the Allies liberated the camps. In 1946 Swedes focused on the stories of the rescue of their near neighbors. Deeper reflection on the Holocaust and its causes was conspicuously absent from political and public debates.

Like many countries in mainland Europe, Sweden moved on from WWII quickly. It had not been physically damaged by the war and it was

looking anxiously at the threat of the Soviet Union. The seeming indifference of its government to the implementation of agreements with the
Allies did not prove to be unpopular or controversial with the majority of
its population. The role of Folke Bernadotte in the rescue of thousands of
Scandinavians from Nazi prisons at the end of the war and his attempts
to end the war were the representative image the country wanted to con-
vey to the outside world. Sweden was a caring and humanitarian society
whose economic miracle of sustained growth was gathering momentum;
the fact that some of that momentum had been created by trade with
the Nazis was not openly discussed. Instead, the country's success was
credited to hard work and careful macromanagement of the economy
by consecutive Swedish governments. Challenges to this narrative were
shouted down by Swedish officials. Trouble, however, was just around the
corner in the form of the story of the rescue of Scandinavians at the end
of the war.

The White Buses mission led by Folke Bernadotte had brought the
country much good international publicity. It helped Bernadotte become
an internationally recognized name. He seemed set for a successful career
outside of Sweden in one of the newly created postwar international institutions. But the mission was fraught with contradictions from the start.

The Swedish government had chosen Bernadotte for the mission because he was senior enough to have credibility with the Germans, but
was not part of the administration. On the surface it appeared a sensible
choice. Bernadotte possessed the organizational skills to handle a delicate
diplomatic and challenging logistical mission. He was far enough away
from the government to provide it with political cover if the mission, as
many expected, failed. He was an ambitious man and his drive and determination to succeed were seen as necessary requirements that might
make the difference between success and failure. He retained a strong
aristocratic belief that the world revolved around him and that he personally had the ability to change minds and convince people. Egotistical
and without the anti-Nazi streak that had ruled out several other people,
he was not afraid to put himself forward. Like many Swedish diplomats,
he would prove acceptable to the Nazis as an honest broker who was not
a stooge of the Allies and their intelligence services. Other personalities

were discussed but either dropped out or were disqualified for various reasons. Bernadotte was not the first choice, but the Swedish government believed him to be the right one.

The diplomatic initiative was supposed to form part of a wider humanitarian effort by Sweden to rescue Scandinavians imprisoned in concentration camps in German-occupied Europe and, if possible, to liberate some Jews from the camps. The latter point was vaguer and more controversial and was not the prime objective. The political aim of the White Buses mission was to position Sweden as a neutral country that had used its position positively—and to deflect any criticism of its trade with the Nazis. After years of trading with the Germans, the Swedes needed to reposition themselves. The reset was deemed necessary for Sweden's prospects in the Allies-led postwar era. In shaping Sweden's legacy from the war, the public relations value of the mission was important. For many Swedish leaders, the launching of humanitarian missions was a much preferable way to fulfill this aim over returning looted gold or making reparation payments.

The key German interlocutor in the diplomatic back channel was Walter Schellenberg. Under interrogation, the head of German intelligence warmly recalled his meetings with Count Bernadotte, whom he came to regard as a friend. Schellenberg articulated the German perspective on the negotiation.[17] While the Swedes viewed the initial contacts and meetings between the two men, and those that later involved Bernadotte and Himmler, as part of the negotiation of a humanitarian rescue operation, the Germans saw it as something altogether different. After the war, the Swedes came to understand more about the wider aims of the Germans in opening the diplomatic channel. Schellenberg saw the contact as part of the attempts of his boss, Himmler, to seek an accommodation with the Western Allies. From a German perspective, the discussions about the return of a modest number of Scandinavians were a confidence-building mechanism for more important negotiations to come.

When pressed by the British in his postwar interrogations, Schellenberg argued that he and Himmler were serious about the potential offer to the Allies to surrender on the Western Front only and believed it could work.[18] This mindset defied several crucial unresolved factors. The war was ending for Germany much faster than most people had foreseen. This applied a time pressure to the talks, which only began on February 10, 1945. Despite Schellenberg's optimism, several obstacles and unknown variables needed to be addressed.[19] Many centered upon the attitude of Himmler himself to the whole process. Schellenberg told Bernadotte that Himmler would agree to the transfer of prisoners to Scandinavia—that he was well-disposed to the Swedes, partially on racial grounds, and did not want them to join the Allies during the final months of the war. From his testimony, it was not altogether clear on what grounds Schellenberg based this assertion.

The negotiations that took place in direct meetings between Bernadotte and Himmler proved less straightforward than Schellenberg suggested.[20] It was far from clear the extent to which Himmler supported the peace offer to the Western Allies. It was uncertain whether Himmler would betray the Führer and seek such an accommodation with the West.[21] Schellenberg was convinced he would, but he did not elaborate on why in Camp 020, nor was he pressed on this point by his interrogators.

Himmler must have understood the perils of making a bold move even as the Nazi empire was crumbling. Probably the best outcome he could have hoped for was to divide the Allies between those who supported his initiative and those who opposed it. But it was unlikely that any potential divisions would have lasted long enough to buy the German military significant time to regroup. Nor was it likely that Sweden would provide Himmler a personal refuge to evade the postwar justice of the Allies. Himmler understood that, as a senior leader of the Nazis, it would be difficult for him to flee when the war was lost. Schellenberg suggested that Himmler might have been able to play a role in bringing the war to an end sooner to spare greater German loss of life.[22] But the memory of the Battle of the Bulge, in which the United States suffered at least seventy-five thousand casualties, was still fresh in the West. The Soviets were implacable in the East. The Allies would inflict more German casualties during the final months than in any other comparable period. Himmler could have done nothing to dissuade them.

Himmler probably wanted to preserve as many of the German assets at home, and those transferred to neutral countries, as possible. Any surrender to the Western powers would not have led to abandonment of German looted goods and gold by the Nazis. The Allies were acutely aware that the Nazis would go to great lengths to prevent their looted treasures from falling into enemy hands, notably the Soviets'. The negotiations involving Schellenberg and Himmler on the one side and Bernadotte on the other were complex and fast-changing as the pace of the war increased. In a further complication, an additional participant emerged who became central to the plot.

Felix Kersten was a Finnish citizen who was Himmler's physical therapist, but his influence went much further. The pain relief that he brought to the ailing Himmler made him indispensable. Toward the end of the war, Himmler's reliance on Kersten's work grew even greater as his ailments worsened. Himmler was not the only man to sing Kersten's praises. Himmler loaned him out to Schellenberg. The head of German intelligence talked about the miraculous healing power of the magical hands of Kersten.[23] Kersten's personality was a curious mixture of arrogance, vanity, self-importance, and desire to help his Scandinavian brethren. He never liked Bernadotte, however, and saw him as an aristocratic snob.

But from the outset he was vital to the mission. Prior to the first meeting between Bernadotte and Himmler on February 19, 1945, Kersten briefed Himmler by phone about the initiative.[24] They decided to keep the rescue of any Jews from the camps away from the agenda. Sweden was not the only neutral country intervening on that issue. Working through Schellenberg, the Swiss president had secured an agreement with Himmler for Switzerland to receive 1,200 Jews each fortnight. When Hitler learned the details of this deal, he was said to have exploded in rage. Bernadotte thought it wise not to provoke a similar reaction that could have led to the whole rescue operation being abandoned. After the war, Kersten alleged that Bernadotte had not wanted to include the Jews in the rescue mission because of his own anti-Semitism. The differing accounts of the story, amid claims and counterclaims of credit by Bernadotte and Kersten, became acrimonious and bitter. Allied intelligence regarded each man's version as dubious and self-serving; Schellenberg

supported Bernadotte. The Swedish government lent its full support to
Bernadotte and dismissed the allegations of anti-Semitism as a groundless slur against the count's good name and the Swedish humanitarian
mission.

Disputes over who was most personally responsible for the rescue mission came to overshadow the operation's success. The February 19 meeting
led to Himmler agreeing to the Red Cross repatriating the weakest of the
Scandinavian prisoners and Swedish residents based in Germany. This
started a race against time to assemble the necessary transportation and
personnel to make the transfer. One hundred buses were requisitioned
from the Swedish army and painted in the colors of the Red Cross—the
white buses. Around three hundred Red Cross workers were assigned to
them. On March 12, the buses entered Germany after a brief delay while
they got Allied permission for safe passage. Two weeks later, on March
30, the Red Cross had assembled the Scandinavian prisoners in the north
of Germany. They got out 4,500, traveling to the camps at great personal
risk. The first phase of the mission was successful. An emboldened Bernadotte met with Himmler again on April 2. During this meeting, the
German agreed to release a further two thousand Danes who had been
imprisoned in Buchenwald as well as several Norwegian students who
had been deported to Germany in 1943.[25]

At this point Norbert Masur, the German-born Jew who had emigrated to Sweden and was its representative to the World Jewish Congress (WJC), became heavily involved in the mission. With the help of
Kersten, he was flown from Stockholm to Berlin on April 19, 1945. The
purpose of his trip was to meet with Himmler to discuss the rescue of a
number of surviving Jews. The following day, Masur had a long meeting
with Schellenberg to discuss the specifics of a rescue plan, and during
this meeting Schellenberg outlined the plan to surrender to the Western Allies and continue the war with the Soviet Union. The meeting was
friendly, but Masur found it difficult to hold back his emotions, knowing
he was meeting the man who was largely responsible for the killing of
several million Jews. Himmler met with Masur for two and a half hours.
For much of the time, Himmler presented the standard Nazi defense,
that the mass murder of the Jews was a necessary and justified action. His

sole concession was to suggest that he wished many things could have been done differently. He stressed that he wanted to move on from the conflict with the Jews and hoped that the Allies would agree to do so. Himmler's reason for taking the meeting was to reinforce the idea of his willingness to open a line of communication with the Allies. Bernadotte, who was in Berlin at the same time, continued to meet with Schellenberg and Himmler in the hope of achieving this aim.

As a result of the meeting, Masur secured the release of a thousand women from Ravensbrück. Many of these women were Jewish but were designated as Poles for their release. Soon after, more women were evacuated from the camp and taken to Denmark and Sweden by road and train. The total number rescued was over 21,000, of which between 3,500 and 6,500 were Jews. Himmler's action cannot be viewed as anything other than a late bribe of the Allies. In making the journey to Berlin at this crucial time, Masur showed his bravery, and his willingness to meet with Himmler helped save the lives of thousands even if there was little chance of the Allies accepting Himmler's proposals for a German surrender.

The Swedish government used the rescue missions to support its policy of noncondemnation of the Nazi atrocities against the Jews. It argued that the rescue would not have happened if the country was vocal in attacking the Nazis. Fewer Jewish lives would have been saved if the Nazis had not been willing to enter negotiations with the Swedes. But the Allies refused to deviate from the agreements they had made with Sweden for the return of stolen gold and reparations from the country's earnings from wartime trade with Germany. To the Allies, the Swedes had ceded the moral high ground when they had formed commercial and industrial links with the Nazis, and a last-minute rescue mission did not change that fact.

The conflict over the White Buses mission became very personal between Bernadotte and Kersten. Both men, for differing reasons, wished to claim the credit. In a brazen attempt to do just this, Bernadotte published his account in a book only six weeks after the end of the war. *The Fall of the Curtain: Last Days of the Third Reich* was his personal account of his experiences at the end of the war.[26] The fast turnaround of the book came down to the ingenuity of its ghostwriter, Ragnar Savanstrom, who

utilized Bernadotte's five successive reports to the Swedish Red Cross
and the Swedish Foreign Ministry. Text linking the reports together was
added, and the little book was soon ready for publication. The timing
of its release could not have been better. It became an immediate international bestseller, translated into eighteen languages and serialized in
the British newspaper the *Daily Telegraph*. Its success made Bernadotte
an overnight star.[27] In a few brief months, Bernadotte had become as
famous as Winston Churchill in the West. Politically, he was viewed as
pro–Western Allies and anti-Soviet, which fitted well with the sentiment
of the immediate aftermath of the end of the war in Europe.

The best-selling book antagonized several people who felt their role in
the rescue operation had been downgraded by Bernadotte. Among those
disgruntled personalities were politicians and diplomats from Sweden
and Norway who believed their efforts had laid the groundwork for the
mission. The most discontented figure, however, was Felix Kersten. The
Finnish-born Kersten applied for Swedish citizenship in 1945. The new
Swedish foreign minister who had taken office in July 1945 regarded Kersten as a pro-Nazi collaborator and refused his application, as did Bernadotte, even though a previous Swedish foreign minister, Christian
Gunther, had been in favor of it. The failed application acted as a catalyst
for a series of attacks against Bernadotte and questions over Sweden's
motives for the rescue missions. The intervention of several international
historians further muddied the waters.

Kersten published his own memoir in 1947, in which he directly attacked Bernadotte and his version of events. Kersten argued that he was
the prime mover in the mission. His attacks on Bernadotte continued in
interviews he gave to publicize the book. In 1953, he went as far as to produce a letter that Bernadotte had allegedly written to Himmler on March
10, 1945, and claimed that it included the line "Jews are not welcome in
Sweden." The Swedish government believed the letter to be a forgery, and
this was confirmed by Scotland Yard in 1978. The police concluded that
the letter had been written on Kersten's own typewriter. Despite the letter
being forged, its impact was significant. The charge that Kersten made on
several occasions was that Bernadotte was anti-Semitic and not interested
in the rescue of the Jews. Instead, he was a self-serving Swedish official

who wanted to save Scandinavians and who made little effort to save anyone else. It was through the work of others that thousands of Jews had escaped from Germany.

Another best-selling book further colored the conflict. The British historian Hugh Trevor-Roper published *The Last Days of Hitler* in 1947, in which he assigned only a marginal role to Bernadotte.[28] This infuriated the count and provoked an unpleasant exchange of correspondence between the two men. More than merely the personal reputations and egos of the two men was at stake. Many of Sweden's postwar narratives were built on its contributions to the rescue missions at the end of the war. Behind the spat was the unresolved question of whether Sweden would repay the gains it had made from wartime trade with Germany. Trevor-Roper's charges that Bernadotte was not responsible for the rescue missions and that he was anti-Semitic were viewed by the Swedish government as an attack on the whole country. The Swedish state dived in to defend Bernadotte and his legacy, arguing that the attacks were groundless and the work of Kersten, whose judgment and morals were severely lacking.

The belligerence of Trevor-Roper toward Bernadotte continued. After meeting Kersten in 1953, the historian published an extended article in the *Atlantic Monthly*, the supporting evidence for which was drawn from discussions with Kersten.[29] In the article, Trevor-Roper gave almost all the credit for the rescue mission to Kersten and described Bernadotte as a mere "transport officer."[30] Even more damaging was his repetition of Kersten's charge that Bernadotte was anti-Semitic. The dispute continued for decades, with the Swedes protesting and Trevor-Roper resisting. The historian's credibility would suffer a near fatal dent when, in 1983, he said that some recently discovered diaries were written by Adolf Hitler. They were soon proved to be forgeries. This false discovery cast a shadow over much of Trevor-Roper's work, which relied on oral histories, such as those provided by Kersten, with all the methodological problems that approach encountered.

The 1945 agreement with the Allies, along with the humanitarian rescue missions led by Bernadotte, must be viewed in the context of the sophisticated game of rebranding the Swedes undertook, which emphasized their cooperation with the Allied cause while they utilized the spoils of war to launch the Swedish economic miracle. The antagonism toward Bernadotte by Kersten and then Trevor-Roper was therefore regarded not only as personal attacks on the diplomat but also attacks on the nation. Internal dissent was hidden and critics were portrayed as malcontented outcasts or communists. When Trevor-Roper was discredited, it helped to confirm the Swedish version of events. But all that came too late to save the legacy and life of Folke Bernadotte. The Swedes adopted a policy of silence toward his legacy for many decades. Any debate on his role in the rescue operations was thought to introduce difficult questions into Swedish politics that few people wanted to discuss. It was only at the start of the twenty-first century that his name came to be more openly recognized by the state. In 2008 a group of leading personalities openly called for the end of silence surrounding his name and that he be honored appropriately.[31]

15

RETURN

IN 1946, WHEN COUNT FOLKE BERNADOTTE WAS ONE OF THE MOST famous men in the world, one overexcited British reporter based in Stockholm wrote that either Winston Churchill or Folke Bernadotte should be placed in charge of rebuilding the European continent.[1] High praise indeed. Amid all the horror stories emerging from the concentration camps as the world learned about the terrible fate of the European Jewry, the White Buses were an image of redemption and bravery. In Palestine, the Zionist movement noted the story of the rescue mission. It was also big news when Kersten attacked Bernadotte. What interested the Zionists were the charge that Bernadotte was an anti-Semite and the comment attributed to him that Jews were not welcome in Sweden. Zionist leaders such as David Ben-Gurion, who went on to serve as Israel's first prime minister, harbored suspicions that the Swedes in general were too close to the Nazis. He also shared the suspicions about Raoul Wallenberg and his business dealings with the Nazis. In short, the Zionists believed there was something wrong with the heroic Swedish narrative of the country's wartime role that focused exclusively on its humanitarian work.

Palestine roiled as an increasingly brutal struggle between the local Arab population and the mostly European Zionists evolved into what amounted to a civil war. British–Zionist relations were deteriorating and threatening to become a major armed conflict as the British moved to tighten Jewish immigration laws. The Zionists wanted a Jewish state where they could bring the survivors of the Holocaust. They launched illegal immigration efforts to rescue the thousands of Jews housed in the Displaced Person (DP) camps. Immigration was the absolute priority and left little time for any other activity, but the Zionists also kept a distant watch on the attempts of the Nazis to flee Europe and extract their looted treasures from the continent. Jewish groups based in Brazil and Argentina helped provide basic intelligence through the World Jewish Council about the comings and goings of Nazis in Latin America.

The Palestine question and the DP camps in Europe became some of the first major points of conflicts between the Americans and the British. It is difficult to assess the negative impact on Safehaven caused by the dispute over Palestine, which threatened to derail postwar Allied relations. Attlee's Labour government included the well-known anti-Zionist Foreign Secretary Ernest Bevin. His opposition to the Zionist struggle in Palestine was well documented. The Foreign Office he led was institutionally pro-Arab.[2] It believed that the Arabs represented Britain's best allies and offered opportunities for British access to lucrative trading markets in the Middle East. The future of British military bases in Palestine was important to preserving British interests in the region. The last thing the British wanted was to allow the Jews in the DP camps to make aliyah to Palestine, altering the demographic balance in the country and antagonizing the Arabs.[3]

British policy toward the survivors of the Holocaust housed in fenced camps in Europe was unacceptable to the Americans. As rescue attempts increased, led by the Zionist groups, the negative publicity for the British increased. Ships carrying survivors the Zionists had liberated were stopped and boarded by the Royal Navy on the high seas. They were then turned around and sent back to Europe. The American press became highly critical of the British actions, calling them immoral and wrong. President Truman and the State Department warned the British about their conduct but were informed that Palestine was a British issue and one that it would resolve. These were foolhardy words given the failure of successive British governments to resolve the Arab–Zionist conflict from the 1930s onward. British diplomats and government officials described the situation as unsolvable. Each of Britain's partition plans to divide Palestine into two independent states had failed to win the support of both sides. In Washington, there were suspicions that America's wartime ally was trying to hold on to Palestine for selfish national or colonial interests. Not for the last time in the postwar era, the United States decided to flex its newly discovered political strength and lean on the British to get them to agree to hand over the mandate on Palestine to the United Nations.

British officials were surprised by the pressure from the Americans, but complied. On May 15, 1947, the United Nations formed a Special Committee on Palestine (UNSCOP), with the intention of preparing a report on the future status of the country for the UN General Assembly. The members of the committee, which included representatives from eleven countries, visited Palestine and met with Zionist leaders. The Arabs chose to boycott the committee. The committee traveled to Europe and spent a week meeting with Jewish refugees in the camps, who expressed their strong desire to go to Palestine. UNSCOP published its report on September 3. Its findings called for confirmation of the British Mandate for Palestine and the division of Palestine into two states: one Zionist and the other Arab. The British announced that they would accept the partition plan, but because the Arabs had rejected it, they refused to enforce it. London also refused to share administration of the country with the UN Palestine Commission during the transition period. In the autumn of 1947, the British government announced that the mandate would end at midnight on May 14, 1948. The proposals of the UNSCOP needed to be approved by the General Assembly by a two-thirds majority.

Prior to the vote, it was clear that there remained deep tensions between London and Washington over the Palestine question. The Foreign Office and the State Department remained jointly skeptical of the partition plan, but President Truman appeared a strong supporter on grounds of the moral need to create a Jewish state in the wake of the Holocaust. The Palestine question became one of the first challenges for the newly created United Nations. Given the failure of its predecessor, the League of Nations, to prevent WWII, the need for the UN to be seen as functioning and efficient in dealing with the issues of the day was important.

The United States and Britain were so fixated by the tense situation in Palestine that, to the governments of Portugal, Spain, Sweden, and Switzerland, it seemed like the Allies' appetite for justice and restitution was fading. There was a growing sense among the governments of these countries that their wartime bounty was safe. The threat of an armed confrontation with the Soviet Union in Europe appeared to be growing by the day as the Iron Curtain started to close over Eastern Europe. The mandarins who were still employed on the Safehaven program continued their work, but out of the limelight.

Britain was not the only country to experience an awkward relationship with the United States in the postwar period. Brazil became frustrated with Washington. Many Brazilian leaders were already looking back on the era of President Roosevelt as a golden age that was not mirrored by the Truman administration's treatment of the country. The deterioration in the relationship had an adverse effect on the efforts of Safehaven officials to persuade the Brazilians to cooperate with their investigations. Allied intelligence reported that Germans continued to enter Brazil with looted art most likely using fake identities or false passports.[4] Nazis such as Herberts Cukurs were able to bring whatever looted treasure they could carry into Brazil. The chaos and confusion at Brazilian ports and airports intensified after the war because the facilities were in the process of being modernized, with building works everywhere. Customs officials maintained a liberal attitude toward inspection of luggage; smuggling by Nazis and local criminal gangs was widespread. Cooperation from the Brazilian government was sporadic, and information relating to Nazi arrivals, movements, and exits from the country came too late, in many cases, to make much of a difference.

However, Brazil was enjoying a period of political progress. The democratic and free elections held in 1945 resulted in the election of Eurico Dutra. That Dutra, a deeply conservative former military officer, decided to run had surprised many people, who cited his lack of campaign skills and poor oratory. His election was initially viewed with suspicion in Washington, which was aware of his close links to the German military during the 1930s. His pro-Nazi stance, which he openly exhibited during the early stages of WWII, was said to have been supplanted once Brazil joined the war on the side of the Allies.[5] He was known to be a late convert to democracy, preferring the Brazilian authoritarian model. Brazilians, he believed, could not understand the complexity of the issues that they were being asked to vote on. It was only because participation in the war had led to popular calls for democratization that it became impossible for the government to resist elections.

After assuming power in January 1946, Dutra cooperated with the Americans. He was not under much pressure to deal with the arrival of Nazis in the country, not least because their paperwork indicated they were in transit to Argentina or Paraguay. British intelligence noted that a few low-level Nazis did try to remain in Brazil. They had existing family in the country among the large German immigrant population or were hosted and hidden by this group. Dutra showed little interest in them. Instead, he concentrated on pushing ahead with a major program of economic modernization, at the center of which was making improvements to Brazil's notoriously rudimentary transportation infrastructure. As the Nazis grew more sophisticated in extracting looted treasures from Europe, less was smuggled through Brazil. The use of transfers by Spanish Argentine bankers became the main way to move funds into South America.

The first many Brazilians heard about any potential Nazi issue in their country was when the film *Notorious*, directed by Alfred Hitchcock, was released in 1946. The movie, starring Cary Grant, Ingrid Bergman, and Claude Rains, follows the fictional story of a US agent who persuades the daughter of a convicted Nazi war criminal to travel to Brazil to help infiltrate a Nazi commercial network hiding out in Rio de Janeiro. Shot in late 1945 and early 1946, it became one of the first big-budget movies to depict the postwar era. The plot centers on the uncovering of uranium ore in the house of the Nazi, Sebastian (Claude Rains), and the deepening romance between the American agent, Devlin (Cary Grant), and Alicia (Ingrid Bergman). The film was critically well received in America and Europe, said to mark a creative watershed for Hitchcock. In Brazil, the film was seen as an insult. Brazilian diplomats who viewed the movie in

North America and Europe were shocked at the reaction of audiences—who came to see Brazil as a haven for Nazis. The consensus of opinion among Brazilian critics was that Hitchcock should have chosen Argentina for the location of the film.

The image of Brazil as a pro-Nazi redoubt stuck in the minds of the audience just in the same way that Lisbon became the city of escape in *Casablanca*. The presence of two of the big stars—Bergman and Rains—from *Casablanca* added to the unease of many Brazilians, who felt their country had been unjustly targeted. Newspaper articles published in Rio and São Paulo sought to remind Americans that Brazilian forces had fought and died in the war for the Allied cause. The Brazilian government's indignation was all the stronger because Argentina escaped any such scrutiny. After the international success of the film, Brazil was never able to free itself from the West's belief that it was pro-Nazi during and after the war.

President Dutra's ratification of the appointment of his old political nemesis, Oswaldo Aranha, as Brazil's delegate to the United Nations in 1947 was seen as a signal of Brazil's continued pro-American policy. Hollywood movies aside, the Brazilian government continued to do as much as possible to press its international credentials. The decision to send Aranha to the United Nations was astute. Aranha, in addition to serving as minister of foreign affairs under Vargas, had served as the country's ambassador to the United States. He took up his post at the UN in the spring of 1947. His popularity among the Western powers helped him get selected as the first president of the UN General Assembly on May 5, 1947. In Brazil this was considered an honor for the country. However, it did not fully compensate for the disappointment over the breaking of President Roosevelt's so-called promise to give Brazil a permanent seat on the UN Security Council. At the UN, Aranha and Folke Bernadotte would become intertwined in a way that neither of them could have foreseen.

Arguably the most historically important event during Aranha's time as president occurred in November 1947. His pro-American sentiments were well-known, but fewer people knew about his pro-Zionist leanings. During the war, his office was involved in the granting of visas to Jewish refugees entering Brazil despite the country's tight restrictions on immigration. It was, however, at the United Nations that Aranha made his greatest contribution to the Jewish people with his handling of the debate and vote on the UNSCOP proposal to partition Palestine into two states. The two-thirds majority required to pass the recommendation was proving problematic for the Zionist lobbyists at the UN. In the hours leading up to the vote, scheduled for November 26, it was clear that the Zionists had secured a bare majority to support the plan, but not the two-thirds majority needed to pass it, whereupon Aranha persuaded his allies in the chamber to extend the length of their speeches. It was a classic filibuster to run down the clock to make sure the vote would not take place that day. The next day was a holiday and this allowed the Zionist diplomats to lobby the undecided countries. Three days later, on Saturday, November 29, the partition plan was approved 33–13, with 10 abstentions and 1 absent. Brazil voted in favor of the plan; Argentina abstained. A road in Israel would later be named after Oswaldo Aranha in appreciation of his support and diplomatic maneuverings.

The dilemma that Aranha helped to create in Palestine would be left to Bernadotte to try to fix the following year, after he was appointed as the UN's special envoy to Palestine.

The Nazis did not choose South America as a port of refuge by accident or through a complete lack of choice of other locations. One of the first lessons they learned in trading with Brazil and Argentina was the importance of a network to the whole process. The culture of trade was different in the two countries, but what was consistent was the presence of pre-existing networks that kept business activities within their known group. These included fixers, such as government officials and police officers who could deal with the necessary paperwork and granting of licenses. The Nazis liked dealing with these networks because they delivered what they promised without unnecessary bureaucratic delays. Hush money, or the buying of silence, which was a central feature of trade, impressed German exporters, who imported their goods into Brazil while bypassing a lot of red tape that put off American and British trading partners.

Nazi leaders were not prepared to be idle in South America. They wanted political influence to match their commercial activities. Walter Schellenberg talked about the German backing of the Brazilian Integralism movement founded by Plínio Salgado in 1932.[6] The movement was similar to European fascism, with the usual mixture of ultra-nationalism and anti-Semitism. Its supporters included several army officers, but it was strongest among the officer class in the Brazilian Navy, many of whom rejected the leadership of Vargas and the high-profile role of Aranha, whom they regarded as an American stooge.

Throughout WWII, the Germans had continued contact with a Brazilian armed faction, the Integralistas, that had attempted a coup against Vargas in 1938. Several were living in exile in Portugal.[7] The quality of the personnel of the Integralistas did not impress the head of German intelligence, who spent time with several of them on his visits to Lisbon during the war.[8] The break between Vargas and Germany can be viewed as one of many reasons most Nazis fleeing Europe at the end of the war chose Argentina, not Brazil, for their hideaways.

The blurring of Brazil's role in WWII continued for decades and was later further muddied by the film *The Boys from Brazil*, whose bizarre plot included the cloning of a new Hitler. Despite the title, much of the plot centered on a Nazi network in Paraguay, and it was in fact shot in Lisbon. Nevertheless, it reinforced the belief held by many that the Nazis retreated to Brazil after defeat in the war, where they planned for a new Reich. The wider implication was that a common South American political identity existed, one that was morally ambiguous and that approved of the influx of old Nazis. This was far from accurate but typified the times and particularly reflected the influence of Hollywood. From Carmen Miranda, a Portuguese-born Brazilian actress and songstress nicknamed the "Brazilian Bombshell," to Walt Disney's chatty green parrot, Zé Carioca, Americans were encouraged to believe there was a homogenous South American entity.

In Hitchcock's film *Notorious*, even when the Brazilian police force is shown to be cooperating with the American intelligence agencies, the viewer is left with the impression that the sinister Nazis—who live in large houses in the leafy suburbs of Rio and in the Imperial City

Petrópolis—must have been allowed to reside in Brazil only with the permission of the government.

During the war, the officials from Operation Safehaven, who were dealing with the realities of Nazi smuggling, were also prejudiced against Brazil. Reports talked of the country as if it were, at best, an unreliable neutral or, at worst, a hostile member of the Axis powers. In retrospect, the mindset of Allied officials and the American and British intelligence agencies toward Brazil was close to racist. The country, considered backward, was seen as not having conditions for advancement and modernization.

The postwar exodus of Nazis from Europe to South America was not one the continent invited. Not even the Argentines appeared ready, at first, to deal with the newly arriving Germans. In Brazil, Nazis transited through the country on fake passports not because the authorities welcomed their arrival but because a central directive banning Germans' entry was lacking. As in Portugal and Spain, low-paid customs officials were easily bribed. Inspections of baggage and cargo were deferential: much of the customs culture in postwar Brazilian ports was based on the premise that if the Allies had let the passengers and the cargos sail from Europe, then the paperwork must be good. Inspections were carried out simply to meet the requirements of local taxation, not on the basis of any intelligence information from the Americans or the British.

Despite the military cooperation of the United States and Brazil during the war on issues such as the use of airbases in northern Brazil, intelligence sharing was poor. The OSS did not trust the Brazilians with details of Nazis fleeing Europe. When they did share information, it was retroactive and too late for the Brazilians to act on. Even though the country had fought with the Allies and shifted toward democracy under Dutra, Brazil remained a distant neighbor of the United States.

Although the United States did not deliver in full on its wartime promises to Brazil, it did take strong action against Brazil's regional rival, Argentina. Reports from Safehaven cataloged a series of postwar transfers from banks in Spain to Argentina. The United States continued to regard Argentina with great suspicion in the postwar order. Argentina's intention to follow a third way, or Cold War nonalignment, did not fit with American plans for the region to become a solid continent of pro-Western sentiment. Washington accused the Argentines of meddling in the internal politics of other South American countries, such as Bolivia. During the war, Winston Churchill and Franklin Roosevelt were deeply divided over how best to handle the Argentines. The United States adopted policies toward Argentina that the British felt were overly harsh. Churchill was prone to reminding the Americans that Britain depended on receiving goods from Argentina and that thousands of Argentines had fought for the Allies despite their country being officially neutral in the war.

Argentina, like Brazil, possessed a large German immigrant population, people who had emigrated in the latter part of the nineteenth century. The political complexion of the Germans in Argentina was mixed. The Nazis in this group were often very vocal during the 1930s, when Nazism was ascendant, but they were in the minority. Among the immigrant population were German Jews, liberals, and socialists, too. In Berlin, Argentinian Nazis were regarded as an oddity. Schellenberg belittled them and indicated that German intelligence did not regard them as influential players in Argentine political society or commercial activities.[9] Nonetheless, at the end of the war, escaping Nazis making their way to Argentina were thankful for the presence of this large German colony that would provide cover for their arrival. It was not strange to hear German spoken in the street cafés of Buenos Aires before, during, and after the war.

During the war, the German colony in Argentina was left alone and allowed a lot more autonomy than their German counterparts in Brazil, who were brazenly persecuted by the Brazilian authorities. Indeed, Brazil could claim the dubious title of oppressor of both Brazilian Germans and Jews in the war. Following the failed coup of the Integralistas in 1938, President Vargas moved to secure a more authoritarian rule in which Brazilian nationalism was central to the development of a strong federal state.[10] Minorities no longer had the right to pursue their own customs and languages. The German colony in Brazil, along with the Jewish population, became an obvious target. The German language was banned in schools (although there is evidence that the Germans ignored this decree and continued to teach courses in their mother language in German schools). Radio stations that broadcast in German and Yiddish were closed. Several Yiddish radio broadcasters refused to comply before they were eventually taken off the air.[11]

Germans fleeing Europe in the years after the war did not feel like they had arrived in a friendly state when they docked in Rio or landed at one of the country's American-built airports.

The television images of Oswaldo Aranha in his gruff, smoky, heavily accented English introducing the dramatic vote on the partition of Palestine in November 1947 would have further confirmed this point. Here was a distinguished Brazilian diplomat presiding over the creation of a state for the Jews. To many Nazis in Brazil, this must have looked like as close to a total defeat of Nazism as possible. Few Nazis arriving in South America chose to stay long in Brazil. By 1947, it had become apparent that Nazis exiting Europe were choosing Argentina, where there was a more friendly regime.

16

OPPORTUNISTS

THE VICTORY OF JUAN PERÓN IN THE 1946 PRESIDENTIAL ELECTION heralded a new era in Argentina and opened a more institutionalized escape route for Nazis who still wished to flee Europe. From late 1946 on, there was a second wave of Nazi exits, including that of Kurt Waldemar Tank—a famous airplane designer in Germany who had worked on many designs for the Luftwaffe. Josef Mengele, known as the Angel of Death, arrived in Argentina in July 1949 after traveling along an Italian ratline via Genoa using a fake identity and passport. Arguably the most notorious Nazi who remained at large, Adolf Eichmann, arrived in Argentina as part of this wave on June 17, 1950. The first groups had slipped out in a clandestine manner, using the ensuing chaos at the end of the war as cover to make their escape through the neutral countries. The networks that aided their flight did not fold but developed into more sophisticated and well-financed operations as time went on. The bribing of local officials did not stop at the end of the war. The list of other Nazis arriving in Argentina in this second wave makes for chilling reading:

Walter Kutschmann, an SS officer and member of the Gestapo in Galicia, arrived in Argentina in January 1948 with a Spanish passport under the name of Andrés Ricardo Olmo.

Eduard Roschmann, commander of the ghetto of Riga, better known
as "the Hangman from Riga," entered Argentina in October 1948
using the name Federico Wegner.

Erich Priebke, an SS officer involved in the execution of over three
hundred Italians near Rome in 1944, arrived in Argentina in
November 1948.

Josef Schwammberger, the commander of the Przemysl Ghetto, arrived in Argentina in March 1949.

Gerhard Bohne, who took part in the killing of people with mental
illnesses and disabilities, moved to Argentina in 1949.

Klaus Barbie, known as the "Butcher of Lyons," passed through
Buenos Aires on his way to Bolivia in 1951.[1]

Additional Nazi networks operating in Sweden and Switzerland deep-
ened their connections with domestic authorities, who showed few signs
of actively moving against the remaining Nazis. In Sweden, networks
continued to be built on the commercial ties in place since the 1930s. In
Switzerland, connections between Swiss intelligence and Nazi networks
remained strong. The main problem Switzerland reported with the large
numbers of Nazis living in the country was not an ideological issue but a
complaint about them occupying well-to-do country villas that otherwise
would have been occupied by Swiss citizens.

For Nazis who either chose not to flee to South America or were unable
to do so, Switzerland was first choice for temporary residence. Its strict
privacy laws in banking and the ease with which the Nazis could transfer
funds from Germany made it an obvious choice. Many Nazis who moved
to Switzerland believed they were in no imminent danger of being handed
over to the Allies. They lived in the country using false documents, while
others retained their identities, confident that the Swiss would not give
them up. The many stories that circulated about Nazis hiding out in Switzerland contained a common thread: they hinted that the displaced Nazis
were in a holding pattern, waiting for one of two developments to happen,
either an improvement in the international situation stemming from the
start of the Cold War and the conflict with the Soviet Union, or the potential rise of a new Nazi empire linked to and based in a third country.

The arrival of Perón in power in Argentina offered the possibility of realizing the dream that many diehard Nazis retained since Germany's defeat in 1945. This group of fanatical Nazis would not have said they were "hiding out" in Switzerland; they were waiting for the call to arms.

Like Schellenberg, who appeared baffled by Allied questioning about the mass murder of European Jewry, many senior Nazi officers downplayed the importance of the Jewish issue.[2] They appeared to separate it from any strategic thinking about the conduct of the war. When pushed by his interrogators at Camp 020 on how much he knew about the atrocities and the conditions in German concentration camps, Schellenberg replied,

I am fully aware of the significance of the Allied propaganda.[3]

When he was told that the British descriptions of what the liberating Allied troops had found in the camps were facts, not propaganda, he replied defensively:

I had nothing whatsoever to do with the executive, but I would not be the least bit surprised if the competent people who have always caused trouble, have perpetrated deeds which will be put to the discredit of the whole German people.[4]

This proved to be one of Schellenberg's most evasive answers during his entire interrogation.[5] Officers closer to the top, such as Himmler and Eichmann, understood the centrality of the Jewish question to how the Allies would deal with the defeated regime. Himmler's apparently humanitarian offer to Bernadotte, which Schellenberg had instigated, was little more than an attempt to buy favor with London and Washington. Hiding out in northern Germany after his escape, Adolf Eichmann understood full well what was in store for him if he were recaptured by the Allies. The damning evidence given against him at the Nuremberg trials by, among others, Rudolf Höss, the commandant of Auschwitz, sealed Eichmann's fate.

Lower-ranking officers believed that the Western Allies would eventually come to their senses and see the need to incorporate Nazis with key skill sets into the conflict with the Soviet Union. Central to this thinking was the belief that their help would be required to secure and rebuild the Allied-held parts of Germany. They were right.

One of the first confirmations that new alliances between the West and the Nazis were being made was known as Operation Paperclip. This program saw over 1,500 Nazi engineers, scientists, and technicians transported from Germany to the United States between 1945 and 1959. Once in America, they worked in aeronautics and rocket science and the early US space program to help give the United States an advantage over the Soviet Union. Unsurprisingly, the Soviets launched their own program with the same aim, Operation Osoaviakhim. Some 2,500 German specialists from the eastern sector of Germany and Berlin were taken on October 22, 1946, to be resettled in the Soviet Union. Many of those hiding out in Switzerland were hoping for a return to Germany, where they could take up positions related to their wartime duties. At the head of this group were ex-Nazi intelligence agents, among whom several would be involved in the creation of the new German intelligence service. Many would spend the rest of their careers working for the interests of the Western powers in what eventually became West Germany.

They were among the large majority of Germans who did not flee Germany at the end of the war but chose to remain and take their chances under Allied occupation. A central attribute of those recruited to the postwar German intelligence service was their attempts to cover up their role in committing the atrocities of WWII.[6] General Reinhard Gehlen is arguably the most important example. By most accounts, he had an uninspiring career in German intelligence during the war. A charmless character with limited intellectual skills, he owed his upward career path to his work ethic and a strong support network among the most senior officers in the Third Reich.

One of his key allies was Schellenberg, who held Gehlen in high esteem.[7] In March 1945, Gehlen asked Schellenberg for a meeting during which he became the most senior officer to raise the topic of a likely defeat of the Germans and questions related to postwar planning.[8] He (rightly) forecast that German military resistance would only last a couple of months and asked Schellenberg to approach Himmler with the idea of seeking an agreed surrender with the Western Allies.[9] Part of this plan involved Himmler taking over from Hitler. Following the meeting, Schellenberg repeated the discussion to Himmler, who appeared reluctant to initiate the move and instead attacked Gehlen's motives.[10] Following Gehlen's advice, Schellenberg did not tell Kaltenbrunner of their discussion.[11] Gehlen had recently been fired during one of Hitler's violent tantrums brought on by continued German losses on the battlefield. On learning of Gehlen's sacking, Kaltenbrunner said in Schellenberg's hearing, "Bye, bye, little piggy." But, although relieved of his duties, Gehlen was by no means finished. He continued to order detailed intelligence surveys of the political situation in Eastern Europe and of the advancing Red Army.

Unusually for an intelligence officer, Gehlen had no prior experience with espionage or counterespionage and spoke no foreign languages.[12] Despite these limitations, with strong American support, Gehlen became the dominant force in West German foreign intelligence until the end of the 1960s.[13] His rise revealed much about the changing political realities in the postwar period and how shrewd Nazis could carefully reposition themselves and sell their services to the Western Allies as useful assets in the fight against communism.

General Gehlen had a great amount of information that the Western Allies desperately wanted after the war. For a man with a mediocre reputation, Gehlen was astute in preparing his own insurance policy in the event of the Reich's defeat. During the war, he collected military and political intelligence, much of it from Red Army prisoners of war. He gathered an enormous amount of material about the Soviet Union and its workings. When he realized that the Nazis were going to lose, he ordered all the intelligence material to be microfilmed. His men then placed the original documents in sealed watertight barrels and buried them in the Austrian Alps. At the end of the war, Gehlen, along with his men, was handed over to the Americans. When Gehlen offered the archive of papers, essentially in exchange for his and his fellow intelligence officers' freedom, the Americans quickly understood his value. Once the Allies agreed, he delivered the papers and was freed from Allied custody in July 1946.

Later that year, on December 6, he started anti-Soviet espionage operations under the umbrella of what became known as the Gehlen Organization. It initially employed around 350 ex-Nazi officers and eventually had around four thousand agents working for it. The scope of the organization was very wide. Between 1947 and 1955, it interviewed almost every German prisoner of war who had returned from the Soviet Union to West Germany. It established contacts with other anti-communist groups and put together a detailed picture of the workings of the Soviet Union and its military and economic capacity. The Soviets did not stand idly by and watch the growth of the Gehlen Organization. The East German Stasi tried to infiltrate it, with a few notable successes that were highlighted in the Western press. Despite these setbacks, on April 1, 1956, the Americans formally transferred the Gehlen Organization to the authority of West Germany, making it the official intelligence service of the country. Gehlen became the president of the Bundesnachrichtendienst (BND), the Federal Intelligence Service. It was an extraordinary resurrection of fortune for a former Nazi Allied prisoner of war.

Many postwar Nazis could be labeled as opportunistic pragmatists. At the heart of their plans lay self-preservation. They believed that they had done little wrong. They took their chances hiding out in Germany in the belief that, if they were apprehended by the Allies, they would be able to sell their services. Those who made their way to Switzerland had looted assets they hoped would be more secure there. Few of the exiles in Switzerland believed that conditions in the near future would be advantageous for the return of the Nazis. Their best hope for Germany was throwing in their lot with the Allies to help defeat the Soviet Union and free the European continent of the threat of communism. Figures such as Gehlen were by no means unique. Several key Nazis planned to cooperate with the Allies in the postwar order. Elements in the highest echelons of the Third Reich viewed the war as impossible for Germany to win. This left a long period for senior Nazis to obtain lifeboats and prepare for the collapse of the German state.

A hard-core group of Nazis refused to accept the inevitable defeat of Nazism and saw the end of WWII as merely a loss on the battlefield in a longer ongoing struggle. Within this number hoping for a resurrection of the Nazi movement, there were two types. Some senior Nazis had nothing to lose by seeking exile in Argentina. If captured by the Allies, they would face trial and likely death or long prison sentences. Nazis in hiding carefully noted the sentences handed down at the Nuremberg trials. The second type viewed the relocation to Argentina as a tactical retreat during which they could reorganize and secure investments in new armaments. The hard-core resistance attracted the Hollywood filmmakers and later writers such as Frederick Forsyth, who wrote fictional accounts of ODESSA (Organization of Former SS Members), which the Nazi hunter Simon Wiesenthal claimed was founded in 1946. Forsyth's book *The Odessa File*, which was subsequently made into a film, brought some names into the public domain and resurfaced the ongoing stories of Nazis trying to reach Argentina.

Three networks were said to be influential in working with ODESSA to aid escaping Nazi war criminals. The first was South American, mainly Argentine diplomats based in Europe. During WWII, large numbers of South American diplomats were on the books of German intelligence. Schellenberg described the use of both bribes and honeytraps to create dependency ties to Germany. The diplomats in Berlin were encouraged to live beyond their means while the intelligence services picked up their debts, often from gambling.[14] Schellenberg employed eight or nine women to entice the South American diplomats into sex and relationships that could subsequently be used to blackmail them.[15] This crude tactic worked surprisingly well.

Diplomats from South American countries based in the neutral countries were viewed as useful and were targeted by German intelligence using similar methods. Schellenberg claimed the Chilean ambassador to Portugal was a German spy who passed on to Berlin information about his embassy's interactions with the Portuguese authorities and the Allies.[16] Thanks in part to the efforts of South American diplomats in Lisbon, Berlin was able to intercept Portuguese diplomatic cables sent to several of its embassies, including the one in the United States.[17] The greatest value of these diplomats, however, was not as intelligence gatherers but as suppliers of travel documents: passports, travel visas, and health records that were required for entry into South America.[18] In the postwar period, many of these connections continued. The Argentine embassy in Madrid remained a hotbed: the issuing of Argentine passports and travel documents for wanted Nazi war criminals was commonplace. The embassy had instructions to issue different types of passports, ranging from documents issued in the real name of the German to documents issued after a German name was adapted to make it sound more Spanish to cases of issuing wholly fake identities.[19] Though it is impossible to verify exact numbers, most Germans arriving in Argentina after the war carried genuine officially issued passports in their own name (or the Spanish equivalent—*Karl* became *Carlos*, for instance).

Senior members of the Catholic Church in Argentina, Spain, and Italy were involved in founding and running ratlines. Two Argentine names came to prominence later in this context: Antonio Caggiano and Agustin Barre flew to Rome in January 1946, where the former was due to be made a cardinal. When in Rome, he passed a message to a French cardinal stating that Argentina welcomed French citizens who had cooperated with the Nazis. Over the spring of the same year, several French war criminals made their way to Argentina via Italy. The role of individual members of the Argentine Catholic Church with good close connections to the political elite in the country was important. They provided cover for the organization of the ratlines and used their offices to obscure the movement of war criminals to Argentina. Together with the diplomats based overseas, they could travel in Europe without arousing suspicion and enjoyed the political cover of the Vatican.

The Gehlen Organization played a role in helping key Nazis escape, too. Its staff included war criminals.[20] Their wartime record was glossed over in the recruitment process, and the Allies chose to overlook the basic fact that the Gehlen Organization was a haven for Nazis, many of whom were unrepentant. One example was Otto von Bolschwing, whose record was truly appalling. He had served as an SD (the intelligence agency of the SS) agent in the Middle East, where he reported on the activities of the Freemasons and the Zionists in the mid-1930s. After this, he worked for Adolf Eichmann in dealing with looted Jewish property in the post-Anschluss Austria. He then served as Himmler's SD representative in Budapest, where he worked on the uprising in 1941 and the resulting pogrom against the Jews in which 125 Jews were killed.[21] Bolschwing was only one example among many in the Gehlen Organization whose records were equally disturbing and who were willing and able to help Nazi fugitives escape to South America in the postwar period. Bolschwing worked for the CIA, which eventually relocated him to the United States, where he worked for a series of drug and chemical companies. Despite knowing of his involvement in the Holocaust, the CIA promised that, as reward for his past work for the Allies, his whereabouts would not be revealed to the Israelis.

Questions were raised by Jewish Nazi hunters about Gehlen himself. His preparation for the postwar era and his curation of the detailed archive on the Red Army and politics of the Soviet Union appeared too neat. He was accused of hiding out to evade arrest, perhaps ahead of an escape through a ratline to Argentina. After his capture, Allied opinion about him was divided. Several officers who questioned him saw little more than an unrepentant Nazi who was trying to save his own skin. In the postwar years, he did little to shake this image and kept closely connected with underground Nazi movements and militia groups.[22] The Americans were deeply suspicious of the Gehlen Organization even after the founding of West Germany, when Gehlen became the legitimate leader of the new state's intelligence service. Despite these anxieties, the intelligence the organization gathered on the Soviet Union and its assessments of this information were considered more important than any other concerns.

The lure of Argentina depended on the political elite there. Although Argentine politics during WWII were characterized by periods of instability and political turnover, for much of the time the main power broker was Perón, who was pulling the strings as early as 1943, when he took part in a military coup by the GOU (United Officers Group) against the civilian conservative government. The offices he held in various governments included the influential positions of secretary of labor and social security and minister of war. In 1943, on the basis of German intelligence reports originating from the German embassy in Buenos Aires, Schellenberg identified Perón as the key man to help further German interests in Argentina.[23] This choice turned out to be a wise and

far-reaching one. Schellenberg would not have understood in 1943 just
how far the pragmatically corrupt and manipulative Perón would go to
further his own political and financial interests. The ultimate marriage of
convenience between the Nazis and arguably the most important political
figure in twentieth-century Argentine politics was created.

The relationship between the Argentine military and the Nazis was
formalized by Schellenberg in 1943.[24] The German consented to a deal
in May that brought important benefits for both sides. German agents
would not be arrested, their identities would be added to the Argentine
Secret Service, they would use the Argentine diplomatic pouch to import
classified material, and an early warning system would help them escape
if there was a change of government.[25] Schellenberg promised in return
Argentine access to the powerful Nazi radio communications service of
the German Secret Service. The information from these communications
included intelligence gathered by German agents from neighboring countries, including Brazil.[26] The Germans agreed to help establish and support the creation of an Argentine-led South American bloc of countries
that included Bolivia, Chile, and Paraguay, among others.[27] A few weeks
after the agreement was implemented, the army colonels made their move
and staged the coup that brought them to office. The power behind the
scenes was Perón.[28]

Argentina wanted arms to strengthen its military position against its
old rival, Brazil. Despite the advent of the Good Neighbor Program in
Washington, the United States proved reluctant to sell weapons to Buenos
Aires as a result of a lack of spare arms and the political consideration that
Argentina was not a stable and reliable ally. Despite promises of weaponry
from Germany during the war, Perón was left disappointed. The Germans
looked to maximize their leverage with the Argentines without supplying
them with arms. Cooperation between the two countries led to a coup in
Bolivia on December 20, 1943, which Perón helped organize and which
Schellenberg monitored from Berlin.[29] The Germans hoped to turn another state in South America against the United States. The OSS documented the involvement of the Argentines and Nazis in the coup.

The Allies used the threat of releasing this information and other
damning evidence of the links between the Nazis and the military rulers

in Argentina to pressure Buenos Aires into cutting official ties with Berlin in January 1944. Argentina remained neutral until a month before Hitler's death, when it made a token declaration of war on Germany. Later, Perón confirmed that Buenos Aires had sent secret messages to the Nazis through General Franco in Spain and the Swiss authorities. The message was clear: Argentina would not cut ties with Nazi Germany. Instead, Buenos Aires, as a belligerent to the Allies in the war, could send its ships and planes to Germany when the war finally ended, offering a great service to the Nazis. Perón was thinking already of helping wanted Nazis to get out. Later, he confessed that this was how several Nazis came to Argentina in the immediate aftermath of the war.[30]

In the final months of the war, several Argentine agents arrived in Spain to prepare an escape line. Many of them were members of the German community in Argentina, with strong Nazi sympathies. Few attracted the attention of the Spanish authorities, and those who did were not picked up by the local police. Fluent in Spanish (albeit with South American accents), they quite often also spoke German as well as English and French. Many were blond and blue-eyed with a good grasp of what was required to set up an escape line. They practiced using different passports to enter the various countries in the line from Switzerland and France to Spain and into Portugal. Their plans were politically supported and well funded. This was not an amateur operation, and they expected many customers. Nazis with an international warrant for their arrest would be taken directly by plane from Madrid to Argentina if possible. By 1947, the flight had become a regular escape route, with Argentine officials waiting at the airport in Buenos Aires to greet the fugitives. It was the Nazi equivalent of the Pan Am Clipper that had flown Jewish refugees escaping Europe from Lisbon during the war.

Assessing the numbers of Nazis who landed in Argentina in the postwar period is difficult. Around eighty thousand Germans and Austrians arrived in Argentina in the decade after the war. Most did not stay. They either went on to neighboring countries, such as Bolivia, Chile, and Paraguay, or returned to Europe. Estimates suggest that at least nineteen thousand Germans and Austrians remained in Argentina.[31] Not all of these people were Nazis, and pinning down an exact number of

Nazis in the country has eluded even the most experienced Nazi hunters. The Simon Wiesenthal Center claims to have tracked down the names of twelve thousand Nazis who lived in Argentina during the 1930s, but postwar numbers have been more difficult to establish.[32] Nevertheless, it is clear that Argentina was the chosen location for the majority of Nazis who fled the European continent after the war.

The warm greeting offered by the Perón administration was an important reason for their choice, and the large German immigrant population made it possible for them to blend in. Many of the Nazis in Argentina wanted nothing more to do with any groups that sought a revival of the Reich. They wanted to retire and see out the rest of their days living quiet lives away from political and military interference. Many used, or resorted to, their original name, believing they were secure in Argentina. For a time, this strategy worked, and they enjoyed little interference from the authorities. The support network from the German population in Argentina was strong, regardless of the political affiliations of individual members.

The other major factor confirming Argentina as a good choice was the country itself. Buenos Aires was one of the most European cities in South America. The architecture and culture are European influenced; the city is known as the Paris of South America. Also known as the intellectual and literary capital of South America, in 1947 Buenos Aires could have been a city based on the European continent. The climate is relatively mild by South American standards: much of the year is pleasant with little cold weather or snow. While such considerations might appear superficial for a group of Nazi war criminals on the run from the Allies, they did matter. Most Nazis hiding in Argentina were middle aged or older. An additional bonus feature of Buenos Aires was its size and the number of gentrified, leafy suburban areas, where it was easy to pick up discreet properties at reasonable prices. Nazis who ventured further afield into other cities and the countryside were attracted to their remoteness; they believed they would never be discovered there, and for many that was undoubtedly the case. Several took jobs, often basic ones aimed at keeping up appearances of living normal lives.

Buenos Aires held an extra incentive for many Nazis with looted treasure. The vibrant art markets provided the perfect cover for sales of looted

art. Several Nazis arriving in the city from 1947 onward brought a large
amount of looted artworks and treasures from Europe or had the loot
delivered separately. The sophistication of the Argentine network made it
easier to get artworks out of Europe than it had been during the war. No
naval blockades were in place and the documentation required to import
the works into Argentina could be arranged for a fee. The auction houses
in Buenos Aires were awash with sales of looted art in the second part of
the 1940s as auctions in Lisbon had been during the war.

Argentina under Perón cared little about the damage to its international standing caused by the influx of Nazis. Instead, it focused on becoming the dominant military and political power in South America. For
a time, this proved a successful policy for Argentina. By 1947, Operation Safehaven had become a toothless tiger whose time was fast running
out. The United States viewed South America through the prism of the
Cold War and wanted to develop economic and political ties with South
American countries to help reduce the threat of Soviet penetration in
the region. For this reason, despite some harsh rhetoric and warnings
directed at Argentina, Perón believed that the old wartime Allies would
eventually focus on the present and not the past.

This belief set had been shaken by the State Department's publication
of the *Blue Book on Argentina* on February 12, 1946.[33] The book represented an attempt by the United States to discredit Perón, whom Washington regarded as the major anti-American agitator in Argentina. There
were two important points about the book: the strength of its attack on
Argentina and Perón, and the timing of its release. The latter coincided
with the national elections in Argentina, which took place twelve days
later, on February 24.[34] The specific intention was to cause maximum
damage to Perón's electoral prospects. An additional factor was whether
the Argentines should be admitted to the inter-American security committee that was scheduled to meet mid-March to mid-April of the
same year.

The *Blue Book* was a clumsy attempt to interfere in national politics—
one that evidently failed when the voters of Argentina elected Perón
as president. To not look like a personal attack, the text claimed that
the State Department had consulted with other South American states

about the Argentine situation,[35] implying that the *Blue Book* was a compilation of broadly held concerns across South America. The report also distinguished between the people of Argentina and their leaders. The harsh criticism in the book was directed solely against the latter. In making the distinction between voters and leaders, the State Department hoped the message would get through to the electorate that Argentina would be regionally isolated if Perón won the presidential election.

The middle third of the book used material gathered from wartime Allied intelligence operations in Argentina and interrogations of captured Nazis. Once again, the interrogation of Walter Schellenberg was central. Sitting in his prison cell in Germany, the German had little idea of how useful his testimony about Argentina was in making the case against Perón.[36] The three charges made against Argentina were taken from his answers and elaborated with the intelligence reports of the OSS and SIS in Argentina. The first accusation concerned the Argentine attempt to buy weapons from the Nazis that they could have used against neighboring countries.[37] Brazil was not named explicitly but was considered the most likely target. The second charge was about Argentina's strategic goal in WWII, which the State Department argued was to undermine pro-Allied governments in South America and persuade them to join a pro-Axis bloc headed by Argentina.[38] The third allegation focused on the collaboration of Argentina and the Nazis in espionage activities, assistance to pro-Nazi press in Argentina, and the preservation of Nazi commercial power in the country.[39]

The final part of the book contained a scathing attack on the fascist character of the Argentine regime,[40] which was described as undemocratic and authoritarian and bankrolled by the Nazis. This charge was an exaggeration, but not wholly untrue. The use of the Secret Police against opponents of the regime was highlighted, as was the close connection of the military with the Nazis. The common theme of the *Blue Book* was that Argentina under the military regime was little more than a Nazi outpost in South America.[41]

The book failed not only in terms of impact on the Argentine election but also in winning support for the American position among the other countries of South America. There was general hostility toward the book. After its publication, Perón launched a strong counterattack on the State Department, accusing it of intolerable interference in the internal politics of Argentina. Cunningly, Perón then published his own book entitled *The Blue and White Book*.[42] It amounted to a point-by-point rebuttal of the American allegations. Central to Perón's defense was the charge that the evidence presented by the Americans was flawed and based on the testimony of disgruntled diplomats and others. He talked about the need to make a distinction between the contemporary government and the government during WWII, citing that several key players in the old government had been removed. Perón's response to the *Blue Book* was effectively a manifesto of his agenda for Argentina—and it was received in Argentina and South America much better than the State Department publication.

The State Department, however, felt vindicated by its actions. It argued that it had made the world aware of the Nazi connections to Argentina. The potential for a Third World War emanating from that country's activities with Nazi war criminals made the headlines in international newspapers, but did little to swing countries against Perón. Although it caused an image problem for Argentina, the *Blue Book* contained little key policymakers in the United States and Western Europe did not already know or suspect.

An unforeseen problem the book's publication caused related to the Gehlen Organization and the uneasy evidence that several of its members had been involved in setting up Argentine–Nazi relations during the war. American policy on Nazi war criminals appeared, at this stage, driven by two contradictory goals: actively seeking regime change in Argentina, and taking a more nuanced approach that considered the thorny overlap in how Nazi war criminals had created strong anti-Soviet organizations in postwar Germany.

The *Blue Book* made for uncomfortable reading for Nazi war criminals living in Argentina, who preferred to remain out of the limelight, but Perón's robust response went some way toward reassuring them. Always cautious about overstaying their welcome, and resentful of the protection money they paid to the Argentine regime, several started to look for alternative South American countries in which to live. Some Nazi war criminals, however, noted a more positive development in their long-term prospects.

In 1947, there was little Nazi hunting by Jewish groups and individuals seeking justice and restitution for everything the Nazis had done to the Jews—that would come later. After the declaration of the State of Israel on May 14, 1948, the Israelis focused on establishing the borders of their new country and fighting off attacks by Arab armies. This situation continued until after the 1956 Suez War, the second major Arab–Israeli war. Only then, over a decade after the founding of the state, did Israel's first prime minister, David Ben-Gurion, prioritize tracing Nazi war criminals by its intelligence service, the Mossad.

17

VISITORS

EUROPEAN NEUTRALS KEPT A CAREFUL EYE ON DEVELOPMENTS ACROSS the Atlantic Ocean in South America. For General Franco and Spain, the State Department's attack on Argentina had implications. Spain, diplomatically isolated by the Americans since the end of the war, feared the State Department might use similarly aggressive tactics against it. There was a sense of relief when Spanish diplomats based in South America sent dispatches to Madrid outlining the failure of the *Blue Book on Argentina* to achieve its intended aims. Arguably, what the Spanish regime feared the most was disclosure of the enormous amounts of money it had received from the British—a bribe to not join the war on the side of the Axis powers. Franco's dealings with Hitler, German commercial links to Spain, and the Nazi ratlines in the country would have made for unpleasant reading as well. Spain, however, unlike Argentina, was actively looking to quickly return to membership in regional organizations, even though the United States had made it clear that it would not be permitted to become a trusted member of the Western alliance for the foreseeable future.

Central to the Spanish strategy of gradual integration into the international fold were the efforts of the Portuguese to do the bidding on their behalf with the Americans. Salazar moved carefully, reminding American and British diplomats of the geographic importance of Spain and arguing that Franco could be a trusted member of the Western powers in the fight against communism. Though the Portuguese were happy to assist Spain, they, too, were keen to consign the events of WWII to the past and to persuade the postwar leadership in London and Washington to look forward. The events in Argentina led to a fear in Portugal that the State Department would take a strong line in the eventual negotiations over Nazi gold held in the country. The Portuguese tried to postpone the opening of the negotiations for as long as possible in the belief that the further into the future talks took place, the less likely the Americans would be to demand full compliance with the terms of Operation Safehaven.

Salazar noted the slow disintegration of the Safehaven program and the political changes that had taken place since the end of the war. He believed time was on his side. As part of the slowing-down process, he instructed Portuguese officials to be politely evasive in helping the Americans estimate the amount of gold Portugal had received from Germany. The Allies had transaction details from communications between Berlin and Lisbon they had intercepted, but the transfers made through the complex system of payments facilitated by the Swiss banks were still a black hole. Salazar believed it was unlikely that the State Department would ever be able to come up with anything more than a loose estimate of the gold without the full cooperation of the Bank of Portugal, which would not be forthcoming. At the heart of Portugal's approach to the gold was the belief that it had the right to hold on to all the gold it had received from Germany as payment for wolfram. Questions over the origins of the Nazi gold were of no concern to Portugal. Not even the discovery that some gold had been plundered from the Jewish victims of the Holocaust moved Portugal to consider restitution or reparation.

Efforts to discuss Portugal's involvement in looted art were met with stony silence in Lisbon as well. Promises were made to investigate specific examples the Allies highlighted, but no plans were made for any internal investigations. Looted art was cast off as a side issue. Salazar understood the issue of restitution but instead moved the country's wartime narrative about the Jews to focus on how it permitted thousands of Jewish refugees to transit through Portugal to escape Europe. Because most sales of looted treasures in the auction houses of Lisbon had been unofficial, the government argued there was not much it could have done. It asked for detailed Allied intelligence reports of these activities, which were not always forthcoming. A certain unease about sharing detailed intelligence with the Portuguese remained for the Allies, especially when the reports also included details of operations in Spain. The Allies, not wanting to share any information with Franco and his regime in Madrid, feared Salazar would pass on key points to Franco during their summit meetings.

Instead, the Portuguese concentrated on appearing useful to the Americans and the British on issues relating to the Cold War. They pursued a full-on policy of cooperation—on all issues except those related to WWII and specifically the Nazi gold and looted treasures. The question of continued American access to the Azores airbase was kept quietly in the back pocket for Lisbon's use when the time came. The subtext of this tactic involved Portugal's stance on the expected publication of the American plan for European reconstruction, which became known as the Marshall Plan. Although Portugal had not been physically damaged by the war, there was a debate in the Portuguese government over whether it should seek funds from the plan to modernize the country. Salazar was initially against the idea, but many in Portugal saw it as a golden opportunity to receive aid and further relations with the United States.

In the aftermath of the publication of the *Blue Book on Argentina*, Lisbon went on a public relations offensive. From Britain, Salazar hoped for one of two developments: a royal visit from the king or one of the princesses, or a visit from the former prime minister, Winston Churchill, who was hugely popular. Regarding the United States, a presidential visit appeared unlikely, but the plans for the reconstruction of Europe offered possibilities to engage with Washington. Central to the strategy was talking up the threat of the Cold War, the personality of Salazar, and the attractiveness of Portugal to foreigners.

During 1947, Salazar used every opportunity to remind the world that his assessment of WWII—it being a forerunner of the Cold War—had proved correct. In a speech at the opening of the National Assembly on November 25, 1947, in Lisbon, he spoke in detail of the problems the European continent then faced:

I realise that it is easier to criticise the past than to take decisions for the future, but in a few years' time it will no longer be possible to dispute that the war policy of the Anglo-Saxon powers was wrong. Most people will see that all the mistakes made derive from two fundamental errors: the doctrine of unconditional surrender, and the priority given to the European theatre of operations, though I can well understand the occupied and devastated countries of the west being of a different opinion.[1]

He then moved on to the consequences of the war in damaging Germany and the implications for Europe:

The positions taken by the powers on these points led to the crushing of Germany to a point at which she is no longer able to function as a productive power, a defensive force, or a factor of balance in the concert of Europe; worse than this, they also led inevitably to the advance of Russia into the heart of Europe, and the occupation by her of key positions.[2]

The onset of the Cold War led to a polarization of international politics into the two camps headed by the United States and the Soviet Union. Portugal's oldest ally, Britain, watched its power on the international stage decline as its economy struggled to pay for its WWII exploits. Relations with the United States, as a result, became much more important for Portugal.

For its part, the British Foreign Office commissioned a major research report on Portugal to gain a deeper understanding of the situation in Lisbon and the rest of the country.[3] Lisbon saw this as an opportunity to help the country move forward and away from WWII. The arrival of British Foreign Office officials in 1947 at least provided an opportunity for Salazar to talk up Portugal and control the narrative about its role in the war. The extensive visit was led by the strangely named Horsfall Carter from the research department of the Foreign Office. During his twenty-five-day stay in Portugal, he spent twenty days in Lisbon interviewing key political and financial personalities and sat down for a lengthy meeting with Salazar. Carter was extremely impressed by both Salazar and the Portuguese people.[4] In the conclusion of his wordy report, he made an astute observation:

The impression of a nation with deep roots in western civilisation comes out unmistakably, I think, in the character of the people; there is an innate civilisedness in their ordinary day-to-day behaviour which makes one forget that the illiteracy figure is still forty-nine percent. . . . By comparison, the Spaniards are a race of charming savages. It is a mistake, by the way, in my judgement, to think of Portugal in terms of its affinity with Spain, despite the accident of geography—though there is no denying the fact that Salazar's Portugal has become fatally tied to the fate of Franco's Spain through the insistence of the Spanish Civil War.[5]

The report then went on to make a comparison with another of the wartime European neutrals, Ireland:

A closer parallel, as I see it, is with [Eamon] de Valera's Eire [Republic of Ireland], with the difference, of course, that Portugal must fulfil herself through her empire, whereas Eire could only do so through breaking the ties of empire.[6]

The linkage of Salazar's Portugal to de Valera's Ireland was a very interesting one because the two leaders shared many similar personal characteristics, not least the importance of the Catholic Church in their lives. Salazar held de Valera in extremely high esteem. When de Valera visited Lisbon in September 1953, on a private trip, Salazar returned early from his late-summer break to meet with him. As he left Lisbon, de Valera sent a warm thank-you to Salazar, wishing both Portugal and Salazar well and offering his prayers that Portugal's authoritarian leader would long continue to lead the country.[7]

From a Portuguese perspective, the Foreign Office delegation from London and the resulting report were important. Lisbon wanted no *"Blue Book"* type of accusation. The final report provided the clearest indication that the British government wished to move on in its relations with Portugal.[8] Crucially, no details of the unresolved issue of the Nazi gold held by Portugal were mentioned, nor any rebuke for Portugal's wartime actions.[9] The main target was General Franco, whose influence in Portugal the report overstated.[10] Also absent from any discussion were the postwar events in Portugal and the use of Portuguese ports by individual Nazis with looted treasures.[11] The warm diplomatic exchanges between London and Lisbon helped create the impression that Portugal would be able to retain its Nazi gold without undue damage to its diplomatic relationships. The Portuguese government breathed a huge sigh of relief. It looked for all intents and purposes that London's silence meant the Labour-led government in Britain, which had plenty of other foreign issues to worry about, would overlook the gold.

Portugal was not the only country trying to improve its postwar image. The Argentines were determined to do something about their pariah status. Like Salazar, Perón considered the problem of his country's role in WWII to have been one of a public relations failing. Buoyed by the success of his strong rebuke to the State Department's *Blue Book*, he devised a strategy to combat Washington's attacks on his regime. He argued that the American position was based on its favoritism of Brazil over Argentina and that this was an attack on the people of Argentina. He reminded the world that he was a democratically elected leader of a country with a long and proud history. Perón's wife, Eva, was dispatched to Europe to present a more positive side of the country to the outside world.

In 1947, Eva Perón (better known as Evita), the first lady of Argentina with political ambitions of her own, undertook an important tour of Europe (known as the Rainbow Tour), which transformed her into an international star, complete with an appearance on the cover of *Time* magazine. A small-framed woman with dyed-blonde hair and sad, deep brown eyes, Eva was always immaculately dressed in the latest fashions from Paris, which she often topped off with a wide-brimmed hat. Evita talked about the poor people among whom she had been born, but she dressed like a queen. At twenty-eight years old, with a charisma that melted even the heaviest of hearts, she transmitted a sense of confidence and sexuality—unusual traits in the gray and drab years in Europe as the continent tried to recover from the physical and economic wounds left by WWII, let alone in spouses of heads of state. In 1947, Evita was well ahead of her time—her personality and charisma made her one of the first celebrity politicians. For a few short years, as her candle burned brightly, she was arguably the most famous woman on the planet.

Eva Perón arrived in Lisbon in the middle of her tour on July 17, 1947, and stayed for five nights at the Aviz, one of the most exclusive hotels in the city, also home to the oil trader and art collector Calouste Gulbenkian.[12] The choice of the most luxurious hotel in Lisbon was very much in keeping with the tone of extravagance that characterized the whole tour. Eva's welcome in Lisbon was somewhat subdued in comparison with her send-off from Buenos Aires, when around five hundred thousand cheering Argentinians showed up for her departure to Madrid. The Argentine press heralded her tour as one of the most important moments in the history of the country. When she arrived in the Spanish capital, around three hundred thousand people greeted her at the airport and along the route into the city.[13] While she was in Madrid, she met with General Franco, who was a strong supporter of Juan Perón. Franco presented her with a prestigious award, Isabel the Catholic. For Franco, Eva's visit was also a chance to remind the world that Spain still had an important role to play in the affairs of South America.

After touring Spain, where huge crowds followed her, Eva Perón traveled to Rome, where, on June 27, she was received by Pope Pius XII. Her trip to Italy, however, did not progress smoothly. Prior to her arrival a bomb had been detonated in the Argentine embassy in the city, and small crowds of anti-fascists jeered her at official engagements. To make matters worse, a proposed visit to Britain was canceled following a campaign in the London press alleging that she was coming to arrange arms deals for the fascist Argentine government.[14] The British royal family made it clear that she would not be received, and King George VI went on holiday to Scotland to make sure the Argentines got the message loud and clear.[15]

From Italy she went straight to Lisbon, where she was politely welcomed without the same rapture that the Spanish had shown her. By this stage of the trip, Eva was in poor health and she enjoyed the relief of the Atlantic breeze. While in Lisbon, she met with local artists and writers and was the guest of honor at a lunch hosted by President Carmona on July 18, where Salazar was also present. The frugal Portuguese leader, who would have been shocked at the price tag of Perón's new dress, appeared a little distracted and bored. Eva Perón's greatest attribute was her charisma—she did not dwell on details and costs—whereas Salazar was meticulous but short on small talk. Perón did her best, however, to charm Salazar, who, in turn, pressed her for information on the state of the Argentine economy. From Lisbon, Perón's tour continued to France and Switzerland before returning to Portugal. She departed Lisbon on the SS *Buenos Aires*, leaving behind a continent that remained suspicious of her husband's fascist regime but that was smitten with his first lady. After stopping off in Rio de Janeiro, she arrived in Buenos Aires on August 23, 1947, where for the sake of the assembled press, she dramatically fell into the arms of her husband.

The Eva Perón who arrived back in Argentina was different from the one who had departed for Europe at the start of the summer. She had lost a lot of weight and looked more like a European model. Gone, too, were the flamboyant clothes, replaced by a more classic style of dress. Her hair had changed too. The curls had disappeared and instead it was carefully combed back and tied in a bun at the back.[16] "Evita" had arrived.

The Rainbow Tour of Europe that made Eva Perón an international star was a very successful diversion from the less savory activities dominating Argentine politics. Eva succeeded in helping to cement Argentina's return to international respectability. Opposition figures charged that the tour was a cover for the regime to deposit funds in Swiss bank accounts, but this went unproven. They claimed that the funds would have been generated from fees the Perón government imposed on Nazi exiles in Argentina. This type of protection money was said to be a major source of income for the Perón regime.

Although personally uninterested in Eva, Salazar saw the public relations value of the tour for Argentina and the tour's success in resetting the international debate about the country. He waited in vain for a British royal visit to Portugal, and when that was not forthcoming he tried to flatter the newly engaged British princess and heir to the throne: Elizabeth. Salazar was keen to mark the wedding in November 1947. Events were organized by the British embassy in Lisbon to commemorate the occasion. The highlight was a formal dinner hosted by the ambassador to which President Carmona, Salazar, ministers, and business leaders were all invited. In the end, the president came down with the flu and was unable to attend. The embassy was then informed that Salazar would also not be attending. The British took this as something of a snub, even though Salazar was known to think very highly of Princess Elizabeth and had sent her a warn message of congratulations. The embassy reported back to London:

> Once he was satisfied that the president would not attend, Salazar decided to spend a happy evening at home picking over the details of the various ministries' budgets, which he has insisted he must himself go through with meticulous care. To the western mind it would have appeared all the more necessary that the prime minister should attend the dinner if the president could not, but here apparently the process of thought is quite different.[17]

In the end, the formal dinner was a success and was attended by the six leading members of the Portuguese cabinet. The meal, however, according to the British ambassador, was almost "shipwrecked" when Nicolas Franco, the Spanish ambassador, arrived forty-five minutes late.[18] Nicolas Franco was one of the most unsavory pro-German figures in Lisbon during WWII. Portuguese officials hoped that his brother, General Francisco Franco, would recall him to Madrid sooner rather than later. His continued presence in Lisbon did not contribute positively to the image the Portuguese wanted to transmit to the world.

There was a serious side to the British criticism over Salazar's no-show at the dinner. There were rumors circulating in Lisbon that the Portuguese leader was unwell, or simply suffering from exhaustion. Unusually, he had retreated to his small country house in Santa Comba Dão for nearly two months that summer. There is no entry in his diary for the period from September 7, 1947, to October 7. A worried British ambassador noted:

> Salazar is still extremely tired and derived no benefit from his six or seven week holiday in the country. Indeed, I have the impression that he has now reached a point of fatigue at which he has not the strength of mind to resist the temptation needlessly to do all over again the work submitted to him by minor subordinates.[19]

For his hard work during WWII, Salazar was finding it something of a struggle to procure a place in the world for Portugal. His speech at the opening of the National Assembly reflected his sense of dissatisfaction over the consequences of WWII. In a clear sign of the changes that the war had brought to Europe, Salazar interrupted his period of rest and recuperation in Santa Comba Dão to return to Lisbon to meet with the American ambassador and attend a parliamentary mission on October 9, 1947. Only one item was on the agenda: the Marshall Plan, or the European Recovery Program (ERP).[20] The origins of the plan lay in President Harry Truman's appointment of George Marshall as secretary of state in January 1947. Working around the clock, Marshall, with help of two key State Department officials, William Clayton and George Kennan, produced the Marshall Plan concept, which he revealed to the world in a speech at Harvard University on June 5, 1947. Its publication was keenly noted in Lisbon as an attempt by the Americans to secure their control and domination over Europe in the postwar order. This was the scenario Salazar had feared would follow on from a total defeat of Germany. It was not one that Portugal was comfortable with. Lisbon hoped that debates about the plan would at the very least distract American attention away from its continued work on tracing Nazi gold: here was a plan to invest in Europe. It made no sense at the same time to pursue the objective of Operation Safehaven—to clean the treasuries of Portugal and Spain of loot that was not properly theirs. The Marshall Plan was the clearest sign yet that the Americans were strategically moving on from the world war to the Cold War.

While the Marshall Plan was still in the planning stage, Salazar rejected the need for such an economic stimulus. He believed that economic solutions for Europe should come from Europeans and that the continent did not need what was effectively massive American aid. He remained deeply suspicious of American intentions. There were rumors circulating in London, which reached Lisbon, that the United States wished to develop major military bases in Spain.[21] This, the British argued, would lead the United States to take an even greater interest in Portugal as well.[22] The rumors turned out to be premature. Washington was not ready to let General Franco's Spain back into the international fold. Both Spain and Argentina continued to be excluded from postwar debates.

Later, due to an economic crisis in Portugal, a more pragmatic Salazar changed his mind about the Marshall Plan and asked for aid amounting to $625 million.[23] Much to his disappointment, the United States provided Portugal with much less: $140 million (US dollars) between 1948 and 1951. Despite the shortfall, the government and most Portuguese economists argued that the aid made a lasting positive contribution to the finances of the state. During the financial crisis in the late 1940s, it was interesting that no internal or international calls came for Portugal to sell part of its rich reserves of gold to alleviate the impact. Salazar let it be known that he was saving the gold for a rainy day, meaning during times of economic crisis. Nobody was quite sure exactly what he meant by this, but several economists wondered, *If not now, then when?* At the center of Portugal's economic policy since the 1930s was Salazar's desire to balance the books every year. He did not like to introduce into the economy elements that he felt would distort it. "Only buy what you can pay for" was the policy.

As part of Portugal's public relations efforts, Salazar's propaganda team asked him to put himself forward for a series of interviews with the foreign media. During 1947 alone, both the *Times* of London and the *Daily Telegraph* ran extensive flattering interviews with the Portuguese leader supported by detailed background information about the country. The interviews represented a key component in the strategy of deflecting world attention away from the issue of Nazi gold. The tactic received a boost from the booming US media.

Life magazine, the world's highest-selling glossy weekly, was particularly kind to the country. During WWII, the magazine ran several photo-essays centered on Lisbon, Portugal's role in the war, and Salazar himself. Unlike *Time*, the more news-centric weekly that adopted a rather more critical line with Salazar and Portugal's alleged lack of progress, *Life* magazine's coverage was more positive.[24] The major rival publication to *Life* was *Look* magazine. In the summer of 1948, it dispatched a young photographer to Lisbon along with the magazine's editor, Jonathan Kilbourn, to put together a photo-essay entitled "Holiday in Portugal." In essence, it was a golden opportunity for some free propaganda for the Estado Novo, and Salazar also liked the idea of promoting Lisbon and its coastline as an upmarket holiday resort. The local PIDE agents were to closely monitor the photographer and the crew during their brief stay in the country. The idea was that they would shoot only in preapproved locations in and around Lisbon.

This was the photographer's first overseas assignment, and he arrived in Lisbon bubbling with a mixture of excitement, nervous energy, and determination to take a reel of memorial photographs of Lisbon. This type of overseas travel essay was extremely popular with photographers, who saw it as a chance to make extra money on their expense accounts, to experience different types of light, and to build up an international portfolio of work.[25] As was typical for the era, the photographer was accompanied by a couple of actors who would form the basis of his photo-essay. The theme was simple: a good-looking American couple enjoying a vacation in Portugal, with the photographs providing an attractive backdrop. In retrospect, it was supposed to be a routine shoot, which was why it was given to one of the magazine's younger staffers.

The young photographer was Stanley Kubrick, who went on to become one of the best exponents of the photo-essay and arguably one of the most important filmmakers of the twentieth century. He directed such classic films as *2001: A Space Odyssey* (1968), *A Clockwork Orange* (1971), *Full Metal Jacket* (1987), and *Eyes Wide Shut* (1999). Kubrick and the beautiful light of Portugal were a perfect match. The assignment, however, did not go completely to plan. Kubrick was simply blown away by Lisbon and by his short trip to the fishing village of Nazaré, seventy-some miles north of Portugal's capital. Lisbon and its coast treated Kubrick to a full range of skies, river mists, and storms. The weather for much of Kubrick's visit was unusually unsettled for the time of year, allowing Kubrick, who shot in black and white, to develop a range of tonal textures and drama in his photographs that showed off the area at its most dramatic and beautiful best.

Kubrick's "Holiday in Portugal," published in *Look* magazine on August 3, 1948, followed a married couple from New York to Lisbon and the surrounding countryside. In Guincho, a beach near Cascais, Kubrick captured the couple on the edge of the sand dunes looking out to the ocean. A cloud rolls off the Sintra hills, giving the photograph dramatic impact. It became one of the most iconic images of the largely unspoiled and unpopulated beaches of Western Europe. As Kubrick photographed central Lisbon, particularly the Bairro Alto area at the top of one of the city's seven hills, he became more interested in photographing the locals than the actors. This was not part of the plan. He took pictures of shabby, semiderelict buildings and residents who were from the lower income groups in the city. Salazar wanted chic and modern, but Kubrick often chose to photograph the very opposite.

The most well-known of Kubrick's Lisbon photographs was taken at the Castelo de São Jorge, with the married couple climbing the steps and the city center low in the shot to give it old-world style. The shot makes the city appear as it was, a remarkable time capsule of a bygone era. With many European cities lying in ruins from WWII, and Madrid and Barcelona still recovering from the physical scars of the Spanish Civil War, Lisbon looked like it belonged to a different world. The photograph gives that section of the article its title, "A Last Look at Lisbon." Kubrick's photographs captured the city in a very austere manner. His focus on both the photogenic beauty of the city and the poverty of its inhabitants in areas such as Bairro Alto presented a realistic portrayal of Lisbon as it headed into the 1950s. It might not have been what Salazar and his cronies from the propaganda office wanted or envisaged, but the photo-essay was well received in the United States. Authoritarian Portugal was painted as a progressive mixture of modernity and tradition. No mention was made in the accompanying text of WWII. For Kubrick, this photo shoot served as a springboard to his distinguished career with *Look* magazine, a period that helped him learn many of the techniques that he came to use in his film career.

By the end of the 1940s, the new American military and economic influence was easily detected in Lisbon. In the summer of 1948, in a sign of its military prowess, the United States Navy held a massive exercise in the waters off the Lisbon coast. As a result, fifteen thousand sailors and officers disembarked onshore. For a brief period, the areas surrounding the docks took on the flavor of little America, with sailors enjoying the delights of the city's cheap beers and wines.[26] Thankfully for all concerned, and largely because of the presence of an immense American military police force onshore, the visit of the US Navy to Lisbon passed without any serious disturbance.[27] The following spring, on April 4, 1949, Portugal became one of the founding members of NATO, a sign of the normalization of Portugal's place in the Western alliance against the Soviet Union. Once again, no mention was made of the Nazi gold held by Portugal or of the restitution of looted treasures during negotiations of Lisbon's entry into NATO.

Portugal's role on the Iberian Peninsula continued to be determined largely by Salazar's relationship with General Franco. The Portuguese leader found himself used by Franco in Spain's attempt to get close to the American-sponsored NATO. The American attitude toward Spain was to isolate it politically and economically. Franco, as a result, viewed Salazar as somebody the Americans and the British respected who could influence the Western powers. General Franco spoke in excessive and unconvincingly glowing terms of Salazar in an interview in *Le Figaro* newspaper:

> The most complete statesman, the one most worthy of respect, that I have known is Salazar. I regard him as an extraordinary personality for his intelligence, his political sense and his humility. His only defect is probably his modesty.[28]

Spain's chronic food shortages were getting worse, but Franco refused to introduce the reforms the Western powers demanded in order to receive the vitally needed foreign credits. The Portuguese believed that Portugal's contribution to the development of NATO would be severely limited until Spain became a member.[29]

The British concurred with Salazar's thinking, arguing,

> The territory of metropolitan Portugal is to all intents and purposes indefensible except considered as part of the whole Iberian Peninsula. From the moment when the idea of joining the pact [North Atlantic Treaty] was first broached to her, Portugal preached the necessity of including Spain.[30]

In general, despite Salazar's endorsement of Franco, Portuguese–Spanish relations during this period resembled those of a couple who are overtly nice to one another in public but who, in private, remain deeply suspicious of the aims and intentions of one another. Over the years, Salazar needed to be at his shrewd best in dealing with Spain.

In 1948, plans were made for Franco's state visit to Lisbon. Salazar hesitated a long time before issuing the formal invitation, concerned about the effect of the visit on Portugal's international relations.[31] The visit was to be preceded by the usual public signals of cooperation between the Iberian neighbors with the signing on September 20 of the renewal of the Treaty of Friendship and Non-Aggression between Spain and Portugal of 1939. The treaty was not due to be renewed until 1949, but the signing of the renewal in 1948 extended the treaty by a further ten years.[32]

British and American diplomats welcomed the renewal but were deeply opposed to Franco's official state visit. The Portuguese ambassador in London was summoned to the Foreign Office, which made its displeasure abundantly clear.[33] The British argued that the visit would serve only to strengthen Franco's position before the meeting of the United Nations General Assembly, at which hostile motions toward Spain were to be debated and voted upon.[34] Salazar listened to the British protests but argued that Lisbon's relations with Madrid were an Iberian affair and that this took priority over European or wider international contexts.[35] There was a feeling in Lisbon that the West had left Franco in the doghouse for too long and that it was time to come to terms with Spain and encourage it to become a reliable participant in European affairs and in NATO as well.

Salazar's position on Spain was largely vindicated two years later when, in the latter part of 1950, President Truman took steps to bring Franco into the anti-communist camp. Amid the background of the deepening Korean War, officials in Washington agreed with Spanish assessments that Franco's armed forces needed modernizing. On November 16, 1950, as a result, the Truman administration signed a loan of $62.5 million for Spain. President Truman also agreed to another of Franco's demands: the appointment of a United States ambassador to Madrid, which was made public on December 27.[36] Finally, the United States had welcomed Spain into the anti-communist camp. Washington's moves had been made all the easier by a softening of the British attitude toward the Franco regime and by Salazar's quiet but persistent diplomacy. Franco gloated and

claimed victory over the Western powers in his end-of-year radio broadcast to the Spanish people.

By the middle of 1948, Salazar's strategy had positioned Portugal to
be the best placed of all the neutrals that had traded with Nazi Germany
during WWII. Argentina and Spain were specifically targeted by Britain
and the United States for special treatment, and both Perón and Franco
were seen as personally irredeemable but deeply entrenched in power,
with strong popular support, and therefore difficult to remove. The deep
suspicions about the complicity of Switzerland in the smuggling of Nazis
out of Europe, the laundering of Nazi gold, and the black market trade
in looted artworks remained, especially since the well-meaning promises
of cooperation by the Swiss government were never realized. Sweden's
attempts to hold out on the implementation of its 1945 agreement on the
gold and reparations cast the country in a negative light in Washington
and London, but explicit American criticism of Sweden was tempered by
its geographic strategic importance in the Cold War. Despite this, Sweden was increasingly seen as having been pro-Nazi during the war, and
its wartime record on the Jewish question was coming under greater scrutiny, not least in Palestine, where in the spring of 1948 the Zionists were
getting ready to declare the Jewish state. The new Western alliance fully
embraced Portugal alone.

18

ASSASSINATION

As Allied criticism grew about Sweden's connections to the Nazis during the war and its aftermath, Swedish efforts to highlight a more positive postwar role were placed on the shoulders of arguably its most high-profile statesman, Folke Bernadotte. To many people, not least the Zionists, he was a controversial figure whose impartiality during WWII was increasingly questioned. His relationship with the head of German intelligence, meetings with Himmler, and alleged indifference toward the Jews were all held against him. The close commercial relations between the Nazis and the Swedes, which had been condemned by Winston Churchill, added to the perception that all leading Swedish officials had cooperated with the Nazis. As Nazis continued to use Sweden to escape and sell or launder their looted assets, the country was in danger of falling permanently out of favor with the Western powers, despite its strategic importance in the Cold War. Bernadotte was looking for a new challenge, one that could generate front-page headlines around the world. Besides, he was a man who was unable to decline the offer of a high-profile position, regardless of whether he held the relevant skill sets. In 1948, challenges did not come much bigger than trying to resolve the Palestine conflict between the Arabs and the Zionists.

The partition of Palestine overseen by Oswaldo Aranha at the General Assembly of the United Nations was never going to be smooth. Most Americans knew it, and for a time the Truman administration tried to wriggle out of supporting it. A row between President Truman and Secretary of State George Marshall over the plan reflected the deep divisions between a pro-partition presidency and a more skeptical State Department. The core issue put forward by Marshall was that the plan would lead to endless conflict in the Middle East that would eventually draw American military forces into the region. President Truman argued that the world had a moral responsibility to support the founding of a Jewish state that overrode any other reservations. For a while, it looked like Marshall would prevail in the dispute as Truman backtracked, but after intense lobbying of the White House by Zionist leaders, including Chaim Weizmann, Truman reverted to his original position. Marshall and the State Department did manage to persuade the president to insert two important provisos into the position of the United States, however. If the Zionists went ahead and declared a state at the end of the British Mandate for Palestine on May 14, 1948, that state would fight alone—it could expect no American military or economic aid—and Washington would abide by the UN arms embargo that was in place for Palestine. For Aranha and the United Nations, Palestine would become the first major test for the newly created international organization.[1]

The decision of the Zionist leadership to establish the State of Israel on May 14, 1948, led to the expected confrontation with the Arab world. In addition to the fighting that had been taking place in Palestine, the conflict escalated into a full-scale regional war when the regular armies of the neighboring Arab states attacked Israel. The UN moved quickly to appoint a special mediator to bring about a ceasefire and find a political solution to the conflict. Several names were put forward in private by the five permanent members of the UN Security Council, but none appealed to the two major stakeholders in Palestine, America and Britain.[2] Finally, a name was agreed upon: Count Folke Bernadotte was chosen as the special mediator and commenced his posting on May 20, 1948, some six days after the start of the 1948 Arab–Israeli War. It was at once both an obvious and a strange choice. As president of the Swedish

Red Cross, and with a high public profile, Bernadotte was a top-caliber candidate. He had, however, no detailed knowledge of the intractable conflict he was asked to mediate. It had been presumed that the job of special mediator would be fulfilled by a person with detailed experience in the Arab Middle East and with dealing with Zionists. Bernadotte had neither qualification. Although he was a quick learner, he depended on his staff to provide him with the nuances of the dispute and its long and tragic history. It now appears that his selection for this role was the work of several international diplomatic factors coming together.

Both the United States and Britain did not want a special mediator who would push his own agenda (ironically, Bernadotte did exactly this once he took up the job).[3] They believed selecting the Swede would make it easier for London and Washington to be backseat drivers, a way to retain control over the mediation and diplomatic efforts to resolve the Arab–Israeli conflict. Sweden was keen to push Bernadotte forward as part of its strategy of highlighting its humanitarian role and diplomatic engagement in the world. There was little concern that the personal attacks against Bernadotte connected to his rescue missions at the end of WWII would in any way compromise his mission in the Middle East. Stockholm's policy of deflection away from WWII was neatly served by the publicity surrounding the appointment and resulting work of Bernadotte.

The Swedish diplomat encountered a political minefield in the Middle East. All sides in the conflict were themselves deeply divided. Despite their acceptance of the partition plan in principle, many Zionists rejected it on the ground, arguing that it did not give enough land to create a viable state with defensible borders.[4] Of the two major Zionist movements, it was the Revisionist Zionists who were vocal in their opposition. The Labour Zionists, led by Israel's prime minister, David Ben-Gurion, accepted the partition plan, albeit with the hope that they could expand the boundaries of the state subsequently.[5] The Arab world was equally fractured. Although all the Arab states publicly proclaimed their declarations of war on Israel to destroy the new state and liberate the land of Palestine, this was not strictly true. Both Egypt and Jordan hid their intentions to grab lands in Palestine for their own respective countries. Inter-Arab rivalry was deep, made worse by the fact that King Abdullah of Jordan, who was in charge of the joint Arab efforts to expel the Zionists, was deeply distrusted by neighboring states. Many Arabs held suspicions that the king would cut a secret deal with the Israelis to prevent the establishment of an independent Palestinian state. The Hashemite rulers of Jordan did not want to see a strong, independent Palestinian state emerge, which might pose a threat to the independence of Jordan.[6]

To add to this complex and chaotic conflict, Bernadotte had to contend with the input of London and Washington. It was clear that both governments regarded his role as a facilitator of their policies and not a framer of his own ideas and plans. This might have been easier if London and Washington spoke with a single voice. They did not. British policy led by Ernest Bevin centered on King Abdullah and a desire to strengthen the Jordanians over the Palestinians. The latter were led by the mufti of Jerusalem, a well-known wartime Nazi collaborator who had accompanied Walter Schellenberg during his missions in the Middle East.[7] Despite British opposition to the Zionists, President Truman leaned more to the side of the Israelis. There was an upcoming presidential election and Truman did not want to risk alienating American Jewish voters supportive of Israel. Amid all the agendas, Bernadotte's reliance on his more experienced staff and his political move toward the position of the personally approachable King Abdullah were easy to understand.

Bernadotte was still driven to make his mark internationally. He had been left deeply hurt by the attacks against his rescue mission and the charge that he had not been interested in rescuing Jews. Though the evidence against him was out in the open, articulated at every opportunity by the relentless Felix Kersten, details for the defense were in British MI5 files that would not be released for at least thirty years.[8] The files contained the testimony of Walter Schellenberg on his negotiations with the Swede about the rescue mission. Schellenberg was also present at, or heard firsthand accounts of, the meetings that took place between Himmler and Bernadotte. Although Schellenberg's version might have been colored by his friendship with Bernadotte, he cited on several occasions at Camp 020 that the Swede had demanded that Jews be included in his rescue missions.[9] Bernadotte's insistence on this point had in the early stages complicated talks with Himmler.

Bernadotte hoped he could use his work on Palestine to entrench his reputation as a humanitarian and a peacemaker. Once he found his feet in the role, he planned to think and act more independently than the Americans and British had foreseen when they supported his candidacy. The two dimensions of the job were clear: liaising with the UN to help broker an end to the fighting, and putting forward a peace plan that was acceptable to all parties in the conflict. The first aspect was problematic because of the state of the battlefield. Early Arab gains in the war made it harder to convince them to accept a ceasefire. Israel was hoping for a pause in the fighting so that it could launch a wide search of the black market for arms to make up for its lack of weapons in key areas of the newly created Israeli Defense Forces (IDF). The second round of fighting in the 1948 war ended with another ceasefire, with Israel in a much stronger position. A third phase of the war that lasted into early 1949 erupted when the ceasefire between Israel and Egypt broke down and fighting continued in the Negev and spilled into sovereign Egyptian territory in the Sinai Desert.

It was in the arena of peacemaking that Bernadotte came unstuck and his alleged past record of putting the rescue of Scandinavians over that of Jews came back to haunt him. The two peace plans the special mediator put forward were different in content and authorship, and timing. The first was presented in the summer of 1948 and the second, that autumn. The initial plan called for the Israelis to make major territorial concessions in return for peace. The Negev was to be given to the Egyptians and Jerusalem was to be under Arab control. In return, the Israelis were to receive part of Galilee. The plan managed to unify the Zionist leadership in opposition to it. Bernadotte was personally denounced as an Arabophile who had been seduced by King Abdullah.[10] He was additionally accused of having collaborated with the British in the design of the plan.[11] The Israelis believed Britain was not a neutral or disinterested party in the conflict. Both charges against Bernadotte were not wholly accurate. His plans reflected the state of the war on the ground during which the Arab Legion of Transjordan and later Jordan had been the most effective of the Arab armies. Rightly or wrongly, Bernadotte viewed the Jordanian king as the de facto leader of the Arab world. This plan undoubtedly contained British influence, but most of it was the work of Bernadotte and his staff. In the end all sides in the conflict rejected it.

Over the summer of 1948, Bernadotte's mission changed. The crisis of the Soviet blockade of Berlin on June 24 focused the minds of the Western powers. The blockade and resulting airlift represented the first big conflict of the Cold War, and the Americans and Western Europeans wanted to secure a successful outcome. When the Soviet Union cut off all land and water connections between the non-Soviet zones and Berlin, the crisis provided a stark reality check of the clear and present danger of Soviet penetration into Europe and the threat it posed to Western Europe. The Western powers responded with a counter-blockade that prevented all rail traffic into East Germany from the British and US zones. Over the subsequent months, this counter-blockade had a crippling impact on the economy of East Germany. On June 25, the Soviets stopped supplying food to the civilian population in the non-Soviet sectors of Berlin. Motor traffic from Berlin to the western zones was permitted, but required a major detour and a ferry crossing. Electricity supplies to Berlin were cut, using a move that was made easy by Soviet control over the generating plants in the Soviet zone. In response the West launched the airlift program to supply Berlin with foodstuffs and other necessities.

The Berlin crisis prompted the Americans and the British to shift their strategy in Palestine from conflict management to resolution. They did not want to police two active conflicts at once, so one needed to be settled as soon as possible. This placed Bernadotte under pressure. He had to cajole both the Zionists and the Palestinians to yield concessions that they were reluctant to make. This led to an increased direct intervention by both London and Washington in the formulating of proposals; Bernadotte became the salesman of the Western Allies' plans and not the framer of them. His assignment would have been difficult enough during the first part of the war, but over the summer there had been a major shift in the fighting as the Israelis moved to the offensive. The IDF's gains on the ground made Israel much more reluctant to agree to a peace deal that would mean relinquishing lands it had just conquered. The status of Jerusalem remained an intractable issue, and the heavy fighting in the city and along the road corridor to Tel Aviv indicated that the city would remain divided at the end of the war.

Bernadotte's position was made more complicated by what the Israelis believed was the hidden hand of Ernest Bevin behind his every move. The British foreign secretary, along with the governmental departments he led in London, was regarded as anti-Semitic. Ben-Gurion believed that Bernadotte was coming under the spell of Bevin with the result that the UN was adopting increasingly anti-Israeli positions. This led to additional scrutiny of the Swede's record in WWII. The tone of the criticism of Bernadotte over the summer months implied that he and Bevin were natural anti-Semitic bedfellows. The language the Israelis used about Bevin and the Foreign Office used about Israel was emotive, direct, and cutting. Without fully realizing it, Bernadotte was dragged into the bigger conflict between the British and the Zionists that had only intensified with Israel's Declaration of Independence in May 1948. In the summer of 1948, Britain had not yet recognized Israel as an independent state, and the hostilities between the two sides was threatening to turn into a direct military confrontation as the IDF moved closer to the international border with Egypt. Britain and Egypt had a defense pact that meant that if Israel crossed into Egyptian territory, the British army would move to repel any incursion, either by land or air.[12]

Bernadotte presented a second plan to the United Nations on September 16. It was a complex proposal, at the heart of which were several points unpalatable to key participants in the war. There would be no independent state for the Palestinians, with the Arab portions of the original UN Partition Plan for Palestine handed over to Jordan. Jerusalem would be run by the UN, with autonomy given to Jews and Arabs in their respective parts of the city. Israel would be encouraged to take back the Palestinian refugees who had left the country during the war and allow them to return to their homes. The Egyptians would be given the majority of the Negev, with Israel allowed to hang on to Western Galilee. The plan was basically a confirmation of the military situation on the ground in September 1948. Although it carried the name Bernadotte, it was not his work. It had originated in the British Foreign Office and had been approved by the cabinet in London. It reflected key British aims: to enhance

King Abdullah's control over Eastern Palestine, including Jerusalem, and to prevent the establishment of an independent Palestinian state. This was not the first British betrayal of the Palestinian people, but it was the most important. The plan also included the proviso that Britain would offer Israel de jure recognition.[13]

One of the strategies for the plan's presentation was deception. The Arab states were to be misled into thinking that Abdullah was as surprised as the rest of them by the offer of lands originally marked for the Palestinians. The British did not want the plan to appear to have come from London because, the Foreign Office argued, that would reduce the chances of the Israelis accepting it. So, Bernadotte was to be the camouflage; the plan would appear in his name as the UN special mediator. It put the Swede in a difficult situation, but without the support of the British, his mission was effectively finished. The Americans backed the plan, and after getting Bernadotte's approval it was released on September 16, 1948, to be presented to the UN Security Council, which would then seek the acceptance of the Israelis and the Arabs. The British had even sketched out a neat timetable, projecting the whole process would be completed by September 20.

All the British planning and marking of dates overlooked a turn of events in Israel that few people had foreseen. On September 10, the leaders of Lehi, a small paramilitary group attached to the Revisionist Zionist movement, met in a Tel Aviv apartment to work out the arrangements for the assassination of Bernadotte.[14] The decision had been made the previous week after a long campaign against the Swede and the dangers he posed to the newly created Jewish state. Over the long, hot summer of 1948, Lehi had directed a campaign of strong opposition to Bernadotte on the basis that he was hostile to Israel. On August 10, members of the shadowy organization demonstrated close to Bernadotte as he visited Jerusalem. Later, Lehi published a claim in its daily bulletin that Bernadotte was a Nazi agent. His contacts with Himmler and Schellenberg at the end of WWII were used as evidence. The decision to kill Bernadotte was based on the belief that the mediator was little more than a British stooge and would transfer Jerusalem and the Negev out of Israeli control. Lehi believed that such a development would be the first stage of a campaign to eliminate the State of Israel, which still lacked international recognition from, among others, Great Britain. It believed it had to act so that the Israeli government would not and could not be coerced by the United Nations into accepting plans that Bernadotte put forward.

On September 17, the situation in Jerusalem was tense. There were reports of a major Arab military offensive about to start in the city. Bernadotte was in Jerusalem assessing the situation on the ground and meeting with Israelis and members of the Arab Legion. He returned to the YMCA building, which served as the UN headquarters in the Israeli-controlled West Jerusalem, in the middle of the day.[15] After lunch he headed to Government House, which during the British mandate had been the residence of its high commissioner. The building was in the neutral zone and Bernadotte was thinking about making this strategically important location the headquarters for his mission.[16] At around 5:00 p.m. a convoy of three UN vehicles started out on the road back to the YMCA building, following the same route it had taken earlier in the afternoon. Bernadotte was in the third car along with his chief of staff, General Aage Lundstrom, and another member of his team, the French air force colonel Andre Serot.[17]

The convoy passed through two Israeli checkpoints without incident. The UN markings on the cars meant that they were waved through with minimum fuss. While passing through the Qatamon Quarter, the cars came to a halt when a jeep stopped to turn around in the road ahead of them. Three men carrying automatic weapons and dressed in what looked like IDF uniforms got out of the jeep. A fourth man remained at the wheel. An unarmed Israeli liaison officer who was traveling with Bernadotte called out in Hebrew to let them pass. The officials in the cars, believing that this was an IDF patrol, reached for their identity documents. The three armed men looked into the first two cars and then moved to the third. At this point, one of the three opened fire on Bernadotte and Serot. The two others shot out the tires of Bernadotte's car. The convoy driver struggled with the first gunman but was shot. Then the gunmen fled, one leaving on foot after firing shots into the radiator of the car, and his two accomplices returning to the jeep and speeding off. Serot had been shot sixteen times and died instantly, and Bernadotte was bleeding from six bullet wounds, including one to his heart, and he died on the way to the hospital. Later, General Lundstrom recalled the events in more detail in his eyewitness report for the authorities.

In the Katamon quarter, we were held up by a Jewish Army type jeep placed in a road block and filled with men in Jewish Army uniforms. At the same moment, I saw an armed man coming from this jeep. I took little notice of this because I merely thought it was another checkpoint. However, he put a Tommy gun through the open window on my side of the car, and fired point blank at Count Bernadotte and Colonel Serot. I also heard shots fired from other points, and there was considerable confusion. . . . Colonel Serot fell in the seat in back of me, and I saw at once that he was dead. Count Bernadotte bent forward, and I thought at the time he was trying to get cover. I asked him: "Are you wounded?" He nodded, and fell back.[18]

Lundstrom went on to describe the scene at the hospital in Jerusalem:

When we arrived [at the Hadassah hospital] . . . I carried the Count inside and laid him on the bed. . . . I took off the Count's jacket and tore away his shirt and undervest. I saw that he was wounded around the heart and that there was also a considerable quantity of blood on his clothes about it. When the doctor arrived, I asked if anything could be done, but he replied that it was too late.[19]

The deaths of Bernadotte and Serot brought strong condemnation from the member states of the United Nations. The support of the nonaligned countries that had been central to winning the vote of the UN Partition Plan for Palestine in November of the previous year all but evaporated. Israel faced several charges. It had failed to provide an armed escort for the mediator's car as it traveled through Israeli-controlled Jerusalem. More important was the political affiliation of the assassins. At first, Lehi denied involvement in the attack, and only much later admitted responsibility.[20] Israel's prime minister, David Ben-Gurion, and his cabinet banned the group. Hundreds of Lehi members were rounded up by Israeli authorities, but the attackers remained at large. After they had fled the

scene, they were hidden by the Jewish religious community in Shaarei
Pina. A few days later, they were said to have made their way to Tel Aviv
hiding in the back of a furniture truck.

The investigation into the deaths of the two UN men was badly
botched by the authorities, leading to claims of a coverup by Israel. The
police investigation was hampered by local rivalries among the security
agencies in the country and by the failure of the police to secure the crime
scene. Nobody was ever charged with the murders, which has added to
doubts about the extent to which Israel investigated the crime. The Swedish government complained that Bernadotte was assassinated by agents
of the Israeli government. Stockholm did not accept the distinction between the official Israeli government and the paramilitary groups like
Lehi and the Irgun. Sweden made it clear that it blamed Israel for the assassination of Bernadotte and, as a result, tried unsuccessfully to delay its
membership in the United Nations. Relations between the two countries
remained frosty for many decades.

The second Bernadotte peace plan that was published just before his
death was never implemented despite a strong push from the UN to make
it his legacy. The balance of the war changed once again in the autumn
of 1948, with the IDF pushing deep into the Negev Desert, forcing the
Egyptians to retreat toward the international border. Eventually, by the
end of the year and into the first part of 1949, Israeli forces reached and
crossed the international border and were occupying part of the Sinai.
This prompted fears of a major clash between British and Israeli forces,
which was averted only when Ben-Gurion decided to pull Israeli forces
back to the border. This decision helped avert a war between the two
countries, but not before the newly formed Israeli Air Force had clashed
with the British RAF in the skies above the Sinai. The plan to which
Bernadotte had given his name was redundant. The Israelis made it clear
that they were unwilling to hand over their wartime gains in the south
to Egypt and had no wish to allow Palestinian refugees to return to their
homes. The British continued to maneuver to find a resolution to the
problem that the Arabs blamed them for creating.

Bernadotte's role in Palestine was seen in Sweden as an example of the
country's continued contribution to humanitarian work and commitment

to conflict resolution. This makes it all the harder to comprehend the silence of the Swedish government when the allegations against Bernadotte, based on the work of the historian Hugh Trevor-Roper and the evidence of Felix Kersten, continued to be publicized in the 1950s. Without Schellenberg's strong defense of Bernadotte and the Swede's commitment to the Jews—this was still not public knowledge—it was a one-sided argument. The Swedes appeared keen to move on from further debate about their role in WWII, of which Bernadotte had played a central part. Swedish criticism of Israel continued with each anniversary of the assassination. Many Swedes failed to understand why Bernadotte's death had not led to widespread mourning among the Israeli population, but Kersten's continued efforts to blacken Bernadotte's name, widely published in the Israeli media, added to the image of Bernadotte as hostile to Jews.

Swedish unease with Israel grew deeper when Yitzhak Shamir became the prime minister of Israel, serving from 1983 to 1992. In 1948, Shamir was said to have been the Lehi operations officer and was thought to have approved the order for the assassination of Bernadotte.[21] He denied any involvement in the crime, but the Swedes believed him to be guilty. In 1995, Shimon Peres, prime minister of Israel, issued the first official expression of regret for the killing of Bernadotte, seen by many as long overdue. Despite public shows of mutual support, official visits by Swedish prime ministers to Israel were infrequent. There were none between 1962 and 1999. Since 1999, the number has increased as Sweden, like its neighbor Norway, attempts to play a more active role in the Middle East peace process.

In Israel, Bernadotte's legacy remains controversial. Local historians have discovered new material that confirms the inefficiency of the investigation into his killing and the lack of a decisive response of Ben-Gurion in dealings with the Lehi and Irgun groups.[22] The names of the four men involved in the crime have become common knowledge thanks to these investigations.[23] It is alleged that the man who fired the fatal shots was Yehoshua Cohen. Cohen, who denied to his dying day his role in the assassination, became one of the founders of Kibbutz Sde Koker in the Negev in 1952. He was later joined at the kibbutz by David Ben-Gurion, who moved there in 1956. At the kibbutz, Cohen, as head of security, was an unofficial bodyguard and friend of Ben-Gurion.[24] The relationship between prime minister and assassin was uncomfortably close.

Many Israelis believed that Bernadotte's death helped unfairly reset the Swedish narrative of its role in WWII. The country moved from being a beneficiary of the massive industrial and commercial trade it conducted with the Nazis to a victim of an attack by a Jewish assassin. At the United Nations there was little criticism of Sweden's role in WWII. In Israel, as the hunt for Nazis became more of a priority in the post–Suez War era, Israeli officials traced and uncovered a lot of uncomfortable information about Sweden's role in helping Nazis flee Europe and raised questions about how much Nazi looted treasure remained in Sweden. During investigations by both Mossad and independent Nazi hunters, the Swedish remained as evasive as ever. For example, the Simon Wiesenthal Center alleged that some twenty-one Estonian and Latvian Nazi war criminals were living in Sweden. These individuals had, on a national level, actively collaborated with the Nazis on security issues and, on a local level, taken part in atrocities against Jews. Among the most prominent Nazis were Aleksandrs Plensners, who headed the Latvian SS-Legion; Karlis Lobe, who worked for the Latvian police in Riga; Arvids Ose, who was heavily involved in the persecution of Jews in Riga; and Alfreds Vadzemnieks, who headed the Latvian Security Service (SD) and allegedly participated in the murder of Jewish civilians. The most important Estonian suspect was Oskar Angelus, who organized the Estonian Political Police, which carried out the murder of the Estonian Jewish population.[25]

19

FATE AND LEGACY

THE BERLIN CRISIS AND THE FIGHTING IN THE MIDDLE EAST DURING 1948 showed the extent to which the postwar priorities had changed and the Western powers had shifted their focus. Operation Safehaven and the search for Nazis, justice, and restitution faded into the background. Officials working on Safehaven had few victories in stemming the tide of the Nazi exodus from Europe and recovering the looted treasure. The operation had not come close to achieving the results its founders had intended. The main reason for the failing was not the Nazis' cleverness and schemes to evade justice but the lack of cooperation of the neutral countries, which was central to the project. The leaders of these countries had reluctantly promised compliance, but did not implement key aspects of Safehaven for complex reasons. A common thread was the suspicion that the Allies were making demands that impinged on their national sovereignty. Sweden and Switzerland made this point on countless occasions as they fought to hold on to their wartime bounty. The Argentines viewed Safehaven as an American colonialist attempt to exert control over South America. Argentina's shift under the military dictatorship, and then under Perón, to become a home for Nazi war criminals was the most direct rejection of the Allies' agenda.

In Iberia, an American desire to punish Spain, and to a lesser degree
Portugal, for its wartime economic gains was tempered by the realities
of the onset of the Cold War. Washington feared Iberia turning communist red, and this meant that both these countries had to be handled
with great care and caution. Distaste for General Franco lingered nonetheless. Stories of the Nazi ratlines through Spain and Portugal became
more publicly known only as the hunt for Nazi war criminals intensified
during the 1950s and with the 1960 kidnapping of Adolf Eichmann
in Argentina by Mossad agents. Most of the careful documentation
put together by the SIS and the OSS on the escape networks remained
under lock for decades. The dubious role of the Catholic Church in the
ratlines was covered up by local political elites worried about challenging the church's hegemony. The political leadership in the neutrals, the
Nazis living in South America, the Catholic Church, and the beneficiaries of treasures stolen from Jews, such as the collectors and galleries accused by the Allies, were all happy that the world had moved on
quickly from the fallout and repercussions of WWII. The new threat of
an aggressive Soviet Union and the distraction of a new global conflict
suited them all.

The first major conflict of the Cold War did not start in Europe, as
many suspected it would following the Berlin crisis, but in Korea. This
enhanced the position of both Spain and Portugal. "All sins forgiven"
best characterized the new American attitude toward the Franco regime in Madrid. Spain was brought in from the cold at a pace not even
the most optimistic internationalists in Madrid could have dreamt of.
Not only was Spain welcomed into the Western alliance, but it was also
made a beneficiary of the rearmament program. The Korean War, and
the resulting international rearmament of which Spain was not the only
Western country to benefit, illustrated the continued dilemma Salazar
faced. The Portuguese leader maneuvered to preserve Portugal's national
identity and independence in a world that was rapidly shifting toward
integration of both the economic and the defense spheres. Nigel Ronald,
the British ambassador in Lisbon, was a shrewd observer of the international problems and choices that Salazar faced at the start of the 1950s.
He summarized the problem:

Portugal is faced with the dilemma, common to all the small countries, that the extreme devotion of resources to war and integration with others which will certainly be required if war breaks out would, if carried out now, require her to submerge many of her national characteristics and special interests in a common organisation over which she would have minimum of control. The Korean war has taught Portugal both the inevitability and the danger of handing over to others decisions which may mean life or death to her as a nation. . . .

One can surmise that Portugal will hold on to her relative isolation for as long as she can, and at any rate until she sees a good prospect of the Atlantic powers being able to stand up to a Russian invasion of Europe and until the plans of the Atlantic Council seem to her to include reasonable provision for the defence of the Peninsula as a whole.[1]

In other words, federalism did not appeal to Salazar. Instead, he argued, national sovereignty should be jealously guarded.[2] International conferences and commitments, which tended to subordinate the interests of small countries like Portugal to the superpowers, needed to be approached, in Salazar's eyes, with great caution.[3]

This thinking was put to the test in 1951 in the negotiations with the Americans over their future use of the airbase on the Azores. The runway was of vital importance to the United States and remained something the Portuguese could leverage with Washington. Naturally, Salazar was concerned about any perceived erosion of Portuguese national sovereignty in allowing the United States a semipermanent position on the islands. The State Department prepared for the negotiations by attempting to reduce criticism of Lisbon's conduct in the talks over Nazi gold, which the Portuguese had made no move to return. Lisbon was the only neutral country in WWII left to settle with the Americans over its wartime trade with the Germans. On this issue, Salazar remained steadfast in his belief that because Portugal had received payment for goods provided (mainly wolfram) to the Germans in good faith, it should be allowed to keep everything.

On February 9, 1951, the US secretary of state, George Marshall, informed the Portuguese government that the United States would be requesting an extension on the use of the airbase in the Azores and that talks should begin immediately in Lisbon. As before, in 1943, Salazar was in no rush to reach an agreement. The longer his team drew out the talks, the more likely the Americans would offer concessions. The two key areas of interest for Portugal were continued noninterference in the affairs of the Portuguese Empire (overseas territories) and the easing of demands for the return of Nazi gold. Neither point was negotiable from a Portuguese perspective. The only question was whether the United States would consider them a price worth paying to retain access to the Azores. The State Department suggested that it had little interest in intervening in the internal affairs of Portugal, which was taken to include all the territories in the world under Portuguese control. The issue of the gold was more complicated. Continued postwar research by officials from Safehaven and, after 1948, from within the State Department pointed to Portugal having received at least double the amount of looted gold than previously estimated, at 356.5 tons on October 31, 1945.

Following a difficult set of negotiations, an agreement was eventually signed in Lisbon on September 6, 1951, that allowed for continued American access to the Azores bases.[4] The deal was preceded by a mutual defense assistance agreement that was similar to those that the United States had happily signed with the other founding members of the North Atlantic Treaty Organization.[5] The Azores deal guaranteed US support for Lisbon. Such was the islands' strategic value to the Americans that Washington was willing to overlook not only the question of the WWII gold but also the fact that Portugal remained a colonial power and was governed by a nondemocratic regime. Indeed, a casual look at the list of original signatories of the North Atlantic Treaty reveals that Portugal was the only nondemocratic country invited to join the club at its formation. Portugal, once again, had maximized its returns from its singular strategic asset located in the middle of the Atlantic Ocean.

Nearly two years later, on June 24, 1953, an agreement was signed to resolve the question of Portugal's gold. The final agreement called for Portugal to return just under 4 tons of gold. International estimates put the figure that Portugal had received from the Germans at nearly 400 tons. At the outset of the negotiations, the State Department proposed that

Portugal should be made to return nearly 95 tons of the gold (94.787 tons).[6] This figure was then dropped to 45 tons (44.864 tons) on the grounds that the Allies could only negotiate on known sources of gold rather than use estimates provided by intelligence agencies.[7] The final agreement represented a colossal victory for Portugal and a vindication of Salazar's refusal to give in to international pressure. The United States would not have agreed to such a one-sided deal in Portugal's favor but for the Azores.

What happened to the vast majority of gold that Lisbon did not surrender is something of a mystery. Salazar was a frugal man and did not sell the gold to help stimulate the Portuguese economy or alleviate poverty and disease. Nor did he invest in modernizing the country or develop new transportation infrastructure to open up parts of the country that had been cut off from the rest. Effectively, he sat on the gold and saved it for a rainy day. Much of the gold remains today deep underground in the vaults of the Bank of Portugal located on the appropriately named road Rua do Ouro (Gold Street).

The agreement over the Azores and the progress toward closure on issues related to WWII led to further improvement in relations between Lisbon and Washington. In an act of goodwill, at the outset of the negotiations over the Azores, General Dwight Eisenhower, the supreme Allied commander in Europe and hero of WWII, visited Lisbon. Eisenhower's plane touched down on a frosty winter's morning, January 16, 1951. The general was on a tour of the capital cities of the founding members of NATO. Eisenhower was keen to see Lisbon, but his schedule was extremely tight. After arriving from London, he left Portugal the following afternoon. Prior to his departure on January 17, he met with Salazar. The *New York Times* reported details of their talks:

> General Eisenhower left here [Lisbon] today with his staff this afternoon in an evident state of high good humor after three hours of talks with Portuguese leaders on Portugal's present and potential position under the North Atlantic Treaty.[8]

As a smiling Eisenhower departed the city he paused at the top of the steps to his aircraft and turned to give his famous smile and wave to the watching public. In January 1953 he would enter the White House and serve as president for two terms. He returned to Lisbon in the twilight of his term in office, arriving in the city in May 1960. At the conclusion of this later visit, he spoke of his warm feelings toward Lisbon, the Portuguese people, and Salazar:

> Twenty-four hours is far too short a time to spend in your lovely country. As in my visit here in 1951, I have been impressed by the beauty of Portugal and by the friendliness and hospitality of the Portuguese people. Equally impressive are the signs of real progress. Today I saw whole communities which in my visit in 1951 did not exist. . . . In the name of the American people, I salute the Portuguese nation, its distinguished leaders, and its wonderful, warm-hearted citizens. My deepest gratitude and thanks go to all who have made this visit so pleasant and memorable.[9]

Eisenhower was by no means the only key figure from WWII to visit Lisbon at the start of the 1950s. Several senior figures from Britain arrived in Portugal in the ensuing years. On February 27, 1951, Lord Halifax, the former British foreign secretary and ambassador to Washington during WWII, visited Lisbon for a holiday. When the British ambassador informed Salazar of Halifax's imminent arrival, the Portuguese leader asked to meet him. The informal meeting took place at the end of February.[10] This was by no means Halifax's first time in Lisbon. During WWII, he was frequently in Lisbon in transit between London and Washington using the Pan Am Clipper service. On one of his stopovers in the city, on September 29, 1941, he had met with Salazar. In private, Salazar had regarded Halifax as one of Britain's best leaders despite—or perhaps because of—the fact that Halifax was one of the main architects of the British policy of appeasement toward Hitler's Germany.[11]

The court in Nuremberg sentenced Walter Schellenberg to six years in prison for his role in the murders of Soviet prisoners of war that had taken place during Operation Zeppelin. His lenient sentence was based on his extensive cooperation with the Allies and his testimony against the SS organization and its key leaders. Because of a deterioration in his liver condition, he was released from prison after only two years. After spending time recuperating in Switzerland, he settled in Italy, where he died in Turin in 1952. His memoir was first published in English in 1956 under the title *The Schellenberg Memoirs: A Record of the Nazi Secret Service*. In later editions the subtitle was changed to the more enticing *The Memoirs of Hitler's Spymaster* and an introduction by the British historian Alan Bullock was added.[12]

The book was received with a great deal of skepticism. While episodic in nature and selective in the topics covered, Schellenberg naturally tried to present himself in the best possible light. The contents remained sensitive to some, none more so than his insights into the German plot regarding the Duke of Windsor. From the British perspective, the book contained nothing new regarding the possible intentions of the duke during his one-month stay in the Portuguese capital in July 1940. If the manuscript contained newly incriminating material on the duke, it was edited out before publication. Despite extensive works on the duke both of academic and populist natures, there remain many gaps in the story where material has not been released into the British National Archives.[13] What was much clearer from Schellenberg's book was the Nazis' concerted attempts to curry favor with the neutral countries in the war, those countries' willingness to trade with the Nazi regime, supplying it with much-needed commodities and other goods, and the wartime networks Schellenberg, among others, set up in the neutral countries that served as excellent support structures for postwar Nazi ratlines and other activities.[14]

The political leaders of the neutral countries experienced different fates. The postwar era in democratic Sweden became known as a great period of reform. This was characterized by the policies of the Social Democrats to introduce pensions, child allowances, healthcare reform, changes in education, and the expansion of higher education. There was a consensus about these advances, many of which were partly funded by the country's economic gains from the war. Sweden stuck to its script about its benign role in the war and focused on developing its global humanitarian efforts. Generations of Swedes were not told about the wartime trade with the

Nazis. Families whose businesses had benefited kept quiet. Restitution of looted treasures held in Sweden was sporadic and unenthusiastic. The policy of collective silence was maintained with the consent, knowing or unknowing, of the Swedish people.

The Swiss followed the Swedish example. The tight privacy laws of the Swiss banking system hampered progress in following the trail of the Nazi gold. The collective ethos remained that the country had done nothing wrong during the war. Its actions were at least in part governed by the perceived threat of a direct Nazi intervention in the country. The use of the country by fleeing Nazi war criminals is still glossed over. The rapid onset of the Cold War allowed Switzerland to navigate around many of the elements of Operation Safehaven that it believed impinged on its national sovereignty. More recent investigations by individuals and international organizations have yielded some results, including a 2022 proposal supported by the upper chamber of the Swiss parliament to set up a so-called independent commission on looted art. However, much of the trail of looted treasure in Switzerland remains obscured.[15]

Brazil underwent further postwar political upheavals. Its wartime authoritarian leader, Getúlio Vargas, who departed politics in 1945, returned to power after winning the 1951 election.[16] He served once again as president, his first term as a democratically elected leader, until a political crisis in 1954 led him to commit suicide on August 24, 1954.[17] He is widely regarded as having been the most influential Brazilian leader of the twentieth century. Political changes and crises led the Brazilian armed forces to seize power following a coup d'état on April 1, 1964. The country that had been a transit port for Nazi war criminals became more attractive as a permanent home for them during the period of military control. Nazis, such as Josef Mengele, who fled to Brazil from Argentina in 1960, enjoyed the partial protection of the Brazilian armed forces, which allowed them to stay in the country provided they did not try to involve themselves in local politics. The Nazis living in the country had little interest in political activity of any sorts and lived out their days quietly.

Argentina and Brazil continued to trade barbs, including over each other's wartime records. Argentina accused Brazil of being an imperialist lacky; Brazil said Argentina was a Nazi collaborator. Nazi war criminals continued to be permitted to live in Argentina for the duration of the Perón era in exchange for the payment of protection money. Wider aims of developing Argentina as a major military power faded. Operation Paperclip helped make the United States the magnet for ex-Nazi scientists, technicians, and engineers. Though Argentina attracted many Nazis, their efforts at building a Fourth Reich were not successful. Argentina's Nazi community was shocked in late 1960 when Mossad agents kidnapped Adolf Eichmann from a Buenos Aires suburb.[18] The publicity surrounding his capture and subsequent trial in Jerusalem prompted a mini-exodus from Argentina of Nazis such as Mengele, who feared they were next on Mossad's list. Many remained, deciding to take their chances in a country whose strong European influence made it the most attractive of South American locations. Juan Perón served two terms as Argentine president before being forced into exile in Spain. He returned in 1973 to briefly lead the country again until his death on July 1, 1974.

General Francisco Franco ruled Spain until his death on November 20, 1975. He remained as uncooperative with postwar investigations into Spain's wartime record as he had been to the Allies during the war. He resisted any suggestion that the Spanish had been involved in the ratlines for the escaping Nazis or that Spanish ports had been used for the export of looted items during and after the war.[19] The close links between several Spanish and Argentine banks continue to be a source of inquiry by researchers attempting to establish how much money was transferred through Spain to South America during and after the war.

Spain's Iberian neighbor, which had been central to the Nazis' efforts to flee Europe, continued to be ruled by the authoritarian leader António de Oliveira Salazar until complications from a stroke incapacitated him in August 1968. He was not expected to recover, and his long-standing deputy, Marcello Caetano, was sworn in as his replacement on September 25. Against all the odds, Salazar awoke from his month-long coma and his mind appeared lucid. For nearly two years, until his death on July 27, 1970, he continued to believe he was still leading the country—nobody was brave enough to tell him that he had been removed from power. His successor tried to introduce some reforms into the Estado Novo, but ongoing colonial wars in Africa and increasing opposition to them at home dominated the political agenda.[20] On April 25, 1974, a revolution mounted by elements of the armed forces who were disgruntled by Portugal's wars brought down the Caetano regime.[21] After eighteen months of political infighting between the communists and socialists, Portugal emerged as a democratic nation.[22]

Narratives of the country's role in WWII are intermixed and clouded by perceptions of Salazar. Investigations highlight Portugal's positive role toward Jewish refugees. Much is made of the interventions of specific Portuguese diplomats in saving the lives of Jews by issuing visas for them to enter Portugal against the will of Salazar. The pro-British nature of the people is highlighted, as is Salazar's decision allowing the Allies access to the Azores airbase in 1943. The pro-Nazi sentiment of the PVDE is attributed to the police force's closeness to the German forces of repression, notably the Gestapo. Everything becomes hazier when issues such as the Nazi gold are discussed. The inauguration of President John F. Kennedy in January 1961 shifted the debate from Portugal's relationship with the United States to the decolonization of the Portuguese Empire. The Nazi gold was forgotten, seemingly consigned to the dustbin of history.

A Portuguese state inquiry led by its democratic politicians and academics unsurprisingly cleared Portugal of any wartime wrongdoing. The central conclusion was that the country had received the gold in good faith. This policy has formed the basis of Portuguese responses to international investigations into the subject. The fact that Salazar chose not to spend the gold adds to the contemporary importance of this debate regarding the economic plight of the country. Portugal was poor in WWII and remains in the same economic position nearly eighty years later. With one of the lowest average incomes in the European Union and close to the highest amount of state debt, the country's economic position remains perilous. But the gold continues to sit in the vaults of the Bank of Portugal.

The country remains keen to flag its positive role in WWII with exhibitions, publications, and tours for tourists, including Jewish visitors to Portugal. The issues covered in this book have received much less attention—there is virtually no debate about Portugal's role in assisting

Nazis to escape through Iberian ratlines. Except for stories of the former German ambassador to Portugal, Oswald von Hoyningen-Huene, there has been no coverage of the alleged Nazis who remained in the country to see out their days in such areas as Cascais and Estoril along the Lisbon coastline.

Investigations into looted treasures and the role of individuals, collectors, and institutions in this racket in Portugal fall far behind those of any other neutral country, including Switzerland. Processes of restitution are almost unheard of in Portugal, whose response is best characterized as a deafening silence.[23] Internationally recognized organizations such as the Commission for Looted Art in Europe have been able to gather extensive material on artworks in many European countries that has led to restitution of several works to their rightful owners. On Portugal, their work has drawn a blank.

The amount and value of the treasures that the Nazis transported through Portugal near the end of the war remain uncataloged by local customs officials and by Allied intelligence, despite the best efforts of Operation Safehaven to track and trace gold, silver, diamonds, rare artworks, valuable antiques, and the rest of the treasure that passed through Lisbon. We will never know the exact answers to the questions of how many and how much it was all worth. Increased cooperation from democratic Portuguese politicians would at least help provide more accurate estimates of this lucrative trade, but Portuguese democracy remains fragile nearly fifty years after the revolution brought about an end of the dictatorship.[24] Difficult questions are often not asked. To this day, Portugal remains the country that has said the least and got away with the most.

ACKNOWLEDGMENTS

There are many people who have been kind enough to help with the research and writing of this book. My wife and literary agent, Emma, has provided enormous support to the project, helping narrow down the wide-ranging subject of the Nazis, their attempts to evade capture, and the flawed efforts at bringing them to justice. Her help in transforming the subject matter into its present form went far beyond that of an agent. My children provided a great deal of assistance in the research for the book. Both are historians in their own right, Benjamin, with a BA in History from Porto University, continues with his MA in history and international relations. Hélèna is currently studying history at University College London. Although this was not my plan, we are developing into a family business in history. Like so many of their generation, both my children remain fascinated by WWII. The strategies of the war, the diplomacy, and, most of all, the espionage games continue to intrigue them. Their interest in the subject matter of this book helps to reassure me that the younger generations will not forget about "the crime of the century" and the need for greater progress in dealing with often complex issues of restitution and justice.

A very special note of thanks goes to Clive Priddle, the publisher of PublicAffairs and my editor. His positive input to the project has been enormous. We have developed the book together from the outset of the proposal through the planning and writing of the script. His feel for the topics of WWII that interest the reader is spot-on. As always, it is great to work with New York and even better when this is with "an Englishman in New York." Clive is supported by a great team whose attention to detail and care in the publication stage of the book are so important. This was the case when they worked with me on the predecessor to this book, *Lisbon: War in the Shadows of the City of Light, 1939–1945*. From the editing through to the book's physical creation, rights, sales, and marketing, this is a well-oiled machine of efficiency and positive energy. Special mention must go to Melissa Raymond, group managing editor, and Jaime Leifer, VP, associate publisher, and director of publicity, who both worked so hard on the Lisbon WWII book and this one. And also to Pete Garceau, who produced the visually stunning cover designs for my two books with PublicAffairs.

I am a professor at University College London (UCL), where I have been based for the best part of a quarter of a century. It is a wonderfully supportive environment in which to work. Several of my colleagues have provided insights and helped in framing this research project and its outputs. I would like to thank Seth Anziska, Michael Berkowitz, Mark Geller, Shirli Gilbert, Francois Guesnet, Lily Kahn, Willem Smelik, and Sacha Stern for their help with the project. We run a weekly departmental research and graduate seminar at which faculty and research students present their ongoing research. The discussions from this seminar have been important in shaping the range of topics and countries that I have focused on. It is always good to hear feedback and to reassess which aspects of this topic needed work. I have been lucky enough to have supervised several PhDs and post-docs who have focused on the Scandinavian side of the project and Israel–Palestine aspects of the story. To all those research students, I remain grateful for your input over the years.

I would like to thank my BA students in the Nazi Gold and Looted Art course at UCL for their perceptive questions and for helping confirm to me that these topics remain of great interest to younger generations. I find it very reassuring that these issues will not be dropped as the generation from WWII passes away.

The research for this book took me on a long and winding road across the world. In London, I remain hugely grateful to the staff at the National Archives (Public Records Office) in Kew. Their good nature and efficiency in helping find the relevant documents is always much appreciated. The same goes for National Archives II in Maryland, where it is always a pleasure to be based for an extended visit. In Brazil the head of the National Archives, Jaime Antunes de Silva, kindly introduced me to the archive and helped me navigate around its documents. The archive is housed in one of the most beautiful buildings in downtown Rio de Janeiro. I would like to thank the members of the team at O Centro de Pesquisa e Documentação de História Contemporânea do Brasil (CPDOC) for their time in answering my questions and replying to inquiries.

In Brazil, it has been a pleasure hearing from the relatives of the late Oswaldo Aranha. The stories about Sergio Corrêa da Costa, the distinguished Brazilian diplomat who was ambassador to the UK, United Nations, and United States, were fascinating to hear. His time stationed in Buenos Aires during WWII produced a wealth of material about Argentina in the war and the relationship between the Perón government and the Nazis dating back to a time earlier in the war than previously thought. His efforts to take copies of the key documents in the Argentine archive while operating undercover were courageous.

I would like to express my sincere appreciation to the staff in Portugal at Torre do Tombo (the National Archives). The collection of twentieth-century documents housed there remains one of the most interesting and sadly underused in Europe. The documents provided me with many new leads, not least about specific Nazis who were based in the country during WWII. Likewise, a big thanks to the team at the Foreign Ministry Archives in Lisbon and the Municipal Archives in Lisbon and in the second city of Porto.

Many people also gave their time to speak to me about their wartime experiences in Portugal, Spain, Sweden, and Switzerland. I hope this book does justice to the incredible stories they told me about the Nazis and their efforts to sell or export looted treasures and escape justice. I would like to thank them all for reminding me of the human aspects of this story, both good and bad.

Neill Lochery
London

NOTE ON SOURCES

THE RESEARCH FOR THIS BOOK HAS INVOLVED THE CONSULTATION OF public and private archives in several countries. The most striking feature of the documentation on a key element in the book, Operation Safehaven, was its sheer volume. The Allies' attempt to track and trace Nazis and the official and unofficial trade between Germany and the neutral countries was complex. Its focus on detail and the fact that it was managed by bureaucrats mean that the documents are, on the whole, often not easy to read. There is a great deal of overlap in the records of the operation and a lack of contextualization. That said, Operation Safehaven documentation proved to be a central source for the book.

From the documentation, it is possible to understand better the huge task the investigators faced. They were confronted with conflicting evidence from the American and British intelligence services. Embassies in the neutral countries intervening in the operation adds a further layer of complication. An additional confounding element was the failure of Operation Safehaven officials to connect the dots on key pieces of evidence. Perhaps this resulted from the scale of the task at hand or more likely was because of the compartmentalization of the investigation, with officials focused on specific neutral countries.

Another striking feature of the British and American diplomatic and intelligence documentation is its tone. The British were more direct, sometimes using language that would be considered unacceptable in the twenty-first century. This is most apparent when dealing with the Zionists. In terms of the neutral countries, the British were softer on the Portuguese and its leader, Salazar, than were the Americans. Conversely, State Department and American intelligence documentation was generally less critical of Sweden than that of the British. On Spain and Franco, there was a negative consensus. The efforts of Samuel Hoare, the British ambassador in Madrid, to keep Spain from joining the Axis powers shine through in the correspondence between Madrid and London.

Attitudes toward South American countries were different. Efforts of the United States to seduce the Brazilians into joining the American camp come across even prior to America's entry into war. Conversely, Washington's negative attitude toward Argentina is clearly reflected from 1941 onward. Because of prewar British interests in South America, London adopted a much less critical line toward Buenos Aires than did Washington. Likewise, the Foreign Office was much more skeptical of the Brazilian regime led by President Vargas than was the State Department. Gaining an understanding of these key differences from the information available in the archives has been central to setting up this book.

Several document series posed serious challenges. This was the case with the papers from MI5 and Camp 020. Two major problems arose: the first, the aggressive nature of the interrogations, and the second, the report write-ups. I had to factor in how much testimony was given under the duress of mental torture. The threat of physical torture, although not actually used, was ever present in many interrogations. This must add to questions about the validity of the material collected from Nazis interrogated at Camp 020. Reports on the interrogations are laced with Camp 020's staff comments that indicate disdain for and a lack of belief in the testimony of the Nazis. Though understandable, this skepticism does detract from the importance of the testimonies. One thing I found most interesting in the papers on Camp 020 was the questions the interrogators did not ask. There appears to be a lack of systematic input from Operation Safehaven officials to the interrogation of key Nazis in the camp.

I used the detailed testimony of Walter Schellenberg at Camp 020 in different parts of the book. From a methodological perspective, there are obvious dangers in using this evidence. Having cross-checked much of Schellenberg's accounts with British and American files, I found them to be on the whole a pretty accurate and detailed recounting of the organization and operation of the German intelligence service during the war. I compared his testimony with local documentation in Portugal and Brazil and found it to be similar. Schellenberg did not always get the details correct in his responses to Allied questions, but his mistakes are largely down to memory rather than any attempt to mislead the Allies. His blistering attack on his major rival, Kaltenbrunner, must be seen as an effort to further discredit the man and push his own narrative with the Allies. Indeed, we must apply caution to interpreting Schellenberg's testimony about inter-Nazi politics because he had a tendency to use his responses to settle scores and enhance his own credentials as the chief instigator of the Nazi peace feelers to the Allies from 1943 until the end of the war.

I ran into the usual problems associated with referencing oral interviews. Many of the people I spoke to "off the record" clearly embellished their roles in helping the Allies during the war. The British port families in Porto (Portugal) are a perfect example: keen to talk about their efforts for the Allies, but in seeming ignorance of the fact that ships carrying their port wines to Brazil after the war were also used to export looted treasures from Europe. Key families in the neutral countries, like the British port families, often split their loyalties between the Allies and the Axis powers. These differences were connected to divisions and disputes within the families that had little to do with the war.

The threat of the Soviet Union and communism hangs over the papers of the Western Allies and those of the neutral countries. A lot of the documentation from 1944 onward contains elements of forward-looking analysis regarding the Red Army and the Soviet Union, reflected in this book with the decisions made by the Western Allies on Operation Safehaven and in their postwar treatment of various neutral countries. Finally, a lot of the papers were written by leaders with an eye on the future. In

Portugal, Salazar carefully wrote his diplomatic papers premised on the fact that future historians would read them and make judgments based on their contents. This knowledge tends to make leaders more conservative about what they include in their papers and what they leave out. To historians like me, the latter can often prove to be the more interesting.

BIBLIOGRAPHY

UNPUBLISHED DOCUMENTS AND PHOTOGRAPHS

Arquivo Histórico Municipal de Cascais, Cascais, Portugal
AFTG—Arquivos Fotográficos
CAM—Colecção Antiga do Município
CAP—Colecção António Passaporte
CCGC—Colecção César Guilherme Cardoso
CFCB—Colecção Família Castelo Branco
CSAG—Colecção Sérgio Álvares da Guerra

Arquivo Municipal Lisboa, Lisboa, Portugal
Photographs of Lisbon, 1939–1945

Arquivo Nacional, Torre do Tombo (ANTT), Lisboa, Portugal
AOS—Arquivo Oliveira Salazar
Diários 1936–1946
Comissão do Livro Branco do Ministério dos Negócios Estrangeiros Correspondência
    Diplomática, 1935–1946
Correspondência Oficial (CO), 1928–1946
Correspondência Oficial Especial, 1934–1946
Correspondência Particular, 1928–1946
Papéis Pessoais, 1936–1946
PIDE (Secret Police)
Arquivo Geral
Direcção dos Serviços de Estrangeiro
Gabinete do Director
Propaganda Apreendida, 1936–1946
SPD Subdelegação de Ponta Delgada, 1942–1945

Centro de Historia BES, Banco Espírito Santo, Lisboa, Portugal
Documentation about World War II
Photographic archive of the family
Transcripts of excerpts of the diary of Salazar, 1933–1946

National Archives (Public Records Office [PRO]), Kew, London

ADM—Records of the Admiralty, Naval Forces, Royal Marines, Coastguard, and related bodies, 1939–1948

AIR—Records created or inherited by the Air Ministry, Royal Air Force, and related bodies, 1939–1948

BT—Records of the British Board of Trade and successor and related bodies

BW—Records of the British Council, 1943

CAB—Records of the British Cabinet Office, 1939–1950

CO—Records of the Colonial Office, Commonwealth and Foreign and Commonwealth Offices, Empire Marketing Board, and related bodies.

DEFE—Records of the Ministry of Defence

DO—Records created or inherited by the Dominions Office, Commonwealth Relations Office, and Foreign and Commonwealth Office, 1939–1950

FO—Records created and inherited by the Foreign Office, 1938–1950

GFM—Copies of captured records of the German, Italian, and Japanese governments

HO—Records created or inherited by the Home Office, Ministry of Home Security, and related bodies, 1939–1950

HS—Records of Special Operations Executive, 1939–1945

HW—Records created and inherited by British Government Communications Headquarters (GCHQ), 1939–1945

KV—Records of the Security Service, 1939–1946

PREM—Records of the British Prime Minister's Office, 1939–1950

T—Records created and inherited by HM Treasury, 1939–1945

WO—Records created or inherited by the War Office, Armed Forces, Judge Advocate General, and related bodies, 1939–1945

Rio de Janeiro, Brazil

Arquivo Geral da Cidade do Rio de Janeiro
Arquivo Histórico do Exército
Arquivo Histórico do Itamaraty
Arquivo Nacional
O Centro de Pesquisa e Documentação de História Contemporânea do Brasil

US Holocaust Memorial Museum (USHMM), Washington, DC

General Correspondence—Jewish refugees in Lisbon and officials and relatives

Series RG-60—Video footage of Jewish refugees in Lisbon and Caldas da Rainha (the Port of Lisbon), the Pan Am Clipper arriving, and António de Oliveira Salazar holding political meetings

Steven Spielberg Film and Video Archive at USHMM

US Holocaust Memorial Museum Photograph Archive, Washington, DC, W/S/59581–86458—Photographs of Jewish refugees in (and departing) Lisbon during World War II

US National Archives (NARA), College Park, Maryland

FRUS (Foreign Relations of the United States)—Relevant parts of volumes on Argentina, Brazil, Portugal, Spain, Sweden, and Switzerland, 1939–1950. Also available online at http://digicoll.library.wisc.edu.

RG 56-2—Notes on the Political Situation in Portugal, July 31, 1944

RG 84—Classified Records of the US Embassy in Madrid, 1940–1963

RG 84—Classified Records of the US Embassy in Paris, 1944–1963

RG 84—Classified Records of the US Embassy in Rio de Janeiro, Brazil, 1937–1954

RG 84 Entry 3126—General Records of the US Embassy, Lisbon, Portugal, 1936–1945

RG 84 Entry 3127—Classified General Records of the US Embassy in Lisbon, Portugal, 1941–1949

RG 84 Entry 3128—Top Secret General Records of the US Embassy in Lisbon, 1945–1949

RG 84 Entry 3129A—Top Secret Subject Files Related to Operation Safehaven, 1947–1948, and German External Assets, 1950–1952

RG 84 Entry 3130—General Records Relating to War Refugees, 1942

RG 84 Entry 3131—Files Relating to War Refugees, 1944–1945

RG 84 Entry 3138—Records Relating to German External Assets in Portugal, 1947–1956

RG 84 Entry 3139—Files of the Financial Attachés, James E. Wood, 1942–1945

RG 84 Entry 3195—General Records of the US Embassy, Stockholm, Sweden, 1936–1952

RG 84 Entry 3197—Classified General Records of the US Embassy in Stockholm, Sweden, 1944–1952

RG 84 Entry 3198—Top Secret General Records of the US Embassy in Stockholm, 1943–1952

RG 131-346—Safehaven-Portugal, July 27, 1946

RG 165—Records of the War Department, Military Intelligence Division, Brazil, 1937–1954

RG 169-91—From London to Secretary of State, June 1, 1944

RG 226—Records of the Office of Strategic Services, Relevant files to Argentina, Brazil, Portugal, Spain, Sweden, and Switzerland and Operation Safehaven

RG 256-190—From Naval Attaché in Lisbon to Washington, September 1, 1944

Wiener Library, London

Mf Doc 2—International Committee of the Red Cross: G59 Israélites, 1939–1961

Mf Doc 56—World Jewish Congress: Central Files, 1919–1976

548—Wilfred Israel Papers, 1940s

585—Documents Re: Nazis in Spain, 1933–1936

660—Thomas Cook & Son Ltd.: Storage Record Book, 1914–1969

683—Jewish Refugees in Portugal: Various Papers, 1930s

1072—Reports and Correspondence Re: Gurs and Other French Concentration Camps, 1940s

1100—Nsdap Auswaertigesamt: Papers on Jews in Spain and Portugal, 1930s

1206—Hepner and Cahn: Family Papers, 1874–1950s

1514—Wilfrid Israel: Correspondence, 1937–1943

1579—Frank Family: Copy Red Cross Telegrams

PUBLISHED DOCUMENTS

Allied Relations and Negotiations with Portugal [online report]. https://1997-2001.state .gov/regions/eur/rpt_9806_ng_portugal.pdf.

Camp 020: MI5 and the Nazi Spies. London: Public Records Office, 2000.

Correspondência de Pedro Teotónio Pereira para Oliveira Salazar: Volume 1, 1931–1939. Mira e Sintra: Presidência do Conselho de Ministros, Comissão do Livro Negro Sobre o Regime Fascista, 1987.

Correspondência de Pedro Teotónio Pereira para Oliveira Salazar: Volume 2, 1940–1941. Mira e Sintra: Presidência do Conselho de Ministros, Comissão do Livro Negro Sobre o Regime Fascista, 1989.

Grande Hotel e Hotel Atlântico: Boletins de Alojamento de Estrangeiros. Cascais: Câmara Municipal de Cascais, 2005.

Hotel Palácio: Boletins de Alojamento de Estrangeiros. Cascais: Câmara Municipal de Cascais, 2004.

MAGAZINES, NEWS AGENCIES, NEWSPAPERS, AND TELEVISION NEWS

Associated Press
The Atlantic
BBC News
British Pathé News
Daily Express (London)
Daily Mail (London)
Daily Telegraph (London)
Diário da Manhã (Goiânia, Brazil)
Diário de Lisboa (Lisbon)
Diário de Noticias (Lisbon)
Diario Popular (Sarandí, Argentina)
Diário da República
The Economist
Expresso (Lisbon)
Financial Times (London)
Grande Reportagem (Lisbon)
The Guardian (Manchester)
Harper's Magazine
Jornal do Comércio (Porto Alegre, Brazil)
Life
New York Times
Novidades (Lisbon)
El Pais (Madrid)
O Primeiro de Janeiro (Primo, Portugal)
Reuters
RTP News
Sábado
San Francisco Chronicle
O Século (Lisbon)
O Século Ilustrado
The Tablet (London)
Time
The Times (London)
Visão (Lisbon)

O Voz
United Press
Washington Post

FICTION AND VERSE BOOKS

Fleming, Ian. *Casino Royale*. London: Penguin, 2006.

Gabbay, Tom. *The Lisbon Crossing: A Novel*. New York: William Morrow, 2007.

Koestler, Arthur. *Arrival and Departure*. London: Penguin, 1971.

Mercier, Pascal. *Night Train to Lisbon*. London: Atlantic, 2008.

Pessoa, Fernando. *Poesia Inglesa 1*. Lisboa: Assírio e Alvim, 2000.

———. *Poesia Inglesa 2*. Lisboa: Assírio e Alvim, 2000.

Saramago, José. *Blindness*. Austin: Harcourt, 2004.

———. *The Stone Raft: A Novel*. New York: Harcourt Brace, 1995.

———. *The Year of the Death of Ricardo Reis*. London: Harvell, 1992.

Wilson, Robert. *The Company of Strangers*. London: HarperCollins, 2002.

———. *A Small Death in Lisbon*. New York: Berkley Books, 2002.

NONFICTION BOOKS AND ARTICLES

Afonso, Rui. *Um Homem Bom: Aristides de Sousa Mendes*. Alfragide: Texto, 2009.

Agudo, Manuel Rós. *A Grande Tentacao: Os Planos de Franco para Invadir Portugal*. Alfragide: Casa das Letras, 2009.

Allen, Martin. *Hidden Agenda: How the Duke of Windsor Betrayed the Allies*. London: Macmillan, 2000.

———. *The Hitler/Hess Deception: British Intelligence's Best-Kept Secret of the Second World War*. London: HarperCollins, 2003.

Allen, Peter. *The Crown and the Swastika: Hitler, Hess and the Duke of Windsor*. London: Robert Hale, 1983.

Anderson, James M. *The History of Portugal*. Westport, CT: Greenwood Press, 2000.

Andrew, Christopher. *The Defence of the Realm: The Authorized History of MI5*. London: Allen Lane, 2009.

Araújo, Rui. *O Diário Secreto que Salazar Não Leu*. Cruz Quebrada: Oficina do Livro, 2008.

Asprey, Robert. *The Rise and Fall of Napoleon Bonaparte: Volume 1, The Rise*. London: Little, Brown, 2000.

———. *The Rise and Fall of Napoleon Bonaparte: Volume 2, The Fall*. London: Little, Brown, 2001.

Assor, Miriam. *Aristides de Sousa Mendes: Um Justo Contra a Corrente*. Lisboa: Guerra e Paz, 2009.

Baer, Werner. *The Brazilian Economy: Growth and Development*. Westport, CT: Praeger Publishers, 2001.

Baigent, Michael, and Richard Leigh. *The Inquisition*. London: Penguin, 2000.

Bailey, Rosemary. *Love and War in the Pyrenees: A Story of Courage, Fear, and Hope, 1939–1944*. London: Weidenfeld and Nicolson, 2008.

Beauvoir, Simone de, ed. *Quiet Moments in a War: The Letters of Jean-Paul Sartre to Simone de Beauvoir, 1940–1963*. London: Penguin, 1995.

Beevor, Antony. *The Battle for Spain: The Spanish Civil War, 1936–1939*. London: Weidenfeld and Nicolson, 2006.

————. *D-Day: The Battle for Normandy*. London: Viking, 2009.

————. *Stalingrad*. London: Penguin, 1999.

Beevor, Anthony, and Artemis Cooper. *Paris: After the Liberation, 1944–1949*. London: Penguin, 2007.

Beevor, J. G. *SOE: Recollections and Reflections, 1940–1945*. London: Bodley Head, 1981.

Benoliel, Joshua. *1873–1932: Repórter Fotográfico*. Lisboa: Câmara Municipal de Lisboa, 2005.

Bercuson, David J., and Holder H. Herwig. *One Christmas in Washington: Churchill and Roosevelt Forge the Grand Alliance*. London: Phoenix, 2006.

Bermeo, Nancy Gina. *The Revolution Within the Revolution: Workers' Control in Rural Portugal*. Princeton, NJ: Princeton University Press, 1986.

Bernadotte, Folke. *Last Days of the Third Reich: The Diary of Count Folke Bernadotte*. London: Frontline Books, 2009.

Bethencourt, Francisco, and Diogo Ramada Curto, eds. *Portuguese Oceanic Expansion, 1440–1800*. New York: Cambridge University Press, 2007.

Birmingham, David. *A Concise History of Portugal*. Cambridge: Cambridge University Press, 2007.

————. *Portugal and Africa*. Athens: Ohio University Press, 1999.

The Blue Book on Argentina: Consultation Among the American Republics with Respect to the Argentine Situation. New York: Greenberg, 1946.

Bloch, Michael. *The Duchess of Windsor*. London: Weidenfeld and Nicolson, 1996.

————. *The Duke of Windsor's War*. London: Weidenfeld and Nicolson, 1982.

————. *Operation Willi: The Plot to Kidnap the Duke of Windsor, July 1940*. London: Weidenfeld and Nicolson, 1986.

————. *Ribbentrop*. London: Transworld Publishers, 1992.

————. *The Secret File of the Duke of Windsor*. London: Corgi Books, 1989.

Bower, Tom. *The Full Story of the Fifty-Year Swiss-Nazi Conspiracy to Steal Billions from Europe's Jews and Holocaust Survivors*. New York: HarperCollins, 1997.

Brandão, F. Norton. "Epidemiology of Venereal Disease in Portugal During the Second World War." *British Journal of Venereal Diseases* 36, no. 2 (1960): 136–138.

Brandão, Fernando de Castro. *António de Oliveira Salazar: Uma Cronologia*. Lisbon: Prefacio, 2011.

Breitman, Richard. "A Deal with the Nazi Dictatorship? Himmler's Alleged Peace Emissaries in Autumn 1943." *Journal of Contemporary History* 30 (1995): 411–430.

Brown, Anthony Cave. *The Secret Life of Sir Stewart Menzies: Spymaster to Winston Churchill*. New York: Macmillan, 1987.

Burleigh, Michael. *Sacred Causes: Religion and Politics from the European Dictators to Al Qaeda*. London: Harper Perennial, 2006.

————. *The Third Reich: A New History*. London: Pan, 2001.

Burman, Edward. *The Inquisition: The Hammer of Heresy*. Stroud: Sutton, 2004.

Burns, Jimmy. *Papa Spy: Love, Faith, and Betrayal in Wartime Spain*. London: Bloomsbury, 2009.

Caldwell, Robert. "The Anglo-Portuguese Alliance Today." *Foreign Affairs* 21, no. 1 (October 1942): 149, 157.

Callow, Simon. *Orson Welles: Hello Americans*. London: Vintage Books, 2007.

————. *Orson Welles: The Road to Xanadu*. London: Vintage Books, 1996.

Cannadine, David. *In Churchill's Shadow: Confronting the Past in Modern Britain*. London: Penguin, 2003.

Cantwell, John. *The Second World War: A Guide to Documents in the Public Record Office.* London: National Archives, 1998.

Caron, Vicki. *Uneasy Asylum: France and the Jewish Refugee Crisis, 1933–1942.* Stanford, CA: Stanford University Press, 1999.

Carpozi, George J. R. *Nazi Gold: The Real Story of How the World Plundered Jewish Treasures.* Far Hills, NJ: New Horizon Press, 1999.

Carr, Raymond. *Modern Spain, 1875–1980.* Oxford: Oxford University Press, 1986.

Carrazzoni, André. *Getúlio Vargas.* Rio de Janeiro: Livaria José Olympio Editora, 1939.

Carrilho, M., et al., eds. *Portugal Na Segunda Guerra Mundial.* Lisbon: Dom Quixote, 1989.

Carter, Miranda. *Anthony Blunt: His Lives.* London: Pan Books, 2002.

Caruana, Leonard, and Hugh Rockoff. "A Wolfram in Sheep's Clothing: Economic Warfare in Spain, 1940–1944." *Journal of Economic History* 63, no. 1 (March 2003): 100–126.

Carvalho, Manuel de Abreu Ferreira. *Relatório dos Acontecimentos de Timor, 1942–45.* Lisboa: Instituto da Defesa Nacional, 2003.

Castaño, David. *Paternalismo e Cumplicidade: As Relações Luso-Britânicas de 1943 a 1949.* Lisboa: Associação dos Amigos do Arquivo Histórico-Diplomático. 2006.

Castro, Pedro Jorge. *Salazar e os Milionários.* Lisboa: Quetzal, 2009.

Chandler, David G. *The Campaigns of Napoleon: Volume Two, The Zenith, September 1805–September 1812.* London: Folio Society, 2002.

Charney, Noah. *The Museum of Lost Art.* London: Phaidon Press, 2018.

Chaves, Miguel de Mattos. *Portugal e a Construção Europeia: Mitos e Realidades.* Lisboa: Sete Caminhos, 2005.

Churchill, Winston, ed. *Never Give In: The Best of Winston Churchill's Speeches.* London: Pimlico, 2003.

———. *The Second World War (Abridged Version).* London: Pimlico, 2002.

———. *The Second World War: Volume One, The Gathering Storm.* London: Folio Society, 2000.

———. *The Second World War: Volume Two, The Finest Hour.* London: Folio Society, 2000.

———. *The Second World War: Volume Three, The Grand Alliance.* London: Folio Society, 2000.

———. *The Second World War: Volume Four, The Hinge of Fate.* London: Folio Society, 2000.

———. *The Second World War: Volume Five, Closing the Ring.* London: Folio Society, 2000.

———. *The Second World War: Volume Six, Triumph and Tragedy.* London: Folio Society, 2000.

Claret, Martin. *O Pansemento Vivo de Getúlio Vargas.* São Paulo: Martin Claret Editores. 1989.

Clausewitz, Carl von. *On War.* London: Everyman's Library, 1993.

Conlin, Jonathan. *Mr. Five Per Cent: The Many Lives of Calouste Gulbenkian, the World's Richest Man.* London: Profile Books, 2021.

Corkill, David, and Jose Carlos Pina Almeida. "Commemoration and Propaganda in Salazar's Portugal: The Mundo Portuguese Exposition of 1940." *Journal of Contemporary History* 44, no. 3 (2009): 381–399.

Costa, Fernando. *Portugal e a Guerra Anglo-Boer*. Lisboa: Edições Cosmos, 1998.

Dacosta, Fernando. *Máscaras de Salazar*. Cruz Quebrada: Casa das Letras, 2007.

Damas, Carlos Alberto. "Espírito Santo e Os Windsor em 1940." *Grande Reportagem* (Lisbon), n.d., 96–101.

———. *Hotel Tivoli Lisboa, 1933–2008*. Lisboa: Centro de Historia do Grupo Banco Espírito Santo, 2008.

———. *Manuel Ribeiro Espírito Santo Silva: Fotobiografia, 1908–1973*. Lisboa: Centro de Historia do Grupo Banco Espírito Santo, 2008.

———. "Ricardo Espírito Santo e o Duque de Windsor." *Historia*, no. 62 (December 2003): 46–51.

Damas, Carlos Alberto, and Augusto De Ataíde. *O Banco Espírito Santo: Uma Dinastia Financeira Portuguesa, 1886–1973*. Lisboa: Banco Espírito Santo, 2004.

Davis, Darién J., and Oliver Marshall. *Stefan and Lotte Zweig's South American Letters: New York, Argentina and Brazil, 1940–42*. New York: Continuum Books, 2010.

De Sousa, Maria Leonor Machado, ed. *A Guerra Peninsular em Portugal: Relatos Britânicos*. Casal de Cambra: Calei dos Copio, 2008.

Deakin, F. W. *The Brutal Friendship: Mussolini, Hitler, and the Fall of Italian Fascism*. London: Penguin, 1962.

Dearborn, Mary. *Peggy Guggenheim: Mistress of Modernism*. London: Virago Press, 2008.

Delgado, Humberto. *The Memoirs of General Delgado*. London: Cassell, 1964.

Diamond, Hanna. *Fleeing Hitler: France 1940*. Oxford: Oxford University Press, 2007.

Dias, Marina Tavares. *Lisboa nos Anos 40: Longe da Guerra*. Lisboa: Quimera Editores, 2005.

Disney, A. R. *A History of Portugal and the Portuguese Empire: Volume One*. Cambridge: Cambridge University Press, 2009.

———. *A History of Portugal and the Portuguese Empire: Volume Two*. Cambridge: Cambridge University Press, 2009.

Doerries, Reinhard. *Hitler's Last Chief of Foreign Intelligence: Allied Interrogations of Walter Schellenberg*. London: Frank Cass, 2003.

Duggan, Christopher. *A Concise History of Italy*. Cambridge: Cambridge University Press, 1997.

Dulles, John W. F. *Vargas of Brazil: A Political Biography*. Austin: University of Texas Press, 1967.

Eccles, David. *By Safe Hand: The Letters of Sybil and David Eccles, 1939–42*. London: Bodley Head, 1983.

Eden, Anthony. *Full Circle: The Memoirs of Sir Anthony Eden*. London: Cassell, 1960.

Edmondson, John. *France: A Traveller's Literary Companion*. London: In Print, 1993.

Eisenhower, Dwight D. *Crusade in Europe*. London: Heinemann, 1948.

Eizenstat, Stuart E. *Imperfect Justice: Looted Assets, Slave Labour, and the Unfinished Business of World War II*. New York: PublicAffairs, 2003.

Esdaile, Charles. *Napoleon's Wars: An International History, 1803–1815*. London: Allen Lane, 2007.

Evans, Richard E. *The Third Reich at War: How the Nazis Led Germany from Conquest to Disaster*. London: Penguin, 2009.

Faria, Miguel Figueira de. *Alfredo da Silva e Salazar*. Lisboa: Bertrand Editora, 2009.

Fausto, Boris. *A Concise History of Brazil*. New York: Cambridge University Press. 1999.

Ferguson, Niall. *The Ascent of Money: A Financial History of the World*. London: Penguin, 2007.

———. *Empire: How Britain Made the Modern World*. London: Penguin, 2004.

———. *The House of Rothschild: Money's Prophets, 1798–1848*. New York: Penguin, 1998.

———. *The House of Rothschild: The World's Banker, 1849–1999*. New York: Penguin, 1998.

———. *The Pity of War*. London: Penguin, 1999.

———. *The War of the World*. London: Penguin, 2007.

Ferraz, Francisco Alves. "Brazilian Participation in World War II." *Luso-Brazilian Review* 47, no. 1 (2010): 11–39.

Ferro, António. *Salazar: Portugal and Her Leader*. London: Faber and Faber, 1939.

Figueiredo, António de. *Portugal: Fifty Years of Dictatorship*. London: Penguin, 1975.

Foot, M. R. D. *SOE: The Special Operations Executive, 1940–1946*. London: Pimlico, 1984.

Fralon, Jose-Alain. *A Good Man in Evil Times: The Story of Aristides de Sousa Mendes, the Man Who Saved the Lives of Countless Refugees in World War II*. New York: Carroll and Graf, 2001.

Fry, Varian. *Surrender on Demand*. Boulder: Johnson Books, 1997.

Garcia, Maria Madalena. *Arquivo Salazar: Inventario e Índices*. Lisboa: Editorial Estampa, 1992.

Garnier, Christine. *Férias com Salazar*. Lisboa: Parceria A. M. Pereira e Grasset e Fasquelle, 1952.

———. *Salazar in Portugal: An Intimate Portrait*. New York: Farrar, Straus and Young, 1954.

Gilbert, Martin. *Churchill: A Life: Volume Two*. London: Folio Society, 2004.

———. *Churchill and America*. New York: Free Press, 2005.

———. *D-Day*. Hoboken, NJ: Wiley, 2004.

———. *A History of the Twentieth Century: Volume One, 1900–1933*. London: HarperCollins, 1997.

Gilmour, John. *Sweden, the Swastika and Stalin: The Swedish Experience in the Second World War*. Edinburgh: Edinburgh University Press, 2012.

Ginsburg, Paul. *A History of Contemporary Italy: Society and Politics, 1943–1988*. London: Penguin, 1990.

Glass, Charles. *Americans in Paris: Life and Death Under German Occupation, 1940–1944*. London: Harpers Press, 2009.

Goñi, Uri. *The Real Odessa*. London: Granta Books, 2002.

Greene, Richard, ed. *Graham Greene: A Life in Letters*. London: Little, Brown, 2007.

Guggenheim, Peggy. *Out of This Century: Confessions of an Art Addict*. London: Andre Deutsch, 2005.

Gulbenkian, Nubar. *Pantaraxia: The Autobiography of Nubar Gulbenkian*. London: Hutchinson, 1965.

Gurriarán, José António. *Um Rei no Estoril: Dom Juan Carlos e a Família Real Espanhola no Exílio Português*. Lisboa: Dom Quixote, 2001.

Halbrook, Stephen P. *The Swiss and the Nazis: How the Alpine Republic Survived in the Shadow of the Third Reich*. Newbury, PA: Casemate, 2010.

Hayward, James. *Mitos e Lendas da Segunda Guerra Mundial*. Lisboa: A Esfera dos Livros, 2007.

Henriques, João, Miguel Bettencourt, Olga Bettencourt, and Teresa Ramirez, eds. *The History of Sailing in Cascais: From the First Regatta to the Internationalisation of Sailing.* Lisbon: Edicoes Inapa, 2007.

Henriques, Mendo Castro, and Gonçalo De Sampaio e Mello, eds. *Salazar, António, De Oliveira: Pensamento e Doutrina Politica.* Lisboa: Verbo, 2010.

Herz, Norman. *Operation Alacrity: The Azores and the War in the Atlantic.* Annapolis, MD: Naval Institute Press, 2004.

Hickley, Catherine. *The Munich Art Hoard: Hitler's Dealer and His Secret Legacy.* London: Thames and Hudson, 2015.

Higham, Charles. *Mrs. Simpson: Secret Lives of the Duchess of Windsor.* London: Pan Books, 2004.

Hildebrand, Klaus. *The Foreign Policy of the Third Reich.* Berkeley: University of California Press, 1973.

———. *The Third Reich.* London: George Allen and Unwin, 1985.

Hilton, Stanley E. "Diplomacy and the Washington–Rio de Janerio 'Axis' During the World War II Era." *Hispanic American Historical Review* 59, no. 2 (May 1979): 201–231.

———. *Hitler's Secret War in South America, 1939–1945: German Military Espionage and Allied Counterespionage in Brazil.* New York: Ballantine Books, 1982.

———. "The Overthrow of Getúlio Vargas in 1945: Diplomatic Intervention, Defense of Democracy, or Political Retribution?" *Hispanic American Historical Review* 67, no. 1 (February 1987): 1–37.

———. "The United States, Brazil and the Cold War, 1945–1960: End of the Special Relationship." *Journal of American History* 68, no. 3 (December 1981): 599–624.

Hinsley, F. H. *British Intelligence in the Second World War* (Abridged Version). London: Her Majesty's Stationery Office, 1993.

Hoare, Samuel. *Ambassador on Special Mission.* London: Collins, 1946.

———. *Nine Troubled Years.* London: Collins, 1954.

Holland, James. *Fortress Malta: An Island Under Siege, 1940–1943.* London: Phoenix, 2004.

Holt, Thaddeus. *The Deceivers: Allied Military Deception in the Second World War.* London: Phoenix, 2005.

Hull, Cordell. *The Memoirs of Cordell Hull: Volume 1.* London: Hodder and Stoughton, 1948.

———. *The Memoirs of Cordell Hull: Volume 2.* London: Hodder and Stoughton, 1948.

Hutchinson, Robert. *German Foreign Intelligence: From Hitler's War to the Cold War.* Lawrence: University Press of Kansas, 2019.

Hyland, Paul. *Backwards Out of the Big World.* London: HarperCollins, 1996.

Hynes, Samuel, Anne Matthews, Nancy Caldwell Sorel, and Roger J. Spiller, eds. *Reporting World War II: Part One: American Journalism, 1938–1940.* New York: Library of America, 1995.

Ingrams, Richard. *Muggeridge: The Biography.* London: HarperCollins, 1995.

Jack, Malcolm. *Lisbon: City of the Sea, a History.* New York: I. B. Tauris, 2007.

Jahner, Harald. *Aftermath: Life in the Fallout of the Third Reich, 1945–1955.* London: W. H. Allen, 2021.

Janeiro, Helena Pinto. *Salazar e Pétain: Relações Luso-Francesas durante a II Guerra Mundial, 1940–44.* Lisboa: Edições Cosmos, 1998.

Jardim, Rita. "Memoria Duque de Windsor: Operação Willi." *Grande Reportagem* (Lisbon), n.d., 116–121.

Jeffery, Keith. *MI6: The History of the Secret Intelligence Service, 1909–1949*. London: Bloomsbury, 2010.

Johnson, Paul. *Napoleon*. London: Phoenix, 2002.

Jong, David de. *Nazi Billionaires*. London: William Collins, 2022.

Justino, Ana Clara, ed. *O Século XX em Revista*. Lisboa: Câmara Municipal de Cascais, 2002.

Kaplan, Marion. *The Portuguese: The Land and Its People*. Manchester: Carcanet, 2006.

Kassow, Samuel D. *Who Will Write Our History? Rediscovering a Hidden Archive from the Warsaw Ghetto*. London: Allen Lane, 2009.

Kay, Hugh. *Salazar and Modern Portugal*. New York: Hawthorn Books, 1970.

Kershaw, Ian. *The End: The Defiance and Destruction of Hitler's Germany, 1944–1945*. New York: Penguin, 2011.

Koestler, Arthur. *Scum of the Earth*. London: Eland Publishing, 2006.

Laqueur, Walter. *Generation Exodus: The Fate of the Young Jewish Refugees from Nazi Germany*. London: Brandeis University Press, 2001.

Leal, Ernesto Castro. *António Ferro: Espaço Político e Imaginário Social, 1918–32*. Lisboa: Edições Cosmos, 1994.

Lee, Laurie. *Red Sky at Sunrise: An Autobiographical Trilogy*. London: Penguin, 1993.

Leitz, Christian. *Nazi Germany and Neutral Europe During the Second World War*. Manchester: Manchester University Press, 2000.

———. "Nazi Germany and the Luso-Hispanic World." *Contemporary European History* 12, no. 2 (May 2003): 183–196.

Lesser, Jeff H. "Continuity and Change Within an Immigrant Community: The Jews of São Paulo, 1924–1945." *Luso-Brazilian Review* 25, no. 2 (Winter 1988): 45–58.

Lesser, Jeffrey. "How the Jews Became Japanese and Other Stories of Nation and Ethnicity." *Jewish History* 18, no. 1, Gender, Ethnicity and Politics: Latin American Jewry Revisited (2004): 7–17.

———. "The Immigration and Integration of Polish Jews in Brazil, 1924–1934." *The Americas* 51, no. 2 (October 1994): 173–191.

———. "Immigration and Shifting Concepts of National Identity in Brazil During the Vargas Era." *Luso-Brazilian Review* 31, no. 2 (1994): 23–44.

———. *Welcoming the Undesirables: Brazil and the Jewish Question*. Berkeley: University of California Press, 1995.

Levine, Robert M. *The Brazilian Photographs of Genevieve Naylor, 1940–1942*. Durham, NC: Duke University Press, 1998.

———. "Brazil's Jews During the Vargas Era and After." *Luso-Brazilian Review* 5, no. 1 (Summer 1968): 45–58.

———. *Father of the Poor? Vargas and His Era*. New York: Cambridge University Press. 1998.

———. *The History of Brazil*. Westport, CT: Greenwood Press. 1999.

———. *The Vargas Regime: The Critical Years, 1934–1938*. New York: Columbia University Press, 1970.

Lewis, Damien. *The Flame of Resistance: American Beauty, French Hero, British Spy*. London: Quercus, 2022.

Lewis, Paul H. "Salazar's Ministerial Elite, 1932–1968." *Journal of Politics* 40, no. 3 (August 1978): 622–647.

Lichtblau, Eric. *The Nazis Next Door: How America Became a Safe Haven for Hitler's Men.* New York: Mariner Books, 2014.

Lidegaard, Bo. *Countrymen: How Denmark's Jews Escaped the Nazis.* London: Atlantic Books, 2015.

Lima, Mário João e José Soares Neves. *Cascais e a Memória dos Exílios.* Lisboa: Câmara Municipal de Cascais, 2005.

Livermore, H. V. *A New History of Portugal.* Cambridge: Cambridge University Press, 1966.

Lob, Ladislaus. *Dealing with Satan: Rezso Kasztner's Daring Rescue Mission.* London: Jonathan Cape, 2008.

Lochery, Neill. *Brazil: The Fortunes of War, World War Two, and the Making of Modern Brazil.* New York: Basic Books, 2014.

———. *Lisbon: War in the Shadows of the City of Light, 1939–1945.* New York: PublicAffairs, 2011.

———. *Loaded Dice: The Foreign Office and Israel.* London: Continuum, 2007.

———. *Out of the Shadows: Portugal from Revolution to the Present Day.* London: Bloomsbury, 2017.

———. *View from the Fence: The Arab-Israeli Conflict from the Present to Its Roots.* London: Continuum, 2005.

———. *Why Blame Israel?* London: Icon Books, 2004.

Louça, António. *Hitler e Salazar: Comercio em Tempos de Guerra, 1940–1944.* Lisboa: Terramar, 2000.

Louça, António, and Isabelle Paccaud. *O Segredo da Rua d' o Século Ligações Perigosas de um Dirigente Judeu com a Alemanha Nazi, 1935–1939.* Lisboa: Fim de Século, 2007.

Louça, António, and Ansgar Schafer. "Portugal and the Nazi Gold: The Lisbon Connection in the Sales of Looted Gold by the Third Reich." *Yad Vashem* (Jerusalem), n.d.

Louro, Sónia. *O Cônsul Desobediente.* Parede: Saída de Emergência, 2009.

Lycett, Andrew. *Ian Fleming.* London: Phoenix, 1996.

MacDonagh, S. J. "A Professor in Politics: Salazar and the Regeneration of Portugal." *Irish Monthly* 68, no. 806 (1940): 417–427.

MacDonald, C. A. "The Politics of Intervention: The United States and Argentina, 1941–1946." *Journal of Latin American Studies* 12, no. 2 (November 1980): 365–396.

Machado, F. Zenha. *Os Úlitmas Dias do Governo de Varga.* Rio: Editora Lux Ltda, 1955.

Macintyre, Ben. *Agent Zigzag: The True Wartime Story of Eddie Chapman: Lover, Betrayer, Hero, Spy.* London: Bloomsbury, 2007.

———. *Operation Mincemeat: The True Spy Story That Changed the Course of World War II.* London: Bloomsbury, 2010.

Macmillan, Margaret. *Peacemakers: Six Months That Changed the World.* London: John Murray, 2002.

Makovsky, Michael. *Churchill's Promised Land: Zionism and Statecraft.* New Haven, CT: Yale University Press, 2007.

Manchester, William. *The Last Lion: Winston Spenser Churchill: Alone 1932–1940.* Boston: Little, Brown, 1988.

Matos, Helena. *Salazar: A Construção do Mito, 1928–1933.* Lisboa: Circulo de Leitores, 2010.

———. *Salazar: A Propaganda, 1934–1938*. Lisboa: Circulo de Leitores, 2010.

Mattoso, José e Fernando Rosas. *Historia de Portugal: Sétimo Volume, O Estado Novo, 1926–1974*. Lisboa: Editorial Estampa, 1998.

Maxwell, Kenneth. *The Making of Portuguese Democracy*. Cambridge: Cambridge University Press, 1995.

Mayson, Richard. *Port and the Douro*. London: Octopus, 2004.

McAuley, James. *The House of Fragile Things: Jewish Art Collections and the Fall of France*. New Haven, CT: Yale University Press, 2021.

McCann, Bryan. *Hello, Hello Brazil: Popular Music in the Making of Modern Brazil*. Durham, NC: Duke University Press. 2004.

McCann, Frank D. "Brazil, the United States, and World War II: A Commentary." *Diplomatic History* 3, no. 1 (January 1979): 59–76.

———. "Brazil and World War II: The Forgotten Ally. What Did You Do in the War, Zé Carioca?" *EIAL (Estudios Interdisciplinarios de America Latina y el Caribe)* 6, no. 2 (July–December 1995).

———. "The Brazilian Army and the Problem of Mission, 1939–1964." *Journal of Latin American Studies* 12, no. 1 (May 1980): 107–126.

Mendes, Oswaldo. *Getúlio Vargas*. São Paulo: Editora Moderna, 1986.

Meneses, Filipe Ribeiro de. *Salazar: A Political Biography*. New York: Enigma Books, 2009.

———. *União Sagrada e Sidonismo: Portugal em Guerra, 1916–18*. Lisboa: Edições Cosmos, 2000.

Milgram, Avraham. "Portugal: The Consuls, and the Jewish Refugees, 1938–1941." *Yad Vashem Studies* (Jerusalem) 27 (1999): 123–156.

———. *Portugal, Salazar e os Judeus*. Lisboa: Gradiva, 2010.

Mocatta, Frederic David. *The Jews of Spain and Portugal and the Inquisition*. Whitefish, MT: Kessinger Publishing, 2009.

Monteiro, Armindo. "Portugal in Africa." *Journal of the Royal African Society* 38, no. 151 (April 1939): 259–272.

Moran, Lord. *Churchill at War, 1940–45*. London: Robinson, 2002.

Muggeridge, Malcolm, ed. *Chronicles of Wasted Time: An Autobiography*. Vancouver: Regent College Publishing, 2006.

———. *Ciano's Diary, 1939–1943*. London: Heinemann, 1947.

———. *Like It Was: A Selection from the Diaries of Malcolm Muggeridge*. London: Collins, 1981.

Murilo De Carvalho, José. "Armed Forces and Politics in Brazil, 1930–45." *Hispanic American Review* 62, no. 2 (May 1982): 193–223.

Neillands, Robin. *Wellington and Napoleon: Clash of Armies, 1807–1815*. Barnsley, UK: Pen and Sword, 2003.

Nicholas, Lynn H. *Europa Saqueada: O Destino dos Tesouros Artisticos Europeus no Terceiro Reich e na Segunda Munidal*. São Paulo: Compania Das Letras, 1996.

———. *The Rape of Europa: The Fate of Europe's Treasures in the Third Reich and in the Second World War*. New York: Vintage Books, 1995.

Nogueira, Franco. *Salazar: Volume 1, A Mocidade e os Princípios, 1889–1928*. Porto: Civilização Editora, 2000.

———. *Salazar: Volume 2, Os Tempos Áureos, 1928–1936*. Porto: Civilização Editora, 2000.

———. *Salazar: Volume 3, As Grandes Crises, 1936–1945*. Porto: Civilização Editora, 2000.

———. *Salazar: Volume 4, O Ataque, 1945–1958*. Porto: Civilização Editora, 2000.

———. *Salazar: Volume 5, A Resistência, 1958–1964*. Porto: Civilização Editora, 2000.

———. *Salazar: Volume 6, O Ultimo Combate, 1964–1970*. Porto: Civilização Editora, 2000.

Norwich, John Julius. *The Middle Sea: A History of the Mediterranean*. London: Vintage, 2007.

Nunes, João Paulo Avelãs. *O Estado Novo e o Volfrâmio, 1933–1947*. Coimbra: Imprensa da Universidade de Coimbra, 2010.

Oliveira, Pedro Aires. *Armindo Monteiro: Uma Biografia Política*. Lisboa: Bertrand Editora, 2000.

Orbach, Danny. *Fugitives: A History of Nazi Mercenaries During the Cold War*. London: Hurst, 2022.

Overy, Richard. *The Dictators: Hitler's Germany, Stalin's Russia*. London: Penguin, 2005.

Paehler, Katrin. *The Third Reich's Intelligence Services: The Career of Walter Schellenberg*. Cambridge: Cambridge University Press, 2019.

Page, Martin. *The First Global Village: How Portugal Changed the World*. Cruz Quebrada: Casa das Letras, 2002.

Paice, Edward. *Wrath of God: The Great Lisbon Earthquake of 1755*. London: Quercus, 2008.

Paxton, Robert O. *The Anatomy of Fascism*. London: Penguin, 2005.

Payne, Stanley G. *A History of Fascism, 1914–45*. London: Routledge, 2001.

———. *A History of Spain and Portugal: Volume One*. Madison: University of Wisconsin Press, 1973.

———. *A History of Spain and Portugal: Volume Two*. Madison: University of Wisconsin Press, 1973.

Persson, Sune. *Escape from the Third Reich: The Harrowing True Story of the Largest Rescue Effort Made Inside Nazi Germany*. New York: Skyhorse Publishing, 2009.

Petropoulos, Jonathan. *Goering's Man in Paris: The Story of a Nazi Art Plunderer and His World*. New Haven, CT: Yale University Press, 2021.

———. *Royals and the Reich: The Princes von Hessen in Nazi Germany*. New York: Oxford University Press, 2006.

Philby, Kim. *My Silent War: The Autobiography of a Spy*. New York: Modern Library, 2002.

Picaper, Jean-Paul. *No Rasto Dos Tesouros Nazis*. Lisbon: Edicoes 70, 1998.

Pignatelli, Marina. *Interioridades e Exterioridades dos Judeus de Lisboa*. Lisboa: Instituto Superior de Ciências Sociais e Políticas, 2008.

Pimentel, Irene Flunser. *Cardeal Cerejeira: O Príncipe da Igreja*. Lisboa: A Esfera dos Livros, 2010.

———. *Judeus em Portugal durante a II Guerra Mundial: Em Fuga de Hitler e do Holocausto*. Lisboa: A Esfera dos Livros, 2006.

Pinto, Jaime Nogueira. *António de Oliveira Salazar: O Outro Retrato*. Lisboa: A Esfera dos Livros, 2008.

———. *O Fim do Estado Novo e os Origens do 25 de Abril*. Algés, Lisboa: Difel, 1995.

Preston, Paul. *Comrades: Portraits from the Spanish Civil War*. London: Harper Perennial, 2006.

——. *Franco*. London: Basic Books, 1994.

——. *Juan Carlos: Steering Spain from Dictatorship to Democracy*. London: Harper Perennial, 2005.

——. *The Spanish Civil War, 1936–39*. London: Weidenfeld and Nicolson, 1986.

——. *The Spanish Civil War: Reaction, Revolution and Revenge*. London: Harper Perennial, 2006.

Raby, Dawn Linda. "The Portuguese Presidential Election of 1949: A Successful Governmental Maneuver?" *Luso-Brazilian Review* 27, no. 1 (Summer 1990): 63–77.

Ramalho, Miguel Nunes. *Sidónia Pais: Diplomata e Conspirador, 1912–1917*. Lisboa: Cosmos, 2001.

Rankin, Nicholas. *Churchill's Wizards: The British Genius for Deception, 1914–1945*. London: Faber and Faber, 2008.

Redondo, Juan Carlos Jiménez. *Franco e Salazar: As Relações Luso-Espanholas durante a Guerra Frio*. Lisboa: Assírio e Alvim, 1996.

Reynolds, David. *In Command of History: Churchill Fighting and Writing the Second World War*. London: Allen Lane, 2004.

Rezola, Maria Inácia. *25 de Abril: Mitos de uma Revolução*. Lisboa: A Esfera dos Livros, 2008.

Roberts, Andrew. *Churchill and Hitler: Secrets of Leadership*. London: Phoenix, 2003.

——. *A History of the English-Speaking Peoples Since 1900*. London: Weidenfeld and Nicolson, 2006.

——. *The Holy Fox: The Life of Lord Halifax*. London: Phoenix, 1991.

——. *Masters and Commanders: The Military Geniuses Who Led the West to Victory in World War II*. London: Penguin, 2009.

——. *Napoleon and Wellington*. London: Phoenix, 2001.

——. *The Storm of War: A New History of the Second World War*. London: Penguin, 2010.

Rodrigues, Luís Nuno, ed. *Franklin Roosevelt and the Azores During the Two World Wars*. Lisboa: Fundacao Luso-Americana, 2008.

——. *Salazar e Kennedy: A Crise de uma Aliança*. Lisboa: Casa das Letras, 2002.

Rohr, Isabelle. *The Spanish Right and the Jews, 1898–1945*. Brighton, UK: Sussex Academic Press, 2008.

Ronald, Susan. *Hitler's Art Thief: Hildebrand Gurlitt, the Nazis and the Looting of Europe's Treasures*. New York: St. Martin's Press, 2015.

Rosas, Fernando. *Lisboa Revolucionaria: Roteiro dos Confrontos Armados no Século XX*. Lisboa: Tinta-da-China, 2007.

——. *Portugal entre a Paz e a Guerra, 1939–1945*. Lisboa: Editorial Estampa, 1995.

——. "Portuguese Neutrality in the Second World War." In *European Neutrals and Non-Belligerents During the Second World War*, ed. Neville Wylie, 268–282. Cambridge: Cambridge University Press, 2002.

Rosas, Fernando, and Júlia Leitão de Barros e Pedro de Oliveira. *Armindo Monteiro e Oliveira Salazar: Correspondência Politica, 1926–1955*. Lisboa: Editorial Estampa, 1996.

Russell-Wood, A. J. R. *The Portuguese Empire, 1415–1808: A World on the Move*. Baltimore: Johns Hopkins University Press, 1998.

Ryan, John J. M. "Election in Portugal." *Irish Monthly* 74, no. 872 (1946): 52–58.

Sands, Philippe. *The Ratline: Love, Lies and Justice on the Trail of a Nazi Fugitive*. London: Weidenfeld and Nicolson, 2020.

Saraiva, António José. *Politica à Portuguesa: Ideias, Pessoas e Factos*. Cruz Quebrada: Oficina do Livro, 2007.

Saraiva, José Hermano. *Portugal: A Companion History*. Manchester: Carcanet, 1997.

Saramago, José. *Journey to Portugal: In Pursuit of Portugal's History and Culture*. San Diego: Harvest, 2000.

———. *The Notebook*. London: Verso, 2010.

———. *Small Memories: A Memoir*. London: Harvill Secker, 2009.

Scammell, Michael. *Koestler: The Indispensable Intellectual*. London: Faber and Faber, 2009.

Schellenberg, Walter. *The Memoirs of Hitler's Spymaster*. London: Andre Deutsch, 2006.

Schwarz, Reinhard. *Os Alemães em Portugal, 1933–1945: A Colónia Alemã Através das Suas Instituições*. Porto: Antilia Editora, 2006.

Sedgwick, Ellery. "Something New in Dictators: Salazar of Portugal." *Atlantic Monthly*, January 1954: 40–45.

Selby, Walford. *Diplomatic Twilight: 1930–1940*. London: John Murray, 1953.

Shepherd, Naomi. *A Refuge from Darkness: Wilfrid Israel and the Rescue of the Jews*. New York: Pantheon Books, 1984.

Shirer, William L. *The Rise and Fall of the Third Reich: A History of Nazi Germany: Volume Three*. London: Folio Society, 1995.

Shrady, Nicholas. *The Last Day: Wrath, Ruin and Reason in the Great Lisbon Earthquake of 1755*. New York: Penguin, 2008.

Sinclair, Anne. *My Grandfather's Gallery: A Family Memoir of Art and War*. New York: Farrar, Straus and Giroux, 2014.

Skidmore, Thomas E. *Brazil: Five Centuries of Change*. New York: Oxford University Press, 1999.

———. "Brazil's American Illusion: From Dom Pedro II to the Coup of 1964." *Luso-Brazilian Review* 23, no. 2 (Winter 1986): 71–84.

———. *Politics in Brazil, 1930–1964: An Experiment in Democracy*. New York: Oxford University Press, 2007.

Smallman, Shawn C. *Fear and Memory in the Brazilian Army and Society, 1889–1954*. Chapel Hill: University of North Carolina Press, 2002.

Smith, Alfred. *Rudolf Hess and Germany's Reluctant War, 1939–41*. Lewes, UK: Book Guild Limited, 2001.

Smith, Richard Harris. *OSS: The Secret History of America's First Central Intelligence Agency*. Lanham, MD: Lyons Press, 2005.

Soutar, Ian, ed. "History Notes: Nazi Gold: Information from the British Archives." Historians LRD, Foreign and Commonwealth Office, rev. ed., January 1997.

———. "History Notes: Nazi Gold: Information from the British Archives: Part II, Monetary Gold, Non Monetary Gold and the Tripartite Gold Commission." Historians LRD, no. 12, Foreign and Commonwealth Office, May 1997.

Stanger, Cary David. "A Haunting Legacy: The Assassination of Count Bernadotte." *Middle East Journal* 42, no. 2 (Spring 1988).

Steury, Donald. "The OSS and Project Safehaven." *Studies in Intelligence*, no. 9 (Summer 2000). www.cia.gov/static/0dc1101a66291d07d66a2729ec768bd7/oss-project-safehaven.pdf.

Stevens, Edmund. "Portugal Under Salazar." *Harper's Magazine* 205, no. 1227 (August 1952): 62–68.

Stone, Glyn A. "The Official British Attitude to the Anglo-Portuguese Alliance, 1910–1945." *Journal of Contemporary History* 10, no. 4 (October 1975): 729–746.

———. *The Oldest Ally: Britain and the Portuguese Connection, 1936–1941*. Woodbridge, Suffolk, UK: Boydell Press, 1994.

———. *Spain, Portugal and the Great Powers, 1931–1941*. New York: Palgrave Macmillan, 2005.

Strachan, Hew, ed. *The Oxford Illustrated History of the First World War*. Oxford: Oxford University Press, 1998.

Streeter, Michael. *Franco*. London: Haus Publishing, 2005.

Sweeney, J. K. "The Portuguese Wolfram Embargo: A Case Study in Economic Warfare." *Military Affairs* 38, no. 1 (February 1974): 23–26.

Tarling, Nicholas. "Britain, Portugal and East Timor in 1941." *Journal of Southeast Asian Studies* 27, no. 1 (March 1996): 132–138.

Taylor, A. J. P. *A History of England, 1914–1945*. London: Folio Society, 2000.

———. *The Origins of the Second World War*. London: Penguin, 1991.

Taylor, Julie. *Eva Perón: The Myths of a Woman*. Chicago: University of Chicago Press, 1979.

Teixeira, Nuno Severiano. "From Neutrality to Alignment: Portugal in the Foundation of the Atlantic Pact." *Luso-Brazilian Review* 29, no. 2 (Winter 1992): 113–126.

———. *O Poder e O Guerra, 1914–1918: Objectivos Nacionais e Estratégias na Grande Guerra*. Lisboa: Editorial Estampa, 1996.

Telo, António Jose. *A Neutralidade Portuguesa e o Ouro Nazi*. Lisbon: Quetzal Editores, 2000.

———. *Portugal na Segunda Guerra, 1941–1945*. 2 vols. Lisboa: Vega, 1991.

Thomas, Bob. *Walt Disney: An American Original*. New York: Disney Editions, 1994.

Thomas, Hugh. *The Spanish Civil War*. London: Penguin, 1990.

Tota, Antonio Pedro. *The Seduction of Brazil: The Americanization of Brazil During World War II*. Austin: University of Texas Press, 2009.

Trabulo, António. *O Diário de Salazar*. Lisboa: Parceira e A. M. Pereira, 2008.

Tremlett, Giles. *Ghosts of Spain: Travels Through a Country's Hidden Past*. London: Faber and Faber, 2006.

Trevor-Roper, Hugh. *The Last Days of Hitler*. London: Macmillan, 1995.

Tucci Carneiro, Maria Luiza. *O Anti-Semitismo na Era Vargas*. São Paulo: Editora Perspectiva, 2001.

Turner, Ewart Edmund. "German Influence in South Brazil." *Public Opinion Quarterly* 6, no. 1 (Spring 1942): 57–69.

Ullrich, Volker. *Eight Days in May: How Germany's War Ended*. London: Allen Lane, 2021.

Unger, Irwin, and Debi Unger. *The Guggenheims: A Family History*. New York: Harper Perennial, 2006.

Vail, Karole, ed. *The Museum of Non-Objective Painting: Hila Rebay and the Origins of the Solomon R. Guggenheim Museum*. New York: Guggenheim Museum Publications, 2009.

Vargas, Getúlio. *Diário: Volume 11, 1937–1942*. São Paulo: Editora Siciliano/Fundação Getúlio Vargas, 1995.

———. *Discurso de Posse na Academia Brasileira de Letras*. Rio de Janeiro: Americedit, 1944.

Vargas de Amaral Peixoto, Alzira. *Getúlio Vargas: Meu Pai*. Pôrto Alegre: Editora Globo, 1960.

Vicente, Ana. *Portugal Visto pela Espanha: Correspondência Diplomática, 1939–1960.* Lisboa: Assírio e Alvim, 1992.

Waller, Douglas. *Disciples: The World War Two Missions of the CIA Directors Who Fought for Wild Bill Donavan.* New York: Simon & Schuster, 2015.

———. *Wild Bill Donovan: The Spymaster Who Created the OSS and Modern American Espionage.* New York: Free Press, 2011.

Walters, Guy. *Hunting Evil.* London: Bantam Books, 2010.

Weis, W. Michael. "The Fundação Getúlio Vargas and the New Getúlio." *Luso-Brazilian Review* 24, no. 2 (Winter 1987): 49–60.

Welles, Orson, and Peter Bogdanovic. *This Is Orson Welles.* New York: Da Capo Press, 1998.

West, Nigel. *MI6: British Secret Intelligence Service, 1909–45.* London: Panther, 1985.

Wheeler, Douglas L. "And Who Is My Neighbour? A World War II Hero of Conscience for Portugal." *Luso-Brazilian Review* 26, no. 1 (Summer 1989): 119–139.

———. "Fifty Years of Dictatorship by António Figueiredo." *International Journal of African Historical Studies* 10, no. 3 (1997): 486–492.

———. *Historical Dictionary of Portugal.* Metuchen, NJ: Scarecrow Press, 1993.

———. "In the Service of Order: The Portuguese Secret Police and the British, German and Spanish Intelligence, 1932–1945." *Journal of Contemporary History* 18, no. 1 (January 1983): 107–127.

———. "The Price of Neutrality: Portugal and the Wolfram Question and World War II." *Luso-Brazilian Review* 23, no. 1 (Summer 1986): 107–127.

———. *Republican Portugal: A Political History, 1910–1926.* Madison: University of Wisconsin Press, 1978.

Wiarda, Howard J., and Margaret MacLeish Mott. *Catholic Roots and Democratic Flowers: Political Systems in Spain and Portugal.* Westport, CT: Praeger, 2001.

Wigg, Richard. *Churchill and Spain: The Survival of the Franco Regime, 1940–1945.* Brighton, UK: Sussex Academic Press, 2008.

Wilcken, Patrick. *Empire Adrift: The Portuguese Court in Rio de Janeiro, 1808–1821.* London: Bloomsbury, 2004.

Williams, Daryle. *Culture Wars in Brazil: The First Vargas Regime, 1930–1945.* Durham, NC: Duke University Press, 2001.

Williamson, Edwin. *The Penguin History of Latin America.* London: Penguin Books, 2009.

Wills, Clair. *That Neutral Island: A Cultural History of Ireland During the Second World War.* London: Faber and Faber, 2007.

Woodward, Llewellyn. *British Foreign Policy in the Second World War.* London: Her Majesty's Stationery Office, 1962.

Wullschlager, Jackie. *Chagall: Love and Exile.* London: Penguin, 2010.

Wylie, Neville. "An Amateur Learns His Job? Special Operations Executive in Portugal, 1940–1942." *Journal of Contemporary History* 36, no. 3 (July 2001): 441–457.

Ziegler, Philip. *King Edward VIII: The Official Biography.* London: Collins, 1990.

Zweig, Stefan. *Brazil: Land of the Future.* New York: Viking, 1941.

NOTES

INTRODUCTION

1. Walter Schellenberg, *The Memoirs of Hitler's Spymaster* (London: Andre Deutsch, 2006), 141.

2. National Archives Public Records Office (PRO)/Foreign Office (FO), 837-1156-4, Looted Art in Occupied Territories, Neutral Countries and Latin America, 4.

3. PRO/HM Treasury (T)/907-1, 77–82.

4. *New York Times*, October 10, 1940, 3.

5. See Neill Lochery, *Lisbon: War in the Shadows of the City of Light, 1939–1945* (New York: PublicAffairs, 2011).

6. PRO/FO/837-1156-4, 6.

CHAPTER 1. SCHELLENBERG

1. *Camp 020: MI5 and the Nazi Spies* (London: Public Records Office, 2000), 81.

2. *Camp 020: MI5 and the Nazi Spies*, 81.

3. PRO/Security Service [KV]-2-99, Final Report on the Case of Walter Friedrich Schellenberg, Introduction.

4. PRO/KV-2-99, Final Report on the Case of Walter Friedrich Schellenberg, Introduction.

5. PRO/KV-2-99, 118.

6. *Camp 020: MI5 and the Nazi Spies*, 81.

7. PRO/KV-2-99, Final Report on the Case of Walter Friedrich Schellenberg, Jewish Atrocities.

8. PRO/KV-2-95-1, 37.

9. *Camp 020: MI5 and the Nazi Spies*, 12.

10. PRO/KV-2-94-1, D. B. Schellenberg, June 1, 1945.

11. Schellenberg, *The Memoirs of Hitler's Spymaster*, 124–125.

12. Schellenberg, *The Memoirs of Hitler's Spymaster*, 125.

13. Lochery, *Lisbon*, 72.

14. Schellenberg, *The Memoirs of Hitler's Spymaster*, 129.

15. Schellenberg, *The Memoirs of Hitler's Spymaster*, 129.

16. Schellenberg, *The Memoirs of Hitler's Spymaster*, 141.

17. Schellenberg, *The Memoirs of Hitler's Spymaster*, 143.

CHAPTER 2. CAMP 020

1. *Camp 020: MI5 and the Nazi Spies*, 10–11.
2. *Camp 020: MI5 and the Nazi Spies*, 6.
3. *Camp 020: MI5 and the Nazi Spies*, 6–7.
4. PRO/FO-371-70830-CG 2671, June 19, 1948.
5. *Camp 020: MI5 and the Nazi Spies*, 19.
6. *Camp 020: MI5 and the Nazi Spies*, 21.
7. *Camp 020: MI5 and the Nazi Spies*, 18–20.
8. *Camp 020: MI5 and the Nazi Spies*, 19–21.
9. PRO/KV-2-99, Final Report on the Case of Walter Friedrich Schellenberg.
10. PRO/KV-2-95, Progress Report in the case of Schellenberg, 2.
11. PRO/KV-2-95, Progress Report in the case of Schellenberg, 2.
12. PRO/KV-2-94, Minute on Schellenberg's Destination after Capture, June 1, 1945.
13. PRO/KV-2-94, From Milmo to Section V, June 9, 1945.
14. PRO/KV-2-94, From US Embassy in Stockholm to British War Department in London, June 8, 1945.
15. PRO/KV-2-94, From US Embassy in Stockholm to British War Department in London, June 8, 1945.
16. PRO/KV-2-95, Camp 020, Photographs of Walter Schellenberg.
17. PRO/KV-2-99, Personal Particulars of Walter Schellenberg.
18. PRO/KV-2-99, Final Report on the Case of Walter Friedrich Schellenberg, Contents of Report.
19. PRO/KV-2-99, Final Report on the Case of Walter Friedrich Schellenberg.
20. PRO/KV-2-95, Post Defeat Plans, Report on Interrogation of Walter Schellenberg, June 27–July 12, 1945, 1.
21. PRO/KV-2-94, From US Embassy in Stockholm to British War Department in London, June 8, 1945.
22. *Camp 020: MI5 and the Nazi Spies*, 81.
23. *Camp 020: MI5 and the Nazi Spies*, 81.
24. *Camp 020: MI5 and the Nazi Spies*, 365.
25. PRO/KV-2-99, Final Report on the Case of Walter Friedrich Schellenberg, 10.
26. PRO/KV-2-99, Final Report on the Case of Walter Friedrich Schellenberg, 10.

CHAPTER 3. INTERROGATION

1 PRO/KV-2-99, Final Report on the Case of Walter Friedrich Schellenberg, Introduction.
2. *Camp 020: MI5 and the Nazi Spies*, 365.
3. PRO/KV-2-95, Report on the Interrogation of Walter Schellenberg, June 27–July 12, 1945, 2.
4. *Camp 020: MI5 and the Nazi Spies*, 365.
5. PRO/FO-371-40999, Bretton Woods Resolution, November 20, 1944.
6. Lochery, *Lisbon*, 126–127.
7. PRO/KV-99-2, Appendix VI, AMT-Post Defeat Plans.
8. PRO/KV-99-2, Appendix VI, AMT-Post Defeat Plans.
9. PRO/KV-99-2, Appendix VI, AMT-Post Defeat Plans.

10. PRO/KV-99-2, Appendix XXII, The I-Netze in Neutral Countries, 2.

11. PRO/KV-99-2, Appendix XXII, The I-Netze in Neutral Countries, 2.

12. PRO/KV-2-99, Final Report on the Case of Walter Friedrich Schellenberg.

13. PRO/KV-99-2, Appendix XXII, The I-Netze in Neutral Countries, 3.

CHAPTER 4. STOCKHOLM FOG

1. PRO/KV-99-2, Appendix XXII, The I-Netze in Neutral Countries, 4.

2. PRO/KV-99-2, Appendix XXII, The I-Netze in Neutral Countries, 3.

3. PRO/KV-99-2, Appendix XXII, The I-Netze in Neutral Countries, 3.

4. PRO/KV-99-2, Appendix XXII, The I-Netze in Neutral Countries, 3.

5. Winston Churchill, *The Second World War: Volume One, The Gathering Storm* (London: Folio Society, 2000), 478.

6. Churchill, *The Second World War, Vol. 1*, 481.

7. John Gilmour, *Sweden, the Swastika and Stalin: The Swedish Experience in the Second World War* (Edinburgh: Edinburgh University Press, 2012), 125.

8. Churchill, *The Second World War, Vol. 1*, 481.

9. For more information on espionage operations, see US National Archives (NARA) RG 84 Entry 3197—Classified General Records of the US Embassy in Stockholm, Sweden, 1944–1945.

10. Douglas Waller, *Wild Bill Donovan: The Spymaster Who Created the OSS and Modern American Espionage* (New York: Free Press, 2011), 286.

11. Richard Harris Smith, *OSS: The Secret History of America's First Central Intelligence Agency* (Lanham, MD: Lyons Press, 2005), 185.

12. "Eric Erickson, Wartime Spy," *New York Times*, January 25, 1983.

13. "Eric Erickson, Wartime Spy," *New York Times*, January 25, 1983.

14. "Eric Erickson, Wartime Spy," *New York Times*, January 25, 1983.

15. Gilmour, *Sweden, the Swastika and Stalin*, 149. Gilmour also argues that the American ambassador shared the sentiments about the OSS.

16. For more details of these deals, see NARA/RG 84 Entry 3195—General Records of the US Embassy Stockholm, Sweden, 1936–1952.

17. Gilmour, *Sweden, the Swastika and Stalin*, 41.

18. Gilmour, *Sweden, the Swastika and Stalin*, 41.

19. M. R. D. Foot, *SOE: The Special Operations Executive, 1940–1946* (London: Pimlico, 1984), 125.

20. Churchill, *The Second World War, Vol. 1*, 481.

21. Churchill, *The Second World War, Vol. 1*, 481.

22. NARA/RG 84 Entry 3195—General Records of the US Embassy Stockholm, Sweden, 1936–1952.

23. The most detailed account in English of this important rescue mission can be found in Bo Lidegaard, *Countrymen: How Denmark's Jews Escaped the Nazis* (London: Atlantic Books, 2015).

24. Swedish humanitarian missions were viewed by London and Washington as a way of securing a more favorable status among the Allies as the war swung in their favor.

25. On the narratives about these events, see Sune Persson, *Escape from the Third Reich: The Harrowing True Story of the Largest Rescue Effort Made Inside Nazi Germany* (London: Skyhorse Publishing, 2009).

26. See Folke Bernadotte, *The Last Days of the Third Reich: The Diary of Count Folke Bernadotte* (London: Frontline Books, 2009).

27. Bernadotte, *Last Days of the Third Reich*, 104.

28. *Camp 020: MI5 and the Nazi Spies*, 365.

29. Foot, *SOE: The Special Operations Executive*, 123.

CHAPTER 5. DONOVAN VERSUS MENZIES

1. NARA/RG 84 Entry 3197—Classified General Records of the US Embassy in Stockholm, Sweden, 1944–1945.

2. NARA/RG 84 Entry 3197—Classified General Records of the US Embassy in Stockholm, Sweden, 1944–1945.

3. Waller, *Wild Bill Donovan*, 165.

4. Anthony Cave Brown, *The Secret Life of Sir Stewart Menzies: Spymaster to Winston Churchill* (New York: Macmillan, 1987), 453.

5. Brown, *The Secret Life of Sir Stewart Menzies*, 453.

6. PRO/KV-2-99, Final Report on the Case of Walter Friedrich Schellenberg.

7. PRO/KV-2-99, Final Report on the Case of Walter Friedrich Schellenberg.

8. On the Italian attempted surrender in Lisbon in 1943, see Neill Lochery, *Lisboa: A Cidade Vista de Fora* (Lisbon: Editorial Presença, 2013), 99–102.

9. Waller, *Wild Bill Donovan*, 243.

10. Waller, *Wild Bill Donovan*, 245.

11. PRO/KV-2-99, Final Report on the Case of Walter Friedrich Schellenberg, Relations with Portugal.

12. Waller, *Wild Bill Donovan*, 257.

13. For a detailed summary of the transfers and the documentation, see "Half a Million for That Crook Kindelán," *El Pais*, June 3, 2013.

14. "MI6 Spent $200m Bribing Spaniards in Second World War," *The Guardian* (Manchester), May 23, 2013.

15. "MI6 Spent $200m Bribing Spaniards in Second World War," *The Guardian* (Manchester), May 23, 2013.

16. PRO/KV-2-99, Final Report on the Case of Walter Friedrich Schellenberg, Relations with Spain in WWII.

17. PRO/British Prime Minister's Office (PREM)-3-362-3, Minute from Winston Churchill, July 19, 1943.

18. There was some opposition to this policy from the Ministry of Economic Warfare.

19. Arquivo Nacional, Torre do Tombo (ANTT)/Arquivo Oliveira Salazar (AOS)/CO-NE-4, Report on "The New Order" from Portuguese Delegation in Berlin, November 15, 1941.

20. PRO/KV-2-99, Relations with Spain in WWII.

21. See David Eccles, *By Safe Hand: The Letters of Sybil and David Eccles, 1939–1942* (London: Bodley Head, 1983).

22. Eccles, *By Safe Hand*.

23. PRO/KV-2-99, Relations with Spain in WWII.

24. Waller, *Wild Bill Donovan*, 257.

25. Waller, *Wild Bill Donovan*, 160.

26. NARA/RG 84—Classified Records of the US Embassy in Madrid, 1940–1963.

27. Waller, *Wild Bill Donovan*, 161.

28. Waller, *Wild Bill Donovan*, 161.

29. PRO/KV-2-99, Knowledge of Allied Intelligence Organisations.

CHAPTER 6. OPERATION SAFEHAVEN

1. NARA/RG 131-346, Safehaven-Portugal, July 27, 1946.

2. PRO/FO/954-7B-FO-45-13, Correspondence between Anthony Eden and Ronald Campbell, May 28, 1945.

3. NARA/RG 131-346, Safehaven-Portugal, July 27, 1946.

4. Both leaders had written personal letters to Salazar asking him to stop the wolfram sales to Germany.

5. NARA/RG 131-346, Safehaven-Portugal, July 27, 1946.

6. See Samuel Hoare's account in *Nine Troubled Years* (London: Collins, 1954).

7. Lochery, *Lisbon*, 213.

8. Lochery, *Lisbon*, 214.

9. *Allied Relations and Negotiations with Portugal* [online report, n.d.], 13, https://1997-2001.state.gov/regions/eur/rpt_9806_ng_portugal.pdf.

10. *Allied Relations and Negotiations with Portugal*, 13.

11. *Allied Relations and Negotiations with Portugal*, 13.

12. PRO/Special Operations Executive (HS)/6-987, From Campbell to Foreign Office, April 2, 1942.

13. Lochery, *Lisbon*, 214.

14. The ambassador did claim not to know much about the work of German intelligence in Lisbon. He left that area to Schellenberg and the Gestapo. He did recall the visits of Schellenberg to Iberia and his efforts to develop a German intelligence operation in the country. He was short on detail when it came to recalling specific operations.

CHAPTER 7. COLLECTORS

1. NARA/RG 131-346, From Embassy in Lisbon to Secretary of State, March 3, 1943, US National Archives.

2. NARA/RG 169-91, From London to Secretary of State, June 1, 1944, US National Archives.

3. NARA/RG 56-2, Notes on the Political Situation in Portugal, July 31, 1944, 6, US National Archives.

4. NARA/RG 169-91, From London to Secretary of State, June 1, 1944.

5. "Real Estate Deals in France: A Banker in Trouble," *The Times* (London), June 15, 1945.

6. PRO/FO/371-49534, Foreign Office Minute, October 18, 1945.

7. PRO/FO/371-49534, From Lisbon to Foreign Office, July 4, 1945.

8. PRO/FO/371-49534, Foreign Office Minute, October 18, 1945.

9. Nubar Gulbenkian, *Pantaraxia: The Autobiography of Nubar Gulbenkian* (London: Hutchinson, 1965), 209.

10. Gulbenkian, *Pantaraxia*, 210.

11. Gulbenkian, *Pantaraxia*, 210.

12. Gulbenkian, *Pantaraxia*, 215.

13. Gulbenkian, *Pantaraxia*, 209.

14. "Mystery Billionaire," *Life*, November 27, 1950, 81.

15. Gulbenkian, *Pantaraxia*, 214.

16. PRO/British Cabinet Office (CAB)/Freedom of Information Act/List of Honours Not Accepted, December 24, 2012.

17. Gulbenkian, *Pantaraxia*, 209.

18. Gulbenkian, *Pantaraxia*, 209.

19. Gulbenkian, *Pantaraxia*, 209.

20. Jonathan Conlin, *Mr. Five Per Cent: The Many Lives of Calouste Gulbenkian, the World's Richest Man* (London: Profile Books, 2021), 303.

21. Conlin, *Mr. Five Per Cent*, 303.

22. "The Man Who Prefers Everything," *Life*, October 15, 1965, 99.

23. Gulbenkian, *Pantaraxia*, 271.

24. PRO/FO-837-1154-3, From British Embassy Madrid to MEW, December 20, 1944.

CHAPTER 8. VICTORY

1. ANTT/AOS/Correspondência Oficial (CO)/NE-2-54, Reports on Death of Hitler, May 3–5, 1945.

2. ANTT/AOS/O Diário de Salazar, May 3, 1945.

3. ANTT/AOS/O Diário de Salazar, May 3, 1945.

4. PRO/FO-954-21, From Salazar to Churchill, May 17, 1945.

5. PRO/FO-954-21, Prime Minister's Minute, May 17, 1945.

6. PRO/FO-954-45-13, From Campbell to Eden, May 28, 1945.

7. PRO/FO-954-45-13, From Campbell to Eden, May 28, 1945.

8. ANTT/AOS/O Diário de Salazar, June 29, 1945.

9. PRO/FO-371-39596, From Campbell to Foreign Office, November 23, 1944.

10. Quoted from Neill Lochery, *Loaded Dice: The Foreign Office and Israel* (London: Continuum, 2007), 36.

CHAPTER 9. LEARNING CURVE

1. PRO/FO-837-1156, Looted Art in Occupied Territories, Neutral Countries and Latin America, Preliminary Report, May 5, 1945.

2. PRO/FO-837-1156, Looted Art in Occupied Territories, Neutral Countries and Latin America, Preliminary Report, May 5, 1945.

3. PRO/FO-837-1156, Looted Art in Occupied Territories, Neutral Countries and Latin America, Preliminary Report, May 5, 1945.

4. PRO/FO-837-1156, Looted Art, 1.

5. PRO/FO-837-1156, Looted Art, 1.

6. PRO/FO-837-1156, Looted Art, 3.

7. PRO/FO-837-1156, Looted Art, 5.

8. PRO/FO-837-1156, Looted Art, 5.

9. PRO/FO-837-1156, Looted Art, 46.

10. PRO/FO-837-1156, Looted Art, 46.

11. PRO/FO-837-1156, Looted Art, 47.

12. PRO/FO-837-1156, Looted Art, 46.

13. PRO/FO-371-24172, Foreign Office Minutes, November 12, 1940.

14. PRO/FO-371-24172, British Embassy in Washington to Foreign Office, November 18, 1940.

15. PRO/FO-371-24172, Telegram from Gibraltar to Foreign Office, December 4, 1940.

16. PRO/FO-371-24172, Telegram from Gibraltar to Foreign Office, December 4, 1940.

17. Shawn C. Smallman, *Fear and Memory in the Brazilian Army and Society, 1889–1954* (Chapel Hill: University of North Carolina Press, 2002), 74.

18. NARA/Foreign Relations of the United States (FRUS)-832-24-260, Burdett to Secretary of State, November 25, 1940, US National Archives.

19. PRO/FO-371-25807, Annual Report for Brazil for 1940.

20. NARA/FRUS-832-24-287, Burdett to Secretary of State, December 11, 1940.

21. PRO/FO-837-1156, Looted Art, 6.

22. PRO/FO-837-1156, Looted Art, 7.

23. PRO/FO-837-1156, Looted Art, 7.

24. PRO/FO-837-1156, Looted Art, 8.

25. PRO/FO-837-1156, Looted Art, 7.

26. PRO/FO-837-1156, Looted Art, 34.

27. PRO/FO-837-1156, Looted Art, 7.

28. PRO/FO-837-1156, Looted Art, 15.

29. PRO/FO-837-1156, Looted Art, 17.

30. PRO/T-209-26, Looted Art in Occupied Territories, Neutral Countries and Latin America, Revised, August 1945, 9.

31. PRO/T-209-26, Looted Art in Occupied Territories, Neutral Countries and Latin America, Revised, August 1945, 9.

32. PRO/KV-2-99, Final Report on the Interrogation of Walter Schellenberg, Goring and Miedl.

33. Jonathan Petropoulos, *Goering's Man in Paris: The Story of a Nazi Art Plunderer and His World* (New Haven, CT: Yale University Press, 2021), 195.

34. Petropoulos, *Goering's Man in Paris*, 196.

35. PRO/T-209-7-1, Memorandum on Alois Miedl included in correspondence from MEW, November 23, 1944.

36. PRO/T-209-7-1, Memorandum on Alois Miedl, 1.

37. PRO/T-209-7-1, Memorandum on Alois Miedl, 1.

38. Petropoulos, *Goering's Man in Paris*, 196.

39. PRO/T-209-7-1, Memorandum on Alois Miedl, 1.

40. PRO/T-209-7-1, Memorandum on Alois Miedl, 1.

41. PRO/T-209-7-1, Memorandum on Alois Miedl, 1.

42. PRO/T-209-7-1, Memorandum on Alois Miedl, 2.

43. PRO/T-209-7-1, Report on Alois Miedl, November 13, 1944.

44. Petropoulos, *Goering's Man in Paris*, 198.

45. PRO/T-209-7-1, Memorandum on Alois Miedl, 3.

46. PRO/T-209-7-1, SIS Report, November 13, 1944.

47. PRO/T-209-7-1, SIS Report, November 13, 1944.

48. PRO/T-209-7-1, SIS Report, October 16, 1944.

49. PRO/T-209-7-1, SIS Report, October 16, 1944.

50. PRO/T-209-7-1, SIS Report, October 16, 1944.

51. PRO/T-209-7-1, SIS Report, November 13, 1944.

52. PRO/T-209-7-1, SIS Report, October 14, 1944.

53. Petropoulos, *Goering's Man in Paris*, 198.

54. PRO/T-209-7-1, From War Office (WO) to MEW, February 6, 1945.

55. PRO/T-209-7-1, Memorandum from US Embassy in Madrid to State Department, March 29, 1945.

56. There are some indications given in oral interviews with the author that he did not use his real name or employed a nickname during his stay in Estoril and Lisbon.

57. Petropoulos, *Goering's Man in Paris*, 198.

58. Petropoulos, *Goering's Man in Paris*, 198.

59. PRO/KV-2-99, Final Report on the Case of Walter Friedrich Schellenberg.

CHAPTER 10. BOOKSHOPS AND GALLERIES

1. *Allied Relations and Negotiations with Portugal* [online report], https://1997-2001 .state.gov/regions/eur/rpt_9806_ng_portugal.pdf, 11.

2. *Allied Relations and Negotiations with Portugal*, 11.

3. PRO/FO-837-1154, Looted Art in Iberian Peninsula: Portugal, 18.

4. PRO/FO-837-1154, Looted Art in Iberian Peninsula: Portugal, 18.

5. PRO/KV-2-99, Final Report on the Case of Walter Friedrich Schellenberg.

6. *Allied Relations and Negotiations with Portugal*, 14.

7. *Allied Relations and Negotiations with Portugal*, 14.

8. PRO/FO-837-1154, Looted Art in Iberian Peninsula: Portugal, 18.

9. PRO/FO-837-1154, Looted Art in Iberian Peninsula: Portugal, 18.

10. PRO/FO-837-1154, Looted Art in Iberian Peninsula: Portugal, 18.

11. PRO/FO-837-1154, Looted Art in Iberian Peninsula: Portugal, 18.

12. PRO/FO-837-1154, Looted Art in Iberian Peninsula: Portugal, 18.

13. PRO/FO-837-1154, Looted Art in Iberian Peninsula: Portugal, 18.

14. PRO/FO-837-1154, Looted Art in Iberian Peninsula: Portugal, 19.

15. PRO/FO-837-1154, Looted Art in Iberian Peninsula: Portugal, 19.

16. PRO/FO-837-1154, Looted Art in Sweden, 21.

17. PRO/FO-837-1154, Looted Art in Sweden, 21.

18. PRO/FO-837-1154, Looted Art in Sweden, 21, 22.

19. PRO/FO-837-1154, Looted Art in Switzerland, 23.

20. PRO/FO-837-1154, Looted Art in Switzerland, 22.

21. PRO/FO-837-1154, Looted Art in Switzerland, 23.

22. PRO/FO-837-1154, Looted Art in Spain, 3.

23. PRO/FO-837-1154, From Paine Embassy Madrid to Bliss MEW, n.d.

24. PRO/FO-837-1154, From Paine Embassy Madrid to Bliss MEW, n.d.

25. PRO/FO-837-1154-3, Memorandum on the Present State of the Investigation into Enemy Assets, British Embassy Madrid, December 15, 1944.

26. PRO/FO-837-1154-3, MEW, February 3, 1945.

27. PRO/FO-837-1154-3, From Ministry of Economic Warfare to Howgate, Trading with the Enemy Department, February 3, 1945.

CHAPTER 11. POSTWAR LISBON

1. PRO/FO-837-1284-1, From Gallman, US Embassy London, to Roberts, Foreign Office, September 27, 1944.

2. PRO/FO-837-1284-1, Economic Warfare Division, Admiralty, October 2, 1944.

3. PRO/FO-49475, Foreign Office Minute, October 19, 1945.

4. PRO/FO-49475, From Lisbon to Foreign Office, August 2, 1945.

5. PRO/FO-49475, From Embassy in Lisbon to Foreign Office, October 24, 1945.

6. See Varian Fry, *Surrender on Demand* (Boulder: Johnson Books, 1997).

7. PRO/KV-2-99, Final Report on the Case of Walter Friedrich Schellenberg.

8. He was also hoping for greater international legitimacy for the new police force.

9. The charges were in the main directed against Portugal collectively and not specific individuals.

10. NARA/FRUS/2, From George Kennan to Secretary of State, November 22, 1943, 2.

11. The speech by the new foreign secretary, Ernest Bevin, on August 20, 1945, revealed the continuity in British foreign policy and the concentration of the government on domestic issues. See PRO/FO-371-49475, From O'Malley to Secretary of State, August 22, 1945.

12. Lochery, *Lisbon*, 234.

CHAPTER 12. ON THE RUN

1. PRO/KV-2-1326, The case of Adolf Nassenstein, 105.

2. PRO/KV-2-1326, The case of Adolf Nassenstein, 115.

3. PRO/KV-2-1326, The case of Adolf Nassenstein, 11.

4. PRO/KV-2-97-2, Statement by Schellenberg, August 9, 1945, 3.

5. PRO/KV-2-1326, The case of Adolf Nassenstein, 118.

6. PRO/KV-2-1326, The case of Adolf Nassenstein, 118.

7. PRO/KV-2-1326, The case of Adolf Nassenstein, 118.

8. Katrin Paehler, *The Third Reich's Intelligence Services: The Career of Walter Schellenberg* (Cambridge: Cambridge University Press, 2019), 249–250.

9. PRO/KV-2-1326, The case of Adolf Nassenstein, 106.

10. PRO/KV-2-1326, The case of Adolf Nassenstein, 113.

11. PRO/KV-2-1326, The case of Adolf Nassenstein, 117.

12. PRO/KV-2-1326, The case of Adolf Nassenstein, 116.

13. PRO/KV-2-1326, The case of Adolf Nassenstein, 116.

14. PRO/KV-2-1326, The case of Adolf Nassenstein, 116.

15. PRO/KV-2-1326, The case of Adolf Nassenstein, 108.

16. PRO/KV-2-1326, The case of Adolf Nassenstein, 108.

17. PRO/KV-2-1326, The case of Adolf Nassenstein, 108.

18. PRO/KV-2-1326, The case of Adolf Nassenstein, 60.

19. PRO/KV-2-1326, The case of Adolf Nassenstein, 60.

20. PRO/KV-2-1326, The case of Adolf Nassenstein, 60.

21. PRO/KV-2-1326, The case of Adolf Nassenstein, 69.

22. PRO/KV-2-1326, The case of Adolf Nassenstein, 69.

23. PRO/KV-2-1326, The case of Adolf Nassenstein, 69.

24. PRO/KV-2-1326, The case of Adolf Nassenstein, 69.

25. PRO/KV-2-1326, The case of Adolf Nassenstein, 70.

26. PRO/KV-2-1326, The case of Adolf Nassenstein, 72.

27. PRO/KV-2-1326, The case of Adolf Nassenstein, 72.

28. PRO/KV-2-1326, The case of Adolf Nassenstein, 72.

29. PRO/KV-2-1326, The case of Adolf Nassenstein, 72.

30. PRO/KV-2-1326, The case of Adolf Nassenstein, 72.

31. PRO/KV-2-1326, The case of Adolf Nassenstein, 72.

32. PRO/KV-2-1326, The case of Adolf Nassenstein, 73.

33. PRO/KV-2-1326, The case of Adolf Nassenstein, 73.

34. PRO/KV-2-1326, The case of Adolf Nassenstein, 74.

35. PRO/KV-2-1326, The case of Adolf Nassenstein, 74.

36. PRO/KV-2-1326, The case of Adolf Nassenstein, 74.

37. PRO/KV-2-1326, The case of Adolf Nassenstein, 75.

38. PRO/KV-2-1326, The case of Adolf Nassenstein, 75.

39. PRO/KV-2-1326, The case of Adolf Nassenstein, 88.

40. PRO/KV-2-1326, The case of Adolf Nassenstein, 88.

41. PRO/KV-2-1326, The case of Adolf Nassenstein, 82.

42. PRO/KV-2-1326, The case of Adolf Nassenstein, 82.

43. PRO/KV-2-1326, The case of Adolf Nassenstein, 39.

44. PRO/KV-2-1326, The case of Adolf Nassenstein, 35.

45. PRO/KV-2-1326, The case of Adolf Nassenstein, 35.

46. PRO/KV-2-1326, The case of Adolf Nassenstein, 35.

47. PRO/KV-2-99, Final Report on the Case of Walter Friedrich Schellenberg.

48. PRO/KV-2-1326, The case of Adolf Nassenstein, 35.

49. PRO/KV-2-1326, The case of Adolf Nassenstein, 36.

50. PRO/KV-2-1326, The case of Adolf Nassenstein, 37.

51. PRO/KV-2-1326, The case of Adolf Nassenstein, 37.

52. PRO/KV-2-1326, The case of Adolf Nassenstein, 37.

53. PRO/KV-2-399-2, The Case of Erich Schroeder, 28.

54. PRO/KV-2-399-2, The Case of Erich Schroeder, 6.

55. PRO/KV-2-399-2, The Case of Erich Schroeder, 8.

56. PRO/KV-2-399-2, The Case of Erich Schroeder, 8.

57. PRO/KV-2-399-2, The Case of Erich Schroeder, 8.

58. PRO/KV-2-399-2, The Case of Erich Schroeder, 8.

59. PRO/KV-2-95-2, Report on the Interrogation of Walter Schellenberg, June 27–July 12, 1945, 31n151.

60. PRO/KV-2-95-2, Report on the Interrogation of Walter Schellenberg, June 27–July 12, 1945, 31n151.

61. PRO/KV-2-95-2, Report on the Interrogation of Walter Schellenberg, June 27–July 12, 1945, 31n151.

62. PRO/KV-2-95-2, Report on the Interrogation of Walter Schellenberg, June 27–July 12, 1945, 31n151.

63. PRO/KV-2-95-2, Report on the Interrogation of Walter Schellenberg, June 27–July 12, 1945, 31n151.

64. PRO/KV-2–399-2, The Case of Erich Schroeder, 8.

65. PRO/KV-2–399-2, The Case of Erich Schroeder, 8.

66. Paehler, The Third Reich's Intelligence Services, 248–249.

67. PRO/KV-2-99, Final Report on the Case of Walter Friedrich Schellenberg.

68. PRO/KV-2-99, Final Report on the Case of Walter Friedrich Schellenberg.

69. PRO/KV-2-399-2, The Case of Erich Schroeder, 21, 28.

70. PRO/KV-2-399-2, The Case of Erich Schroeder, 21.

71. PRO/KV-2-399-2, The Case of Erich Schroeder, 7.

72. PRO/KV-2-99, Final Report on the Case of Walter Friedrich Schellenberg.

73. PRO/KV-2-399-2, The Case of Erich Schroeder, 2.

74. PRO/KV-2-399-2, The Case of Erich Schroeder, 2.

75. PRO/KV-2-399-2, The Case of Erich Schroeder, 2.

76. PRO/KV-2-399-2, The Case of Erich Schroeder, 4.

77. PRO/KV-2-399-2, The Case of Erich Schroeder, 4.

78. PRO/KV-2-399-2, The Case of Erich Schroeder, 3.

79. PRO/KV-2-399-2, The Case of Erich Schroeder, 3.

80. PRO/KV-2-399-2, The Case of Erich Schroeder, 3.

81. PRO/KV-2-399-2, The Case of Erich Schroeder, 7.

82. PRO/KV-2-399-2, The Case of Erich Schroeder, 3.

83. Lochery, *Lisbon*, 158.

84. PRO/KV-2-399-2, The Case of Erich Schroeder, 2.

85. RG 131-346-Safehaven-Portugal, July 27, 1946, 1.

86. PRO/KV-2-399-2, The Case of Erich Schroeder, 2.

87. PRO/KV-2-99, Final Report on the Case of Walter Friedrich Schellenberg.

CHAPTER 13. GOLD BARS

1. ANTT/AOS-CO-NE-2-16, Records of Meetings on German Payments for Wolfram, April 30–May 27, 1942.

2. ANTT/AOS-CO-NE-2-16, Records of Meetings on German Payments for Wolfram, April 30–May 27, 1942; Lochery, *Lisbon*, 203.

3. Churchill was very dismissive of the Foreign Office's tough line against Portugal.

4. PRO/T-209-26-2, Looted Art in Occupied Territories, Neutral Countries and Latin America, Revised, August 1945, 20–22.

5. PRO/T-209-26-2, Looted Art in Occupied Territories, Neutral Countries and Latin America, Revised, August 1945, 20–22.

6. PRO/T-209-26-2, Looted Art in Occupied Territories, Neutral Countries and Latin America, Revised, August 1945, 20–22.

7. PRO/T-209-26-2, Looted Art in Occupied Territories, Neutral Countries and Latin America, Revised, August 1945, 20–22.

8. "Catholic Shrine Has Nazi Gold Haul," BBC News, May 3, 2000.

9. PRO/KV-2-99, Final Report on the Case of Walter Friedrich Schellenberg.

10. Neill Lochery Archive (NLA), editions of the weekly magazine *O Seculo Ilustrado* from 1933 to 1956.

11. NLA, editions of the weekly magazine *O Seculo Ilustrado* from 1933 to 1956.

12. NLA, editions of the weekly magazine *O Seculo Ilustrado* from 1933 to 1956.

13. PRO/PREM-19-6042, Nazi Gold Histories, 9.

14. PRO/PREM-19-6042, Nazi Gold Histories, 9.

15. PRO/PREM-19-6042, Nazi Gold Histories, 9.

16. PRO/PREM-19-6042, Nazi Gold Histories, Switzerland.

17. PRO/PREM-19-6042, Nazi Gold Histories, Spain.

18. PRO/PREM-19-6042, Nazi Gold Histories, Sweden.

19. PRO/PREM-19-6042, 4.

20. PRO/PREM-19-6042, 4.

21. PRO/PREM-19-6042, 4.

22. NARA/RG 256-190, From Naval Attaché in Lisbon to Washington, September 1, 1944.

23. ANTT/AOS-CO-NE-2-26, US Embassy in Lisbon to Ministry of Foreign Affairs in Lisbon, February 12, 1945.

24. ANTT/AOS-CO-NE-2-26, US Embassy in Lisbon to Ministry of Foreign Affairs in Lisbon, February 12, 1945.

25. PRO/KV-2-95-1, Report of Interrogation of Walter Schellenberg, June 27–July 12, 1945, Post Defeat Plans, 1.

26. PRO/KV-2-95-1, Report of Interrogation of Walter Schellenberg, June 27–July 12, 1945.

27. PRO/KV-2-3159, The case of Frank Koschnick, 9.

28. PRO/KV-2-3159, The case of Frank Koschnick, 9.

29. PRO/KV-2-3159, The case of Frank Koschnick, 9.

30. PRO/KV-2-3159, The case of Frank Koschnick, 9.

31. PRO/KV-2-3159, The case of Frank Koschnick, 13.

32. PRO/KV-2-3159, The case of Frank Koschnick, 25.

33. PRO/KV-2-3159, The case of Frank Koschnick, 25.

34. NARA/RG 84-90, General Records of the Embassy in Lisbon, Gold Imports into Portugal, October 12, 1944.

35. NARA/RG 84-90, General Records of the Embassy in Lisbon, Gold Imports into Portugal, October 12, 1944.

36. PRO/KV-2-3159, The Case of Frank Koschnick, 25.

CHAPTER 14. STORY BUILDING

1. NARA/RG 84 Entry 3197—Classified General Records of the US Embassy in Stockholm, Sweden, 1944–1952. From State Department to Embassy in Stockholm, n.d.

2. Anthony Georgieff, "Europe: Documents Reveal Sweden's Ties to Nazi Gold," Radio Free Europe, January 9, 1997, www.rferl.org/a/1083119.html.

3. PRO/KV-2-99, Final Report on the Case of Walter Friedrich Schellenberg, Sweden.

4. PRO/KV-2-99, Final Report on the Case of Walter Friedrich Schellenberg, Sweden.

5. PRO/KV-2-99-Peacefeelers.

6. PRO/KV-2-99-Peacefeelers.

7. PRO/KV-2-99-Peacefeelers.

8. PRO/KV-2-99, 102–103.

9. Schellenberg believed that the splits were operational and strategic.

10. PRO/KV-2-99, 102–103.

11. NARA/RG 84, Sweden, Records of the Foreign Service Posts of the State Department.

12. NARA/RG 84, Sweden, Records of the Foreign Service Posts of the State Department.

13. NARA/RG 84, Sweden, Records of the Foreign Service Posts of the State Department.

14. NARA/RG 84, Sweden, Records of the Foreign Service Posts of the State Department.

15. NARA/RG 84, Sweden, Records of the Foreign Service Posts of the State Department.

16. NARA/RG 84, Sweden, Records of the Foreign Service Posts of the State Department.

17. PRO/KV-2-99, Final Report on the Case of Walter Friedrich Schellenberg, Sweden.

18. PRO/KV-2-99, End of War.

19. PRO/KV-2-99, 91–96.

20. PRO/KV-2-99, 91–96.

21. PRO/KV-2-99, 98–100.

22. PRO/KV-2-99, 98–100.

23. PRO/KV-2-99, Karsten.

24. Gilmour, *Sweden, the Swastika and Stalin*, 199.

25. Gilmour, *Sweden, the Swastika and Stalin*, 200.

26. Bernadotte, *Last Days of the Third Reich*, 12.

27. Sune Persson, *Escape from the Third Reich: The Harrowing True Story of the Largest Rescue Effort Made Inside Nazi Germany* (New York: Skyhorse Publishing, 2009), 250.

28. Hugh Trevor-Roper, *The Last Days of Hitler* (London: Macmillan, 1995).

29. Persson, *Escape from the Third Reich*, 253.

30. Persson, *Escape from the Third Reich*, 253.

31. Bernadotte, *Last Days of the Third Reich*, 22.

CHAPTER 15. RETURN

1. Bernadotte, *Last Days of the Third Reich*, 12–13.

2. See Neill Lochery, *Loaded Dice: The Foreign Office and Israel* (London: Continuum, 2007).

3. Lochery, *Loaded Dice*.

4. PRO/T-209-7-1, Looted Art to South America.

5. Neill Lochery, *Brazil: The Fortunes of War, World War Two, and the Making of Modern Brazil* (New York: Basic Books, 2014), 214.

6. PRO/KV-2-99, Final Report on the Case of Walter Friedrich Schellenberg.

7. PRO/KV-2-99, Final Report on the Case of Walter Friedrich Schellenberg, Portugal and Brazil.

8. PRO/KV-2-99, Final Report on the Case of Walter Friedrich Schellenberg, Portugal and Brazil.

9. PRO/KV-2-99, Final Report on the Case of Walter Friedrich Schellenberg, Argentina.

10. Lochery, *Brazil*, 21.

11. On the importance of radio stations, see Lochery, *Brazil*, 44.

CHAPTER 16. OPPORTUNISTS

1. Raanan Rein, "Argentina, World War Two, and the Entry of Nazi War Criminals," in *Argentine Jews or Jewish Argentines? Essays on Ethnicity, Identity, and Diaspora Jewish Identities in a Changing World*, Vol. 12, ed. Eliezer Ben-Rafael, Yosef Gorny, and Judit Bokser (Boston: Brill, 2010), 86.

2. PRO/KV-2-99, Jewish Issues.

3. PRO/KV-2-98-3, 14.

4. PRO/KV-2-98-3, 14.

5. PRO/KV-2-98-3, 14.

6. Robert Hutchinson, *German Foreign Intelligence: From Hitler's War to the Cold War* (Lawrence: University Press of Kansas, 2019), 160.

7. PRO/KV-2-1, Report on Interrogation of Walter Schellenberg, June 27–July 12, 1945, Post Defeat Plans, 2.

8. PRO/KV-2-1, Report on Interrogation of Walter Schellenberg, June 27–July 12, 1945, Post Defeat Plans, 2.

9. PRO/KV-2-1, Report on Interrogation of Walter Schellenberg, June 27–July 12, 1945, Post Defeat Plans, 2.

10. PRO/KV-2-1, Report on Interrogation of Walter Schellenberg, June 27–July 12, 1945, Post Defeat Plans, 2.

11. PRO/KV-2-1, Report on Interrogation of Walter Schellenberg, June 27–July 12, 1945, Post Defeat Plans, 2.

12. Hutchinson, *German Foreign Intelligence*, 159.

13. Hutchinson, *German Foreign Intelligence*, 159.

14. PRO/KV-2-99, South American Diplomats in Germany.

15. PRO/KV-2-99, South American Diplomats in Germany.

16. PRO/KV-2-99, South American Diplomats in Germany.

17. PRO/KV-2-99, South American Diplomats in Germany.

18. PRO/KV-2-99, South American Diplomats in Germany.

19. PRO/KV-2-99, South American Diplomats in Germany.

20. Hutchinson, *German Foreign Intelligence*, 182.

21. Hutchinson, *German Foreign Intelligence*, 182.

22. Hutchinson, *German Foreign Intelligence*, 173.

23. PRO/KV-2-99, Argentina and Perón.

24. PRO/KV-2-99, Argentina and Perón.

25. PRO/KV-2-99, Argentina and Perón.

26. PRO/KV-2-99, Argentina and Perón.

27. Uri Goñi, *The Real Odessa* (London: Granta Books, 2002), 16.

28. Goñi, *The Real Odessa*, 16.

29. PRO/KV-2-99, Argentina and Perón.

30. Goñi, *The Real Odessa*, 24.

31. Rein, "Argentina, World War Two, and the Entry of Nazi War Criminals," 80.

32. BBC News, May 5, 2020.

33. NARA/FRUS, Argentina: Documents 142–271, the Issuance by the Department of State of the Blue Book and the Position of the United States on Supplying Arms to Argentina, 1946.

34. A PDF of the *Blue Book on Argentina* can be found at: http://cedinpe.unsam.edu.ar/sites/default/files/pdfs/blue_book_on_argentina.pdf.

35. "Introductory Statement," in *The Blue Book on Argentina: Consultation Among the American Republics with Respect to the Argentine Situation* (New York: Greenberg, 1946), 2–3.

36. PRO/KV-2-99, Argentina and Perón.

37. *Blue Book on Argentina*, 4.

38. *Blue Book on Argentina*, 11–15.

39. *Blue Book on Argentina*, 16–43.

40. *Blue Book on Argentina*, 44–57.

41. *Blue Book on Argentina*; NARA/RG 226—Records of the Office of Strategic Services, Relevant files to Argentina and Operation Safehaven.

42. NARA/RG 226—Records of the Office of Strategic Services, Relevant files to Argentina and Operation Safehaven.

CHAPTER 17. VISITORS

1. PRO/FO-371-67856, Speech by Salazar to the National Assembly, November 25, 1947, 1.

2. PRO/FO-371-67856, Speech by Salazar to the National Assembly, November 25, 1947, 1.

3. PRO/FO-371-67856, Report on Situation in Portugal, Horsfall Carter, December 21, 1947.

4. PRO/FO-371-67856, Report on Situation in Portugal, Horsfall Carter, December 21, 1947.

5. PRO/FO-371-67856, Report on Situation in Portugal, Horsfall Carter, December 21, 1947.

6. PRO/FO-371-67856, Report on Situation in Portugal, Horsfall Carter, December 21, 1947.

7. Filipe Ribeiro de Meneses, *Salazar: A Political Biography* (New York: Enigma Books, 2009), 354.

8. PRO/FO-371-67856, Report on Situation in Portugal.

9. PRO/FO-371-67856, Report on Situation in Portugal.

10. PRO/FO-371-67856, Report on Situation in Portugal.

11. PRO/FO-371-67856, Report on Situation in Portugal.

12. Felipe Pigna, *Evita* (Barcelona: Ediciones Destino, 2013), 286.

13. Julie Taylor, *Eva Perón: The Myths of a Woman* (Chicago: University of Chicago Press, 1979), 44.

14. Taylor, *Eva Perón*, 45.

15. Lesli J. Favor, *Eva Perón* (Singapore: Marshall Cavendish, 2010), 66.

16. Taylor, *Eva Perón*, 46.

17. PRO/FO-371-67856, Ronald to Foreign Office, November 22, 1947.

18. PRO/FO-371-67856, Ronald to Foreign Office, November 22, 1947.

19. PRO/FO-371-67856, Ronald to Foreign Office, November 22, 1947.

20. ANTT/AOS-O Diário de Salazar, October 9, 1947.

21. PRO/FO-371-79627, Annual Report for Portugal for 1948, 5.

22. PRO/FO-371-79627, Annual Report for Portugal for 1948, 5.

23. Meneses, *Salazar: A Political Biography*, 350.

24. See, for example, "Lisbon: Europe's Bottleneck," *Life*, April 28, 1941, 77.

25. Phillipe Mather, *Stanley Kubrick at Look Magazine: Authorship and Photojournalism and Film* (Bristol, UK: Intellect, 2013), 119.

26. PRO/FO-371-79627, Annual Report for Portugal for 1948, 5.

27. PRO/FO-371-79627, Annual Report for Portugal for 1948, 5.

28. Paul Preston, *Franco* (London: Basic Books, 1994), 454.

29. PRO/FO-371-89420, Annual Report for Portugal for 1949, 6.

30. PRO/FO-371-89420, Annual Report for Portugal for 1949, 6.

31. PRO/FO-371-89420, Annual Report for Portugal for 1949, 6.

32. PRO/FO-371-79627, Annual Report for Portugal for 1948, 5.

33. PRO/FO-371-79627, Annual Report for Portugal for 1948, 5.

34. PRO/FO-371-79627, Annual Report for Portugal for 1948, 5.

35. PRO/FO-371-79627, Annual Report for Portugal for 1948, 5.

36. Preston, *Franco*, 602.

Chapter 18. Assassination

1. For background on this, see Neill Lochery, *View from the Fence: The Arab-Israeli Conflict from the Present to Its Roots* (London: Continuum, 2005).

2. Joseph Heller, "Failure of a Mission: Bernadotte and Palestine, 1948," *Journal of Contemporary History* 14, no. 3 (July 1979): 515.

3. Heller, "Failure of a Mission," 515.

4. See Neill Lochery, *Why Blame Israel?* (London: Icon Books, 2004).

5. Lochery, *Why Blame Israel?*, 31–32.

6. Lochery, *View from the Fence*, 50.

7. PRO/KV-2-95, Report on Interrogation of Walter Schellenberg, June 27–July 12, 1945, The Grand Mufti of Jerusalem, 26–27.

8. The testimony of Walter Schellenberg at Camp 020 formed a central part of this defense.

9. PRO/KV-2-99, Final Report on the Case of Walter Friedrich Schellenberg, Prisoner Releases in 1945.

10. Heller, "Failure of a Mission," 521.

11. Heller, "Failure of a Mission," 521.

12. See Lochery, *Loaded Dice*.

13. Heller, "Failure of a Mission," 524.

14. Cary David Stanger, "A Haunting Legacy: The Assassination of Count Bernadotte," *Middle East Journal* 42, no. 2 (Spring 1988): 265.

15. Stanger, "A Haunting Legacy," 262.

16. Stanger, "A Haunting Legacy," 262.

17. Stanger, "A Haunting Legacy," 262.

18. UN Department of Public Information, "General Lundstrom Gives Eyewitness Account of Bernadotte's Death," press release, September 18, 1948, www.un.org /unispal/document/auto-insert-195099.

19. UN Department of Public Information, "General Lundstrom Gives Eyewitness Account."

20. Stanger, "A Haunting Legacy," 263–264.

21. Stanger, "A Haunting Legacy," 264.

22. "Count Bernadotte's Killers Revealed," *Journal of Palestine Studies* 6, no. 4 (Summer 1977): 145–147.

23. "Count Bernadotte's Killers Revealed," 145–147.

24. "Count Bernadotte's Killers Revealed," 145–147.

25. Efraim Zuroff, "Sweden's Refusal to Prosecute Nazi War Criminals, 1986–2002," *Jewish Political Studies Review* 14, nos. 3/4, "Post-Holocaust Issues" (Fall 2002): 88.

Chapter 19. Fate and Legacy

1. PRO/FO-371-96129, Annual Report for Portugal for 1950, 4–5.

2. PRO/FO-371-101954, Annual Report for Portugal for 1951, 8.

3. PRO/FO-371-101954, Annual Report for Portugal for 1951, 8.

4. NARA/FRUS, Editorial Note 352, Negotiations for the Extension of United States Military Base Rights in the Azores, 771.

5. NARA/FRUS, Editorial Note 352, Negotiations for the Extension of United States Military Base Rights in the Azores, 771.

6. NARA/RG 131-346, Foreign Funds Control, Memorandum on Gold Acquisitions by Portugal during World War Two.

7. NARA/RG 131-346, Foreign Funds Control, Memorandum on Gold Acquisitions by Portugal during World War Two.

8. *New York Times*, January 18, 1951.

9. Dwight D. Eisenhower, Remarks at Portela Airport, Lisbon, Before Leaving for Washington, May 20, 1960, the Eisenhower Presidential Library, Abilene, KS.

10. ANTT/AOS/O Diário de Salazar, February 26, 1951.

11. ANTT/AOS/O Diário de Salazar, February 26, 1951.

12. Schellenberg, *The Memoirs of Hitler's Spymaster*.

13. Despite the efforts of several historians, including me, to get them released under the Freedom of Information Act.

14. PRO/KV-2-95, Report on Interrogation of Walter Schellenberg, June 27–July 12, 1945, Post-War Plans.

15. In the third decade of the twenty-first century, Swiss cooperation remains patchy.

16. See Lochery, *Brazil*.

17. Lochery, *Brazil*, 277–288.

18. On Eichmann, see David Cesarani, *Eichmann: His Life and Crimes* (London: Vintage, 2005).

19. "Churchill Ok'd Bribes to Keep Spain Neutral, Papers Show," *Los Angeles Times*, August 5, 1997; Giles Tremlett, "General Franco Gave List of Spanish Jews to Nazis," *The Guardian* (Manchester), June 20, 2010.

20. On these events, see Neill Lochery, *Out of the Shadows: Portugal from Revolution to the Present Day* (London: Bloomsbury, 2017).

21. Lochery, *Out of the Shadows*.

22. Lochery, *Out of the Shadows*.

23. The country's geographic position at the edge of Europe helps it remain away from the fray. Its ruling elite is small and closed and has family ties to people under suspicion.

24. For more information on this, see Lochery, *Out of the Shadows*.

PHOTO CREDITS

1. Horacio Novais, CFT164.160797, Art Library and Archive, Foundation Calouste Gulbenkian, Portugal
2. KV-2-95 British National Archives, Kew, United Kingdom
3. The Royal Gazette, Bermuda
4. Public Domain
5. Mario Novais, CFT164.102487, Art Library and Archive, Foundation Calouste Gulbenkian, Portugal
6. Horacio Novais, CFT164.54947, Art Library and Archive, Foundation Calouste Gulbenkian, Portugal
7. Bundesarchiv, Germany, B 323 Bild-0311-008
8. Bundesarchiv, Germany, Bild 146-1975-041-07
9. Mario Novais, CFT003.50521, Art Library and Archive, Foundation Calouste Gulbenkian, Portugal
10. Library of Congress, United States
11. National Portrait Gallery, London, United Kingdom
12. Mario Novais, CFT003.15223, Art Library and Archive, Foundation Calouste Gulbenkian, Portugal
13. Mario Novais, CFT003.40657, Art Library and Archive, Foundation Calouste Gulbenkian, Portugal
14. Horacio Novais, CFT164.69732, Art Library and Archive, Foundation Calouste Gulbenkian, Portugal
15. Public Domain
16. Imperial War Museum (CA137), United Kingdom
17. United States Holocaust Memorial Museum Photo Archives (#45696), courtesy of Eric Saul

18. United Nations (UN712292)
19. United Nations (UN7479264)
20. Public Domain
21. Britannica, United Kingdom
22. Arquivo MNE, Portugal
23. United States Holocaust Memorial Museum Photo Archives (#80500), courtesy of National Archives and Records Administration, College Park / photographer: Donald R. Ornitz
24. Public Domain
25. Public Domain
26. Buenos Aires Holocaust Museums Collection, Argentina
27. Horacio Novais, CFT164.160811, Art Library and Archive, Foundation Calouste Gulbenkian, Portugal

INDEX

Neill Lochery, PhD, is a world-renowned source on the politics and modern history of Europe and the Mediterranean Middle East. He has authored a series of critically acclaimed books, including the international bestseller *Lisbon: War in the Shadows of the City of Light, 1939–1945*, as well as countless newspaper and magazine articles. He regularly appears on television in the UK, the USA, and the Middle East. He is currently based at University College London and regularly gives talks in the UK, Europe, the Middle East, and North America.